MARGARET
THE TRAGIC PRINCESS

Also by James Brough

MARGARET
THE TRAGIC PRINCESS

JAMES BROUGH

G. P. Putnam's Sons, New York

SBN: 399-12051-3

Library of Congress Cataloging in Publication Data

Brough, James, 1918–
  Margaret–the tragic princess
  Includes Index
  1. Margaret, Princess of Great Britain, 1930–
  2. Great Britain—Princes and princesses—Biography.
  I. Title.
DA585.A5M32 1977   941.085′092′4 [B]   77-21635
          PRINTED IN THE UNITED STATES OF AMERICA

Acknowledgments

Grateful acknowledgment is made for the help generously provided by Michael Malloy; Brian Hitchen; the National Institutes of Health in Bethesda, Maryland; the Medical Library of McGill University in Montreal; librarians of the *Daily Mirror*, London; the men and women of Fleet Street who have been covering the story of the lady in question for the past forty-seven years; Janet Aston, who typed the manuscript; and others who chose not to be identified.

Reference sources include *The Little Princesses* by Marion Crawford (New York, Harcourt, Brace & Company, 1950); *Princess Margaret* by Marion Crawford (London, George Newnes, Ltd., 1953); *Gone With the Windsors* by Iles Brody (Philadelphia, the John C. Winston Company, 1953); *Princess Margaret* by Gordon Langley Hall (Philadelphia, Macrae Smith Company, 1958); *King George VI: His Life and Reign* by John W. Wheeler-Bennett (London, Macmillan & Company, Ltd., 1958); *Thatched With Gold:* The Memoirs of Mabell, Countess of Airlie (London, Hutchison & Company, Ltd., 1962); *Tony's*

Room by William Glenton (New York, Bernard Geis Associates, 1965); *The New London Spy* edited by Hunter Davies (London, Anthony Blond, Ltd., 1966); *Lord Snowdon* by Helen Cathcart (London, W. H. Allen, 1968). *George III and the Mad Business* by Richard Hunter and Ida Macalpine (London, Allen Lane, 1969); *Facets of Genetics:* Scientific American (San Francisco, W. H. Freeman & Company, 1969); *The Royal Family* by Ralphe M. White and Graham Fisher (New York, David McKay, Inc., 1969); *The Queen's Year* by Andrew Duncan (Garden City, Doubleday & Company, Inc., 1970); *Princess Margaret* by Helen Cathcart (London, W. H. Allen, 1974); *The Woman He Loved* by Ralph G. Martin (New York, Simon & Schuster, Inc., 1974); and "Porphyrin Metabolism and the Porphyrias" by Donald T. Tshudy, M.D., included in *Duncan's Diseases of Metabolism* (Philadelphia, W. B. Saunders Company, 1974).

Dulce et decorum est
pro patria mori.

I

The Fine Print

On this July morning, she was up earlier than usual. Having fruit and coffee served on a tray while she lingered in bed was more to the liking of the woman known as "Yvonne" in the argot of the London disco set. Her grandmother used to reprimand her for idleness: "The hours before breakfast are the best part of the day."

The girl had been unrepentant. "One can do a great deal of work lying down," she answered.

The quarters in which she lived now had claims to veneration every bit as valid as those of her sister, Elizabeth, though they were spared only a line or two in the tourist guides. Grandmother was born here in Kensington Palace in 1867. Half a century before that, its rooms served for the birth of another princess, a German like Grandmama, at a time when problems of health threatened to interrupt the supply of Hanoverian rulers for England. The timely arrival of the child Victoria, who became queen and empress, preserved the line and the future of the inheritance. Victoria would not have been amused to learn that "Yvonne" would be the jeering tag applied to one of the multitude of her great-great-great-granddaughters, Her Royal Highness the Princess Margaret. But reverence for royalty was out of date in Britain today; "Brenda" was the name applied in the same spirit of gentle scoffing to the queen, Elizabeth II.

For generations, Kensington Palace had been in use as a kind of royal apartment house. The present landlord was Elizabeth, whose relations were charged no rent, but were expected to pay their own property taxes—"rates" to the English—which in Margaret's case amounted to a little more than £1,000 a year.

The terms could be considered generous even if old floorboards creaked, voices carried through some interior walls, and the chimneys were not all they should be. Minor inconveniences had to be expected when the property was over two hundred years old, the stately handiwork of Sir Christopher Wren. Margaret's three-story apartment, No. 1A, contained a total of twenty-one rooms. Her sister had personally contributed £20,000 and the taxpayers £65,000 to pay for remodeling and repairing wartime bomb damage to make a home for Margaret after her marriage to Tony Armstrong-Jones.

One advantage of the place was its seclusion. It lay off the familiar tracks of tourism, though Buckingham Palace stood less than two crow's-flight miles away across the tree tops of Kensington Gardens, where withered grass provided a skimpy diet for a flock of chomping sheep. In the spring, birdsong sounded over the distant mutter of traffic on Kensington High Street. Outdoors, the atmosphere was of time-faded red brick, smooth cobblestones, and gaslamps. Only dribs and drabs of people came to inspect the Victorian bric-a-brac and funereal paintings in the state apartments next door, open to the public on weekdays from 10 A.M. to 6 P.M., Sundays at 2 P.M.

The mistress of No. 1A, who in stockings measured a trifle more than five feet tall, had seen to it that the scale of furnishings fitted her diminutive height. "I am small myself, so I like small things." A king-size bed in her pink-painted bedroom was out of the question. Like the rest of the rooms, this one reflected eclectic rather than prodigal taste—inherited antiques blended with 1930s-modern, sentimental trinkets, and an abundance of examples of family photography, which had been the pride and passion of royals since the advent of George Eastman.

Three-inch heels on size 2½ shoes would help as Margaret dressed for her outing today. She was due in Tidworth, Wiltshire, headquarters of the 15th/19th King's Royal Hussars. It was one of two British regiments for which she served as nominal colonel-in-chief. Following the custom of bestowing such titles as birthday gifts for adolescent princes and princesses, her father, King George VI, awarded his first martial appointment to her when she reached seventeen.

"In my own sort of humble way, I have always tried to take some part of the burden off my sister," she once told a quizzical reporter, who was not alone in his skepticism. But inspecting the men and tanks of the unhorsed Hussars would mix duty with an uncommon pleasure. She would take along her fourteen-year-old son, David and her daughter, Sarah, aged twelve. She wanted a different, happier life for them than hers had turned out to be. She would not permit them to be idolized by an adoring public yet simultaneously walled off from the world, as she had been. Most of the time, they were away together at Bedales, a private coeducational school in Hampshire, treated like any other boarders, making friends at an age when she had never had that chance. When they were at home with her, she continued the process of preparing them to find their place in society. They impressed most of her guests with the ease of their manners. She took care to treat them as equals, with an equal place in her affections. She was well aware of the damage that favoritism could do.

Applying a shield of makeup for the expedition, she may have reconciled herself to the face in the mirror. The most destructive words she had read in the course of last spring's trouble turned up in an otherwise respectful, conservative Sunday newspaper: "You occasionally see faces like hers alone in a bar, staring at a tumbler of gin as though it were an hour glass."

The gibe held too much truth to be forgotten. Admittedly, the perky prettiness of youth had long since disappeared. The glossy brown hair was becoming foxed with gray, but the skin was nursery-soft and smooth. Until she smiled, the full, downturned lips had a look that could be interpreted variously as petulance, disappointment, or dejection. The reflected image was that of a middle-aged woman who had ventured and failed to shelter herself from hurt.

There was a Hanoverian plumpness in cheeks and jawline that had not been present before. Waist and arms had thickened, too. She had given up the effort to keep girlishly slim. Nine years ago, she had tried too hard and finished up in King Edward VII Hospital, great-great grandfather's, for some days of tests.

For most of her life, she had known the intermittent, raging pain diagnosed as migraine, which makes a toothache a comparative relief. Classic attacks were likely to be preceded by disturbance of speech, vision, and balance; common ones by vague feelings of fogginess and inexplicable irritability. Her own experience prompted her to lend prestige as a patron to The Migraine Trust, which figured about halfway down the list of analogous good causes, ranging alphabetically from the Architects' Benevolent Society to the Zebra Trust.

Medical men outlined the problem. "Migraine is defined as

a periodic vascular headache, usually but not always accompanied by nausea and vomiting. The blood vessels dilate, causing the blood to pound through the head." Severe spells might last for days or weeks. Normal remedies on the order of aspirin had no effect.

A lowering of levels of bloodstream sugar caused by stringent dieting was recognized by the doctors as likely to bring on the spasms. Other triggers were mental stress, changes in hormone balance, variations in the weather, and a taste for artificially tinted drinks like Scotch, rye, rum, and beer.

Staying clear of these was easy for her; she much preferred gin, vodka, or champagne. Following the physicians' advice almost inevitably meant putting on weight. They recommended going no more than five daytime hours without eating, thirteen hours overnight, and nibbling a snack before bed to ward off danger next morning.

The savage Sunday journalist had omitted to mention the feature of her face that made it exceptional. Her eyes' alternating shades of blue matched the mood of the mind behind them. They could be glazed with tedium, icy with arrogance, gentle with compassion, brilliant with amusement, and all in the span of an hour or two.

With the task of making up her face completed, she could review the results, never entirely satisfactory these days. She had changed so much over the past few years. Nothing could hide the puffiness around the eyes, the drooping muscles by the mouth. She looked trammeled, not beautiful as she once had been.

Time had to be spared, of course, for the initial cigarette of the day before she set off; nothing as bland as an English filter tip, but a Gitane, French and forceful, inserted in a long black holder. Everyone knew that smoking did a little to hold down poundage. It had hastened her father's death from lung cancer when he went through several packages a day out of unconquerable nervousness. Elizabeth was forever urging her to break the habit. This was one more subject on which the sisters failed to agree.

The downstairs rooms of the apartment showed the most obvious signs of upset in Tony's wake. He had carried away most of his personal gear by car, in the same fashion as the two of them ferried in their more precious possessions one Saturday morning thirteen years ago. In a spirit of independence, he had stipulated that, besides taking care of the rates, he must pay rent to Margaret for the four rooms earmarked for his use as a top-price professional photographer.

Camera cases no longer dangled over the back of a chair in the hall. The darkroom was bare and his twenty-by-eighteen study in disuse, like his secretary's office. The equipment was gone from the workroom across from the massive front door, including a movie projector set in place behind a hatch concealed by shelves of trinkets. One of the twin bedrooms in their master suite stood empty.

Some marks of the presence of the imaginative, inventive little man were impossible to expunge. He designed the center-piece display of seashells encircled by a towel rail in the white-and-coral master bathroom, as well as the smoke-extractor hood in the brown-tiled kitchen. The choice of Welsh slate and cut-down sidewalk paving for the hall floor was his. She pitched in, a butter-fingered amateur, when he took on the job of refinishing the mahogany double doors opening between drawing and dining rooms to trim the cost of renovations.

"Please remember this is not a wealthy house," he admonished their first, expendable butler, who imagined that only a wine cellar stocked with vintage stuff would satisfy the couple's tastes. Taking into account the incomes of some of the entrepreneurs, lords, and ladies eager for their company at the time, Tony was not to be corrected.

Of all the remembrances, his photographs were unique. They dated back to the start of their days together—Margaret imperious, Margaret joyful, then Margaret maternal against the pillow as she nestled their newborn son. If she thought about them, she could still grow teary and seek a shoulder for consolation.

The morning's newspapers had made uneasy reading. "What have our friends to say today?" was a standard opening as she thumbed through them. They were reluctant to let the embers cool after the fire storm ignited in March 1975, when England was officially informed that a royal marriage was breaking up. The like of it had never been heard in the country's history of sixty monarchs, starting with Egbert of Wessex, who made himself ruler over the seven warring kingdoms of the Anglo-Saxon age before his death in the year of our Lord 839.

Today's *Daily Mail*, anno Domini 1976, fanned the coals by identifying yet another "close friend" of Tony's. The newsroom staff had learned that Tony had a "film production assistant" with him for the six weeks he spent last year in Australia, shooting a television series for the British Broadcasting Corporation. Lucy Lindsay-Hogg, thirty-two-year-old daughter of an Irish clothing manufacturer, was a divorcée, and readers were left to conjure up their own visions of what all this implied.

Tony himself was house-hunting at present. He had told Savills, the agents, that he wanted "something not too grand," but his current earnings, more than £30,000 a year, made it possible to set a top price of £80,000. At the age of forty-six, he had not lost an iota of self-confidence in his ability to pay his way.

He needed, he said, four bedrooms, two baths, and two or three rooms "for entertaining"; he had a host of friends to welcome. A garage would be useful but not essential for his blue Volvo station wagon. The house could be rundown if it were otherwise suitable, as he had enjoyed freshening up Kensington Palace. He had already inspected half a hundred properties in his old haunts in Chelsea, Pimlico, and down-trodden Fulham, and even a few in Kensington, but nothing precisely right had come up yet.

A parting glance around the apartment before she faced the day lent reassurance to a woman of sentiment such as Margaret, clinging to the protective patterns of yesterday. The long, gray drawing room, whose windows overlooked the gardens, emanated a flavor of the past. The grand piano's polished top was arrayed with framed photographs—of herself; her sister; their surviving parent, the widowed Queen Mother Elizabeth; Margaret's children; her nephews and niece, Elizabeth's sons and daughter,. Charles, Anne, Andrew, and Edward. Once upon a time, Margaret enjoyed playing any piano by the hour and had been flattered to hear that, circumstance aside, she would probably have earned a place on concert platforms. That made for another wry remembrance.

The two sofas facing each other in front of the fireplace belonged to early married days; David and Sarah liked to sit on them with their books now. The portable bar was well supplied and the desk against one wall a. cluttered as ever, though her standards of neatness had improved. Elizabeth, on the other hand, who had been obsessively tidy as a girl, was somethi of a backslider; anyone who saw *her* desk knew that.

The summer had brought back to the apartment the young Welshman who was a target of almost unanimous accusation as the supposed case for the failure of Margaret's marriage. After Tony's leave-taking, Roddy Llewellyn had visited this room, personable, fair of skin and hair, twenty-eight years old. He had sat at table with Margaret, but not alone, in the lofty-ceilinged dining room, with its sedate Chippendale chairs and a neon strip above the carved, whitened chimneypiece shining down on a delicate, John Piper impression of Venice. In her memory, Venice belonged to the spring when she was eighteen, fulfilling one romantic fantasy of her life by being allowed four runaway weeks in Italy. There she was called *La Bella Margherita,* and mandolins plinked out serenades of "Santa Lucia." Roddy was out of range for the moment. He had gone to earth across the Welsh border on the country estate of his father, a fox-hunting man.

It was time to leave for Tidworth. Walking through the hall to the front door, heels clicking on the Welsh slate, took her past a favorite portrait. Pietro Annigoni, master painter and Florentine charmer, had completed it to the satisfaction of them both on his second try. In color as glowing as Titian's, he pictured a bareheaded peasant girl with sensuous, vigilant eyes, wearing a shawl across her shoulders.

Tidworth was picked up as spick-and-span as a barracks square. On both sides of the road that runs north and south through it, painted signs identified the offices, quarters, and depots of those units of the dwindling British Army that constituted the community's lifeblood. The road wound down to Salisbury, but sightseeing tours approached the cathedral there by an altogether different route from London, nearly a hundred miles away. Margaret would not be confronted with crowds of strangers today, only by spit-and-polished troopers on parade and hosed-down tanks in clattering exercise on Salisbury Plain, which stretches to the fringes of the town.

Arms and ammunition held no strong appeal for the colonel-in-chief. In her teens, she scoffed at male relatives who enjoyed one staple diversion for "popping horrid guns at silly birds." The army recommended itself to her principally then because it supplied attentive young officers as dancing partners. If she found pleasure on this excursion, it would be in her children's entertainment.

That was arranged for them on customary lines. Sarah donned denims from the quartermaster's stores and was hoisted in through a tank's turret "to take command." Equipped with goggles and a tankman's helmet with built-in intercom, David drove a twelve-ton Scorpion for a few dusty yards across the burned-out landscape under a sky gauzy with heat—"The Royal Action Kid," in the language of tomorrow's headline.

Tony would not have brought himself to joining in such a party, but Mother was doing her best in providing some fun for them. No cannon were fired, however, though a routine request on occasions like this was apt to be, "With permission, Ma'am, perhaps the children would like to have a go?" Margaret was content to leave the fireworks to more extroverted relatives like her niece Anne, colonel-in-chief of another tank regiment, the 14th/20th King's Hussars. Now *she* had shown her spunk by driving a fifty-six-ton Chieftain on a visit to West Germany and then let loose a burst from a Sterling submachinegun held tight against her hip.

"Even the best in the regiment could hardly do much better," said her loyal instructor.

When Tidworth was left behind to a parting snap of salutes, the day's work was done. Tomorrow would be less strenuous and probably more enjoyable. The one official engagement called for Margaret's presence at the Royal International Horse Show at the Empire Pool in the London suburb of Wembley, and she liked seeing experts on horseback. Thursday would be horsy and convenient, too, with no long trips in stuffy closed cars—a performance of the Royal Tournament at Earls Court. Nothing special was demanded on Friday, and after that the weekend would be hers.

Nobody could remember a summer like it. For weeks on end, unconscionable sunlight had baked the city streets. The wind scarcely breathed to dilute the reek of diesel smoke trailing blue from dusty red buses and nimble black taxicabs. In the parks, manicured trees shed yellow leaves and seared grass died at the roots. From the churches, prayers for remission ascended to the heavens. The heavens remained obstinately dry. This royal throne of kings, this sceptered isle, this normally green and pleasant land of England bore the look of somber blight.

London, which had seen no rain since May, was awash with foreigners, drawn as much by the weather as by the lowly state of the pound sterling, which made a cut-price bargain of everything bought for dollars or dinars, Deutsche marks, francs, or yen. Hotels, rooming houses, and youth hostels overflowed with guests, droves of them recruited by advertising placed in European newspapers, promoting cheap package tours to cash in on the benefits obtainable now that the strength of Britain's currency was fading fast.

"There's so much to see and do," exclaimed a British Tourist Board manual. "From the Changing of the Guard at Buckingham Palace, to the Crown Jewels in the Tower of London; from the bright lights of Piccadilly, or a seat at a West End play—to elegant Knightsbridge or a bargain-cluttered stall in Portobello market, London's attractions are endless!"

All day and every day, tour coaches with air brakes hissing inched their way through crawling traffic to unload their cargoes at the stellar attractions—Whitehall, Westminster Abbey, St. Paul's Cathedral, and a dozen other candles certain to lure the moths. Incoming hosts of visitors took command of the sidewalks along major arteries like Oxford Street, where store-window signs tempted shoppers in half a dozen languages, or filtered through side-street capillaries in search of a sweating policeman who might pull from a top pocket a heavily-thumbed directory and steer them to the next assembly point. Waiting patiently in line for a bus or a train ticket, natives of the city grumbled to each other that spoken English was becoming as rare as an angel choir in the surrounding babble of tongues.

The slow onset of evening reduced the temperature by only a few degrees. Crowds began to coagulate in the crisscross of avenues and alleyways around Piccadilly Circus. Neon flared on theater marquees, over the entrances of gambling casinos, at doorways leading down to clubs where ladies of the chorus cavorted between cramped tables in nothing more obscuring than mascara-clotted eyelashes and high heels, while tawny-hued customers watched as though they intended buying an extra wife or two to take home with them. "London," as the guidebook said, "is the place where it's all happening ... London switches on for everyone."

The turnover rate was phenomenal in the arenas of uninhibited entertainment. Seasoned Anglophiles, before setting out to dine, were wise to check whether the flux of change had affected even more demure establishments. Did famous movie people still patronize Mario Galetti's Caprice on Arlington Street? Had Margaret been into Quaglino's on Bury Street lately? Was Annabel's in Berkeley Square a place to be seen these days? Wasn't this disco, Tramp, on Jermyn Street supposed to be *trendy?*

On these brief July nights, it was almost dawn before the terminal skull-hammering blasted out from discotheque amplifiers and addicts left the last-to-be-closed of the hundred and more gaming houses to wave down a cab if they had money left over. Strollers who earlier had abandoned the attempt to sleep in airless rented rooms went back to try again before starting another day.

Not an hour of darkness passed without at least a handful of visitors ambling by the capital's focal enticement—the floodlit, ocher-walled pile of Buckingham Palace. A solitary policeman eyed them from behind the gilded spikes of the black railings. In the forecourt, guardsmen in red tunics, faces hidden under towering black bearskins, stamped to and fro between the sentry boxes. The convention stayed intact over the decades; some sergeant-majors had a habit of creeping out of bed to spy and see that punishment was meted out in the morning for any faltering in the nocturnal, cuckoo-clock performance.

A thin haze arose from the trees and lakes that bracketed the complex of buildings, Green Park to the north, St. James's Park on the east, and forty-five acres of the palace's own gardens behind it on the west. As soon as the sun came up again, the mist would be gone, and the first trickle of the daily flood of spectators would turn up to make sure of front-row positions to observe the rite of changing the guard.

Those who had studied the handbook knew that today they had no hope of catching a glimpse of Elizabeth. "When the Queen is in residence, the Royal Standard is flown at the masthead." The flagstaff was bare. Her Most Excellent Majesty Elizabeth, Queen of the United Kingdom of Great Britain and Northern Ireland and her other Realms and Territories, was off on a visit to what was possibly the most restless region in her entire domain. The French-Canadians of Qúebec, la Belle Province, seemed increasingly eager to be rid of her. In disco argot, "Brenda's gone to Montreal to open the Olympics, and Yvonne's doing more housework."

Pursuing a daily study of the Court Circular, which itemizes the public activities of the family and its upper branches, was a dilettante's pastime when the country had graver matters to consider. More men and women were out of work than had been in the last twenty years. Inflation was unchecked. Factory output faltered. A pound note was worth less than two dollars and seemed likely to drop by perhaps another fifty cents before the year was over. The Labor Government's majority in Parliament was precariously thin. Yet among most of the population a calm optimism prevailed. In general, the drought, which was drying out reservoirs and reducing rivers to sluggish streams, took precedence over all other topics of conversation.

Apart from the weather, the root cause of Britain's troubles was a chronic inability to make ends meet. There simply was not enough money around to pay for everything needed to restore health to the nation. The list of requirements abashed politicians of left and right alike. Welfare-state pensions, child benefits, medical programs, and unemployment allowances. Capital to launch new industries and retool old ones. Funds to satisfy foreign creditors anxious to close out their sterling bank balances before the situation worsened. Cash to meet the Arabs' escalated bills for fuel oil until the miraculous day when underwater wells in the North Sea began pumping nearer capacity. Outlays, never big enough in American opinion, to keep the North Atlantic Treaty Organization up to par. Interest due on an ever growing mountain of debt.

Survival depended on borrowing ever more money. Already the government was adding to the mountain at a rate approaching £19 billion a year, while the average month saw goods imported from overseas costing some £230 million more than British exports sold there. Levying blame for the doleful state of affairs was sport for both prim Mrs. Margaret Thatcher's Tory Party and bluff Mr. James Callaghan's Socialists. One accused labor of greed and idleness, the other charged management with greed and ineptitude. Neither had any clear-cut solution with which to entice the voters.

One of the few things both sides agreed on was that from here on in, every citizen would be obliged to put in a solid day's work for every day's pay. Belts must be notched tight while the country tried to hoist itself by the bootstraps. Britain had no alternative to starting to live within its means.

Should this automatically include the royal family? There was no immediate answer. The question itself was seldom asked outside a small group of anti-monarchists whose mouthpiece was Willie Hamilton, Scottish gadfly, author, and leftist Member of Parliment. The idea of staging a referendum to assess the popularity of Elizabeth and her relatives was unthinkable except to these few. But since only money and its spending would decide the fate of the country, there was increasing interest in just what was the price of maintaining the extraordinary beings whose lives, in the words of one bleak critic, amounted to no more than "comic relief to the death rattle of a nation."

The arithmetic, like the behavior of the Soviet Union as Sir Winston Churchill regarded it, was a riddle wrapped in a mystery inside an enigma. Most members of Elizabeth's court knew more about the Holy Roman Empire than about cost accounting. Comprehensive figures disclosing Elizabeth's finances had never been published, and they were not going to be supplied now. Immediately after Margaret's expedition to Tidworth, her sister let slip a rare clue in a single word.

In lieu of the personal interview he was seeking with Elizabeth, a Canadian columnist named Jim Proudfoot was invited by palace officials to submit written questions and promise to let them vet his typescript when it was completed. One of the several changes made before the article was returned came from her own fastidious hand. He had referred to her as "the richest woman in the world." She amended that by inserting "probably." It was remotely possible that Queen Juliana of the Netherlands deserved the description. Her tax-free allowance of $1,300,000 a year did not compare with

Elizabeth's $3,500,000, but the House of Orange *did* own a hunk of Royal Dutch-Shell, and who knew what that was worth at current oil prices? The best estimates put Juliana's private fortune at $12,000,000, Elizabeth's at "probably" more.

The last detailed calculation by an outsider of the British monarchy's operating expenses was half a dozen years old. It was computed then that they ran as high as an annual $21,000,000, and inflation must have increased the tally. The government paid for the upkeep of the enormous castle at Windsor and the Scottish estates of Balmoral and Holyroodhouse. Besides Buckingham Palace, the most expensive royal residence in the world, the taxpayers were responsible for three more—Kensington Palace; St. James's, offering living space for members of the Household; and Hampton Court, providing more rent-free housing for some three dozen people. The total bill for taking care of the real estate was roughly $3,000,000 a year and rising, causing Elizabeth constantly to dip into her own resources to contribute part of the cost.

The royal yacht *Britannia*, which was carrying the Queen home across the Atlantic, was a $3,000,000-a-year perquisite, half the length of the liner *Queen Elizabeth II* and having a complement of 230 navy men. Elizabeth was provided with a flight of half a dozen private planes and helicopters, flown and serviced by the Royal Air Force, as well as a fleet of automobiles and two royal trains, painted regal purple, with twelve specially designed coaches, including a playroom with bathtub for her younger children.

Her art collection, one of the finest in existence, might at a guess fetch $150,000,000 were it to be offered item by item at auction, but the idea of its disposal was preposterous. Like every other British sovereign, she paid no income taxes or Customs duty on any gift, and she inherited her fortune clear of death duty. Most of it would be passed on in the same condition to Charles, her heir, whose present income of $300,000 was also free of tax.

In contrast with these splendrous rates of pay, Margaret was a poor relation, held on a short financial string. Her state allowance of $70,000 was fully taxable after deductions for expenses, which were unlikely to be questioned by Her Majesty's Department of Inland Revenue.

Britain's family of super-royals cost more than all the other monarchies of Europe put together—Belgium, Denmark, Norway, Spain, and Sweden—according to one Welsh Member of Parliament. Only a minority of Britons bothered about the arithmetic. It was a safe bet that most of those, if asked, would agree that Elizabeth was scrupulous in earning her keep—and that most more and more openly wondered whether the same was true of Margaret.

As soon as Elizabeth arrived back in Buckingham Palace, she worked overtime to catch up with the backlog of work that had accumulated while she was in North America. The closing days of July found her in full swing. Students of the Court Circular could cite that quaint document as proof that she deserved every penny of her income.

Tuesday, July 27. The Queen, Sovereign of the Most Distinguished Order of St. Michael and St. George, this morning attended the Annual Service of the Order in St. Paul's Cathedral ... The Queen gave an Afternoon Party in the Garden of Buckingham Palace ... The Right Honorable James Callaghan, Prime Minister and First Lord of the Treasury, had an audience of Her Majesty this evening.

Margaret was off duty that day. In fact, now that her sister was back, the controvertible little princess had one formal job to perform in the remainder of the week; she opened a hostel for the physically handicapped in faraway Cornwall. Elizabeth maintained the queenly pace. She held an investiture in the palace ballroom, a species of prize day which involved her hanging medals on some of those named on her birthday honors list and giving a deft tap with a sword on each shoulder of others who knelt on a cushioned stool for the more spectacular reward of knighthood.

In chronological order, she received ceremonial kisses on the right hand from a newly appointed ambassador to Damascus, a new high commissioner from New Zealand, a new ambassador to Budapest, and a new high commissioner to Sierra Leone. A new bishop did homage to her as temporal head of the Church of England. She took her two youngest, Andrew and Edward, to see the Royal Tournament and, making the most of the persistent fair weather, had a thousand or so more guests in for tea, sandwiches, and cake at another garden party. Mr. Callaghan's second-in-command, white-maned Michael Foot of the fervent left wing of the Labor Party, came in for a private talk before he trailed her into a council meeting at which the Head of State was brought up to date on the country's frustrated affairs by three more elected Ministers of the Crown.

One not altogether surprising reason for Margaret's dearth of employment was a scarcity of invitations. She was merely second-best choice for dedicating hospitals, laying foundation stones, planting trees, and the rest of those civic occasions where the principal's role was reserved for a royal. Requests for Elizabeth's attendance, on the other hand, inundated the palace, always far too many to be filled. Senior staff there admitted to embarrassment that so few institutions asked for the services of Margaret.

She had left a poor impression at some events she patronized. Royal Windsor, for example, the town that prides itself on being the Queen's real home, recalled a public dinner that Margaret attended. She wore what the burghers' wives considered to be an *unsuitable* green dress with matching shoes and handbag; on occasions like these, a princess' clothes were expected to be decorous rather than dashing. Aloof at the top table, she ate nothing apart from nibbling on a roll. She dismayed the traditionalists by lighting a cigarette before the toast was drunk, "Her Majesty the Queen!" Such a contrast, the citizens clucked, to Prince Charles, who was as friendly as could be when he was the honored guest and joked about marrying an Arabian princess to ease the country's financial bind!

A sergeant of the local constabulary commented, "She's always been the same, spoiled and selfish. I remember us getting a call early one morning when she was staying at Blenheim Palace. They had us send squad cars to shine their headlights on the croquet lawn. She and the rest of them wanted a game before beddy-byes."

At an Oxford dinner party, when the talk turned to Margaret, an indignant wife exploded, "She behaves like a tart. The way she carries on hurts our queen. That sister of hers fails to do her duty. If she insists on acting like a commoner, she ought to abdicate and find herself a decent job."

"What do you suggest she might become—an office temporary?"

"Anything! Or else nothing, like the riffraff she mixes with!"

When she was seventeen, an American magazine called Margaret "Britain's number one item for public scrutiny" and added, "People are more interested in her than in the House of Commons or the dollar crisis." Mothers named their babies after her. Teenage girls copied her clothes, the ankle-strap shoes she wore, and her hairdos. After she visited Canada, a Toronto newspaper editorialized, "This gay child, who was rightly called the Sweetheart of the Commonwealth, has grown into womanhood without losing the charm of her youth."

She had once been a national darling. At present, she was the most vilified woman in England, under attack as heavy as Wallis Simpson suffered when Uncle David abandoned his throne to marry her. If Margaret puzzled over how she fell from grace, she could find part of the explanation in a highly improbable quarter, something once said by Clark Gable to David Niven, whom she rated equally as movie actors.

"We all have a contract with the public," Gable explained. "In us they see themselves as what they would like to be ... We are the standards by which they measure their own ideals of everything—sex, guts, honor, stupidity, cowardice, crummi-ness—you name it. They love to put us on a pedestal and worship us—form fan clubs and write thousands of letters telling us how great we are.

"But they've read the small print, and most of us haven't—they expect us to pay the price for it all ... We have to get it in the end ... that's the payoff, the public feels satisfied."

She was a product, like the rest of us, of her years on earth, of her income, and of humanity's groping for happiness. What were the special circumstances in her case, the setting, the events, the successes, and defeats that turned a jubilant childhood into soured middle age?

The search for answers would need to take into account her ancestry. "Of course," one weekend host of hers once said, "you must remember she's a Hanoverian." Her health would be an inevitable factor, the illnesses she'd had and the treatment for them, though the records were confidential. Indeed some of the family's records had been destroyed in the past. The men she felt drawn toward—father, husband, and admirers—

could provide a clue. Looking for other intangibles would be a job of detection, weighing up the significance of her moodiness, for one thing, against details like the makeup she applied.

Was the hostility that surrounded her justifiable? Well, as things turned out, not exactly.

II

A Family Business

She was more than two weeks overdue for the first of all her appearances. The doctors had anticipated the birth any time after August 6. Here it was the twentieth, and the serene little duchess was not yet in labor. The delay seemed to bother her less than any of those attending her. Her only other child had been late, too, though not to this extent. Her first daughter, who was to be christened Elizabeth Alexandra Mary in honor of her mother, great-grandmother, and grandmother respectively, had been delivered without mishap.

The baby Elizabeth's parents had wondered whether "Victoria" should be included in the list, too, for good luck, since the departed queen's reign had seen England at its peak of power. When they consulted the baby's grandfather, the regnant King George V, he ruled this to be quite unnecessary. After all, Victoria, who was *his* grandmother, had been gone to glory for almost a quarter of a century. So many descendants had been named for her that adding another could increase the confusion he abhorred.

The duchess' first-born, an April child, was now four years old. For reasons of sentiment, and for lack of a house to call her own in London, the young mother had chosen the home of her parents, the Strathmores, for her confinement. The Georgian mansion at No. 17 Bruton Street, near Berkeley Square, would one day be converted into a branch of the First National City Bank of New York.

If the baby turned out to be a boy, he would rank third in line of succession for the crown. The father, Bertie, Duke of York, held second place, following behind his older, bachelor brother, Uncle David, the king's eldest son. The law of primogeniture, which prevailed in the land, assured David, Prince of Wales, the primary right of inheritance. The genealogical aspects of the delivery demanded the personal attention of Home Secretary "Jix," otherwise Sir William Joynson-Hicks. He had proved his evangelical mettle in a recent coal miners' strike by clapping twelve Communists into prison under the Incitement to Mutiny Act, passed in 1797.

With an underling, he showed up on Bruton Street soon after breakfast. He must satisfy himself in accordance with tradition that royal blood lines were not tampered with and that there was no hanky-panky such as, legend had it, when a changeling son of James II was spirited into his mother's bed in a warming pan.

Jix mounted guard within call of the duchess' bedroom all day with time off only for lunch and dinner. At 2:40 the following morning, the vigil turned out to be largely futile. The birth of Princess Elizabeth still left the king without a grandson in the line of succession. Thirty-two-year-old David had been sought out by any number of willing young ladies at home and on his travels, but he had disentangled himself from all of them except one exemplar of constancy in London, and he shied away from marriage.

This time, King George trusted his daughter-in-law to do

right by him and his heritage. *First a girl, and then a boy* had proved to be the case with his mother, Alexandra, and grandmother Victoria, which was enough to make it a royal tradition. The Duchess of York could always be counted on as a conscientious wife and mother. From everything he heard, she and his son had not even considered names for a girl, they felt such confidence in the outcome.

As the days of inaction passed, Bertie had a second reason for concern besides worry over his wife. His father, a stickler for discipline, was not accustomed to being kept waiting. "My father was frightened of his mother," the king boasted, "I was frightened of my mother, and I'm damned well going to see that my children are frightened of me."

The "safety first" Conservative government of pipe-puffing Stanley Baldwin had been out of office for more than a year this August, and Jix had departed with it. The Socialists were back with the golden-tongued Scot, Ramsay MacDonald, as Prime Minister and a new Home Secretary in John Robert Clynes, a one-time mill hand as cautious as Baldwin himself. His was a ticklish job when last October's collapse on Wall Street had hit British exports hard. More than two million British unemployed threatened to stir unrest in the factory towns and set off protest marches to harass Parliament.

The Home Secretary had been hoping that the duchess would want to have her baby in the house at No. 145 Piccadilly, which had been provided on a crown lease for the Yorks after Elizabeth's birth. The duchess, another Scot, had a contrary idea. She would go to Glamis Castle in the county of Angus, Scotland, the home of her family, the Bowes-Lyons, since the fourteenth century, with a history dating back to William the Conqueror. In the interests of primogeniture, Mr. Clynes would have to be on hand there, too.

He took a train north on August 4, which chanced to be the duchess' thirtieth birthday—Bertie was five years older. If

Mr. Clynes expected to have a room provided in the castle, he was disappointed. The country had known only one other Labor government before the present MacDonald team. At the apex of society, Socialists took a lot of getting used to. Though the monarch was not supposed to dabble in politics in any form, he could obviously be selective in the choice of politicians whom he found congenial, and his family accepted his judgments.

Like most people who had dealings with the man, George discovered that his namesake Mr. Lansbury, lowly but influential First Commissioner of Works, was the most lovable of the group. The king and the pacifist commoner who had once edited the pink-hued, poverty-stricken *Daily Herald* liked to swap stories about their health problems when they met.

Tense, terrier-like Mr. Clynes had less winning ways than George Lansbury. "If there have to be gentlemen waiting outside my bedroom door, I hope it's someone we know," the duchess had hinted. He was not to be balked in carrying out his duty, but he would be put up eight miles away in the pocket-sized castle bearing the family name of old Lady Airlie, a good friend of the duchess' mother-in-law, Queen Mary.

His hostess kept him well fed on trout freshly hooked from nearby streams, game pies, and home-made scones while he waited. The ceremonial secretary who had accompanied him, the same civil servant who had stood by for Elizabeth's birth, had become so jumpy by the fourteenth of the month that he begged his master not to leave Airlie Castle lest they miss a sudden summons to the duchess' bedroom door.

By the twentieth, the secretary was so tense that he declined to go to bed that night. News of the baby's reluctance to emerge had brought sightseers to the remote, rural scene. The Home Secretary, with his professional eyes peeled for trouble, noted, "The estate had to be put almost into a state of siege, and some of the sensation-mongering tourists were roughly treated by the dour tenantry." They'd had bonfires built for days, ready for the torch as a welcome for the newborn bairn.

On the evening of the twenty-first, the call came over the strand of telephone cable strung between Glamis and Airlie. The duchess was in labor at last. Mr. Clynes and amanuensis set off helter-skelter in a police car as the sun sank behind piled black banks of storm clouds. They had twenty minutes to linger downstairs while Sir Henry Simpson, the obstetrician, completed his task.

To the roll of thunder, rain began hissing on the weather-beaten tiles of the roof, and lightning flickered around the turrets. Glamis, where Macbeth slew Duncan to steal the Scottish crown and the murderer's wife found her hands perpetually spotted with blood, was the most celebrated of Britain's half-hundred haunted castles.

Mr. Clynes was asked into the billiard room, where Bertie stood with his mother-in-law, the Countess of Strathmore, more doctors, and nurses. The king might feel let down again by the outcome of the evening, but the stalwart man of Labor was stirred by his ritualistic peek at the six-pound eleven-ounce infant, "wide-open eyes looking with apparent interest at the strange new world," as he noted later with more tenderness than medical plausibility. In sight of the bedroom windows, the bonfires spluttered in the storm.

"Yesterday evening at twenty-two minutes after nine o'clock," said the next morning's bulletin, "Her Royal Highness the Duchess of York was safely delivered of a Princess." Her names could not be mentioned, since she had none.

The Times of London under its latest proprietor, the American John Astor, took pride in speaking for England's top people. Its self-preening editor, Geoffrey Dawson, drew information from the highest places. He may have heard rumblings from Buckingham Palace when he composed the editorial that said, "There will be some natural disappointment that the baby is a girl and not a boy, but she is nevertheless sure of a loving welcome." The tenantry at Glamis, less dour now that the siege was over, recalled a tradition which held that a girl born in the castle was sure to be a bride before she reached twenty.

Bertie was hesitant about getting in touch with his father, whose temper was notoriously short. Instead, he dashed off an anxious note to his mother, aiming to calm the situation. "I do hope that you and Papa are as delighted as we are to have a granddaughter, or would you sooner had a grandson? I know Elizabeth wanted a daughter ..."

The duchess concentrated on finding names for the baby that might meet with Papa's approval, disgruntled or otherwise. She was an easygoing woman, stronger in character than her husband and less in awe of his father, a full-blooded martinet. He more than anyone else was responsible for Bertie's nervous stammer, which sometimes made his words hard to understand. Psychologists would trace the defect to his father's insistence that his left-handed son be compelled to learn penmanship with his right.

The king, whose own letters had the look of a schoolboy's, set great store by the appearance of words on paper. "For goodness' sake, teach Margaret and Lilibet to write a decent hand, that's all I ask you," he would boom at the girls' governess. "Not one of my children can write properly. They all do it exactly the same way. I like a hand with some character in it."

He also had knock-knees, which Bertie inherited. Papa's remedy was to have his son's legs clamped in steel braces, causing such pain that his tears on some days made lessons impossible. The frail, browbeaten boy would meekly apologize for his weakness to his parent.

"Ann" was the first choice of the duchess, when her daughter was almost a week old. It "sounds pretty" was the reason she gave her mother-in-law. The king's voice was raised in disagreement. That had not been a royal name for more than two hundred years. The queen who bore it (spelled with a final "e") was a Stuart, the last of them before the first Hanoverian George took over in 1714. The Stuart queen had been a ninny, too, by all accounts, content to be kept under the thumb of Sarah Churchill. His granddaughter must have something more fitting.

The duchess, convalescing in Glamis, was open to suggestions. Scottish kinfolk pressed for "Margaret," a designation of their country's queens almost until the time when an earlier Stuart, James VI of Scotland, became James I of England in 1603 and celebrated himself as the first king of a united Great Britain. "But it has no family links really on either side," the duchess, an indifferent student of history, told her mother-in-law.

The trim-bearded king and his poker-straight queen descended on the castle to inspect their anonymous granddaughter on the ninth day of her life. At this season of the year, the calendar called for them to be in residence at Balmoral, the mock-Gothic castle built to the designs of Victoria's German husband, Albert of Saxe-Coburg-Gotha, the prince consort. Stag roamed as targets in eighty thousand acres of Scottish highland that made up the estate. Wallpaper inside was still embossed with her "VRI" cipher.

The duchess continued to ask approval for "Ann," but Papa would not hear of it. A name, in his unbending opinion, was a kind of talisman. Now "George" fitted a king like a crown. All but one predecessor of his own sex in the House of Hanover who occupied the British throne had been a George. He was fortunate in having been so christened and known always by the name within the family. Of course, interests of expediency sometimes made a change advisable. For instance, his father, Albert Edward, had been called "Bertie" all his life until his mother, Victoria, died, and he succeeded her. He could quite properly have been King Albert I. The excuse he gave for choosing instead to be Edward VII was that there could be only one Albert, his father, bequeathed to history. Recollections of the merciless badgering he suffered from both parents may also have played a part in the decision.

Royals, like the rest of the aristocracy, did not question the fact that their titles would be transformed as one generation replaced another. The death of the father could turn a viscount into an earl or an earl into a duke just as it could elevate a prince into a king. George V had gone one better. From his father, he acquired the identification of Saxe-Coburg-Gotha, a territory of Mitteleuropa no bigger than an English county. It had a disastrously Teutonic ring after the outbreak of war in 1914 brought on a boycott of dachshunds among British loyalists and an epidemic of brickbats thrown through windows of shops carrying German names. An ancient courtier who had served Victoria suggested "Windsor" as a substitution. George liked the sound and symbolism of that. Parliament approved, and before peace was declared, he and his offspring had acquired a brand-new name.

The duchess was not concerned with the past; only with coming up with something appropriate that, for one thing, would clear up the confusion in the mind of four-year-old Lilibet, who had to refer to the newcomer as "baby sister." Time as well as patience was running out. Under penalty of Scottish law, the birth must be registered no later than September 11. The duchess made her own, independent choice. Her husband went along with her in commemorating her closest sister, Rose, even though her name had nothing dynastic about it.

"Bertie and I," his wife informed his mother, cutting off

further debate, "have decided now to call our little daughter *Margaret Rose* ... I hope that you like it. I think that it is very pretty together."

Clocks and calendars received no more than a nod from the duchess. She was chronically late for most appointments and relied on a sunny smile to avoid trouble. The September 11 time limit slipped by. She was not so much above the law as out of touch with it. Not before the last day of the month was the registrar of births and deaths brought to the castle from his village store, source of cigarettes, tobacco, newspapers, confectionery and souvenir postcards. Strictly speaking, Margaret had been a non-person until then.

The baby and bubble-curled Lilibet were in the care of the same stately nanny who had looked after Mummy when she was small. Mrs. Clara Cooper Knight was in command now that the monthly nurse had departed. She was a farmer's daughter, one of an already vanishing species, the servant class prepared to subordinate their existence to a master and mistress. The upbringing of the two sisters would be more her doing than their parents'. She was level-headed and loving, which was their good luck. Tales abounded in the family of childhood terror at the hands of tyrants who pinched and slapped and locked a young charge in a closet for infringing the rules.

What to call her presented the usual, chronic problem between the highborn and the low. "Clara" would be altogether too cosy, "Knight" too stiff for a surrogate mother. The happy solution came by accident from Elizabeth, whose trouble in pronouncing her own name led to "Lilibet." "Clara" emerged as "Alah," which was how this nanny was always addressed. Nicknames were *such* a convenience.

She carried the ten-week-old child into the private chapel of Buckingham Palace for her christening. The robe of cream-colored silk and Honiton lace in which she was enfolded was

ninety years old, another talisman after its first use for
Victoria's baby daughter in 1840. The water poured into the
gold-plated font was imported from the River Jordan in
Palestine, where a halt to Jewish immigration had just been
ordered by the London government. Cosmo Gordon Lang,
Archbishop of Canterbury, who worshipped tradition as he
did God, sprinkled the princess' forehead.

Her grandparents were there, but Uncle David's youngest
brother, George, stood in for him. Slender, golden-haired
David had a conflicting engagement. The following month, at ·
a weekend house party in the fox-and-hounds country of
Melton Mowbray, he would come across a lean, witty, wide-
mouthed American, Mrs. Ernest Simpson, who earned more of
his attention.

One woman in the chapel found it hard to smile. The
king's youngest sister, another Victoria, aged sixty-two, had
no husband; she would die without one five years later. Their
mother, Alexandra, had kept Toria on hand as a glorified
ladies' maid, scurrying to answer the tinkling of a bell
whenever she was wanted. Lord Rosebery, a millionaire
widower who was briefly Prime Minister, was eager for
Toria's hand. Alexandra set her foot down: her daughter could
not be spared at home.

The Royal Marriages Act, which constituted the final word
on the subject, dated back to the reign of the third George. He
conceived it in anger after two of his sons scandalized him by
taking commoners as brides. "No descendant of George II,"
declared the 1772 statute, "shall be capable of contracting
matrimony without the previous consent of the King, and
signified under the Great Seal, declared in Council, and
entered in the Privy Council books."

Without permission in writing for their marriage, a prince
or princess forfeited all rights of succession personally and for
their children and simultaneously had all income and al-

lowances from the state cut off. An earlier law, the Act of Settlement of 1701, passed after priests were burned at the stake in religious warring, stipulated that any royal convert to Catholicism or any royal who married a Catholic lost all claim to the throne. Bloodlines of sovereigns must be kept unsullied, Protestant, and preferably noble. It limited the field unless cousins united as man and wife, but there was no shortage of cousins. Victoria the queen had borne nine children. Her thirty-four grandsons and granddaughters had married into most of the reigning houses in Europe.

Toria was too docile and her mother too possessive for Rosebery to press his suit. Consent was never asked from the throne. Toria's melancholy wore itself out eventually, but she hovered on the fringes of the family as an example of an unfulfilled maiden aunt.

No. 145 Piccadilly stood in a row of tall, narrow, stone-fronted mansions, backed by Hamilton Gardens, which were planted with sooty shrubs and boasted a murky lake where mallards nested, undisturbed by the buzz of traffic passing outside the iron-railed forecourt that led to the front door. From the gardens, a gate opened into Hyde Park. When the weather was warm enough, Alah gave her baby an airing in a pram that had been Elizabeth's.

Indoors, Alah ruled the nursery world on the fourth, top floor. It consisted of two rooms, one on the sunny front of the house, in which a coal fire glowed behind a wire-mesh guard, hung with drying diapers and baby's underwear. There, baby was tubbed and towelled before bedtime. The children slept in a quieter room, at the back, decorated in Mummy's favorite pink and beige. They could see the park through the windows.

The glass-domed center landing provided stable space for Elizabeth's toy horses. There were about thirty in all before relatives in doubt about what she might like best for

Christmas or a birthday stopped adding to the collection. A maxim respected among the upper classes held that at the onset of adolescence a girl's fancy for boys could be curbed by buying her a pony to care for. Young Elizabeth cottoned on to horses of her own accord.

She was taught to share everything with her doll-like sister, including the stuffed animals on four wheels, which had to be unsaddled, fed, and watered every night. Horses seemed somehow to be an obscure part of being royal. Her father and most of her relations were devoted to them. They pulled the carriage that Grandpapa sometimes ordered to be driven over from the Buckingham Palace mews to give his granddaughters a unique outing.

Elizabeth's enthusiasm was contagious. As soon as Margaret could propel herself, she would follow Elizabeth to the day nursery window on winter afternoons to push her snub nose against the glass and stare down at Piccadilly. A brewer's dray on its daily rounds, drawn by a pair of Clydesdales with nostrils steaming, usually pulled up by a traffic light below. The sight of a scrubby pony dragging a costermonger's cart was a mixed pleasure. Elizabeth wondered whether the creature would slip on a wet street. Could it expect a feed of oats? Where would it sleep that night?

From the back windows, they could see Rotten Row. Generations of lords and ladies had ridden there, but these days the tan bark between the wooden railings attracted more humdrum folk on rented hacks. "If I am ever queen," Elizabeth told her sister, "I shall make a law that there must be no riding on Sundays. Horses should have a rest, too."

Buxom Alah was a graduate of downstairs, servant society, which was an exaggerated, pinchbeck copy of the upstairs hierarchy. As a senior, privileged member of a duke's household, she was above boiling diapers, stoking fires, or fetching trays. The menial tasks were left to the undernurse, who had been handed on to the duchess by a fellow Scot, the Marchioness of Linlithgow.

Margaret MacDonald, a lively redhead in her early twenties, was a railroad worker's child, her home a three-roomed cottage in the Black Isle in Inverness. As an apprentice chambermaid in a modest hotel, she had originally taken home six shillings a week in pay. She did not earn a great deal more at present but she felt more than compensated as Elizabeth became more and more her responsibility while Alah gave her time to the baby.

There was already a *Mrs.* MacDonald in the household, the cook, known as "Golly." Once again, Elizabeth's prattle solved any difficulty of identification. The undernurse took her to play hide-and-seek in Hamilton Gardens, calling "boo!" to the child from behind the bushes. "Boo! boo!" she would answer, clapping her hands. Miss MacDonald was henceforth only "Bobo."

Her elevation as companion for Elizabeth called for hiring another girl to do minion's work in the nursery. Bobo recommended her sixteen-year-old sister, Ruby, another redhead, whom the duchess promptly engaged. Perhaps because she ranked so far down the scale that she seldom came within the orbit upstairs society, Ruby escaped being labeled with a nickname.

Bertie, his wife, and their two children were waited on by a platoon of servants. Ainslie, the butler, had an assistant, and Golly her three kitchenmaids. There were housemaids, a valet, a chauffeur, and a living-in telephone operator, all paid at Victorian rates, while workers who held on to jobs in the world outside were better off than they had ever been.

But the king himself, a Victorian at heart, set the pattern for most of his family. His father had been a roué with an

insatiable appetite for food, cigars, and women. He had tried
to blow away some of the cobwebs that accumulated around
the court and adjust to the era of change that replaced horses
with automobiles and made factory owners millionaires.
Edward VII opened palace doors to Jews and gambled with
the new rich. He felt such alarm in the process that he spoke
of his son George as "the last king of England."

Once George was enthroned, he set out to protect his
position from further perilous erosion by reverting to
Grandma's style of living. Respect must be restored for the
monarch, with none of the nonsense of racetrack crowds
milling around, yelling "Good old Teddy!" George preferred
to enjoy orderly, well-staffed comfort like a captain retired
from the sea. His arguments with David arose largely because
his son evidently took after his grandfather in his taste for
novelty and frivolous amusement. His travels overseas as a sort
of salesman for British industry were all very well, and
perhaps darting about all over the place at home *did* make him
popular, but it was so damnably undignified. "You must
remember your position," George told him, but David refused
to listen.

Bertie was much more dutiful. He would not balk at being
sent to Canada as governor-general, the king's permanent
representative in that dominion, where the post was open and
he was favored for it. Margaret and her sister were spared
growing up in the forbidding residence in Ottawa because
John Henry Thomas, once a locomotive driver and currently
Dominions Secretary, was cool to the idea.

Canadians, he insisted, "don't want a royalty." They were
physically too close to the United States, and they prided
themselves on being as democratic in spirit as their neighbors
below the border. "I cannot believe that this is true," sniffed
Sir Clive Wigram, a courtier due to be promoted to Privy

Councillor, but the Ottawa appointment went to Vere Brabazon, Earl of Bessborough.

By way of consolation, the king offered Bertie a country home, the first for the Yorks, when Margaret was one year old. Royal Lodge was built as a shooting box in Windsor Great Park by the Prince Regent, destined to be the fourth of the Georges. He moved in when the great castle itself was converted into a glorified lunatic asylum for his father, the third George, judged insane by every physician who attended him and bound in a straitjacket. George IV continued to live in the lodge as king, secluded and safe from abuse by the laboring classes, who detested him.

Eighteen years and a fortune were spent on "improvements," which went to waste when his brother William succeeded him and had most of the fanciful edifice demolished out of spite. The dilapidated gray-stucco shell had lately housed the manager of the fifth George's racehorses. Bertie, however, could envisage getting the place fixed up as a happy retreat for his wife and daughters.

"It is too kind of you to have offered us Royal Lodge," he told his father. "I think it will suit us admirably." Where the necessary money was coming from to foot the contractors' bills remained to be seen in these hard times.

"Devotion" was the word that best described the feelings of this diffident man toward his children and his wife, "the most marvelous person in the world in my eyes." If he could prevent it, Margaret and Elizabeth would never know the misery of his own childhood. As a junior prince, he was not short of unoccupied time to spend with them on most days. Like their mother, he favored neither one above the other, though the older girl showed signs of developing his kind of sobriety and her giggly sister had more of Mummy's nature. What he wanted for them was happiness, which he had not found until he married.

One thing more was essential to protect them. So long as David stayed single, only two lives, his and Bertie's, stood between Elizabeth and the throne, three in the case of Margaret, who had the shielding of her sister. Accidents had happened before, the last to their grandfather, who would not have been king but for the death of his older brother Eddy six days short of his twenty-eighth birthday. Pneumonia was announced as the cause, but the swan-necked prince, jeered at as "Collars and Cuffs," was notorious for debauchery both with women and boy prostitutes. Syphilis may have been a contributory factor. In the following year, George married May of Teck, to whom Eddy had been engaged. Nowadays, she made the country a most upright queen.

Alah was obsessed with thoughts of her darling coming to harm. She confined Margaret to the pram well past her second birthday. Margaret's first recollection was of the uproar that ensued the day she fell out. "I must have wanted to be noticed." When she would put up with the indignity no longer and Alah lost her last baby to push, the pram was stored away along with the beribboned crib and the basket in which she had been toted from room to room. The nanny persisted in spoon-feeding her, though she could handle the business herself. Some people who knew the Yorks gained the firm impression that husband and wife were planning to have another child and praying for their daughters' sake that it would be a son. That was possibly a further reason for the king's regard for Bertie.

The cross-grained old man was far from being a doting grandfather. Visits with the two children were limited, which was no hardship to anyone. The younger of them was barely eighteen months old when an entry in his meticulously maintained diary indicated the order of importance he set at one meeting: "Lilibet and Margaret came after luncheon. My new little cairn, Bob, was fairly friendly to them."

Bertie was anxious for Royal Lodge to be made habitable, so that the girls had a place of their own to escape to and breathe fresher air than in Hamilton Gardens. The builders' pace was dismally slack. At weekends, he and the duchess would drive their daughters down to Windsor along with Alah and Bobo to picnic in the overgrown gardens and check on what little had been achieved inside the house. He took a hand at hacking away at the wilderness of shubbery. Elizabeth helped the chauffeur tend the fire. Margaret watched her, bundled up in a blanket and installed at least once in a baby carriage Bobo had borrowed from a willing neighbor.

Work went slowly because cash was tight. England was locked into what politicians mistook for a financial crisis. The American depression had infected the world. More Britons were out of work than ever, and their numbers kept climbing. Prime Minister MacDonald was convinced that capitalism itself had broken down.

One newcomer to Parliament confounded his fellow Laborites by publishing a masterly plan for a new deal that anticipated what Franklin Delano Roosevelt was to attempt later in the United States. Sir Oswald Mosley, a rich radical, called for government direction of production, cuts in imports, and massive injections of borrowed money to restore health to industry. When MacDonald rejected his proposals, Mosley quit in disgust to found the New Party, which would shortly be debased into the blackshirted British Union of Fascists, aping the Mussolini model in Italy. Uncle David was intrigued by what he knew of Mosley's thinking.

Margaret was not quite twelve months old when London bankers warned MacDonald that the country was "on the verge of the precipice." The run on the pound threatened to be ungovernable. Frantic foreigners were selling out their sterling holdings, certain that Britain was fated to suffer like post-war Germany, where a pound note would buy 19,000,-000 marks.

Deficits on the fund for relief to the unemployed were creeping up toward the level of £1,000,000 a week. For the moment, this could be reckoned as $4,860,000 precisely. Britain and the western world still clung to gold as a fetish, employing it as the standard measure of one currency's value against the rest, and one pound equaled $4.86.

The Cabinet began four days of writhing on the eve of Margaret's first birthday. A ten per cent reduction in out-of-work benefits was mandatory if the pound was to be saved. but nine of the twenty Ministers rejected this Draconian solution. MacDonald tendered his resignation to the king on August 24.

It was not accepted. The next morning, George commissioned him to form a National Government of all three major parties—Socialists, Tories, and Liberals—with Stanley Baldwin back as Lord President. Churchill was left in the cold. Baldwin had him down as his arch-rival for the Tory leadership.

Britain was tossed into turmoil. Alarmists feared that class warfare was about to erupt. Montagu Norman, trim-bearded governor of the Bank of England, was not to be satisfied unless ration books were printed against the day the pound went the way of the mark and hungry Britons had to barter their household goods for food to eat.

An emergency budget was drawn by Philip Snowden, the whey-faced Welsh Laborite who as Chancellor of the Exchequer was every bit as orthodox as Norman. The unemployed had their benefits lopped as prescribed. And everyone paid from state funds, from the royals down to the lowest ranks of the armed forces, suffered a ten per cent cut, too

Demonstrators had started rallying in city streets, chanting

"For the king a crown, for the workers half-a-crown" (then sixty cents) when George told Bertie, "I am going to give up the shooting in Windsor Park as I can't afford it."

Bertie's own sacrifices included an end to riding with the Pytchley hounds. "It has come as a great shock to me," he said, "that with the economy cuts I have had to make, my hunting should have been one of the things I must do without. And I must sell my horses, too. This is the worst part of it all, and the parting with them will be terrible."

The new hybrid government was granted a few days to breathe when bankers in New York and Paris loaned it £80,000,000. Then the pound came under fresh attack. In the middle of September, seamen of His Majesty's Navy based on Invergordon, Scotland, mutinied in protest against the cuts in their pay. Foreign depositors in British banks took the outburst as signaling the start of a revolution that would convulse the United Kingdom just as the Bolsheviks had seized power from Tsar Nicholas before slaughtering him and his family.

With overseas credits exhausted, the country had no choice but to abandon the gold standard, driving the value of a pound down as low as $3.40. As the depression deepened and unemployment edged up toward three million, it seemed to most of the population that the very foundations of the land were crumbling. One means of shoring up morale was to enlist George as a grandfather figure.

The microphone was specially gilded for his broadcast from Buckingham Palace on Christmas Day, 1932, when turkey and plum pudding were on the table of the luckier households. The tones of the announcer for the state radio monopoly, the British Broadcasting Corporation, were unctuous. George was doing something no king had attempted before—not because it gave him any pleasure but because he took it to be part of his job. "Our duty," he said simply, "is to England always." In the new age that was opening, he and his family would be a well-publicized public institution. Nine out of ten homes had a radio set. Most were switched on to hear his guttural voice evoke memories of past grandeur, when Britain stood as solid as a rock.

Even then Margaret, aged two, was subject to the consequences. Only left-wing hot-heads dared criticize the king, but the rest of his family was not immune. An atavistic desire to level the mighty led a host of his forty-five million subjects to believe the whisper that his granddaughter, poor little thing, was deaf and dumb.

III

Limelight

In those times of stress, Margaret and her sister were cast as performers in a continuing pageant that employed the kingdom as its theater. Its audience was the patriotic middle class, which would provide the strongest safeguard against a radical change of course for England. Idols of steadfast virtue were needed on stage to enthuse every age group.

George served as the idealized grandfather, a decidedly more sympathetic figure after a prolonged bout of bronchial trouble left him weakened and pale. His wife was an image of perfection almost too good to be true. Mary set such lofty personal standards that only paragons like herself could live up to them. High-living, hard-drinking David could scarcely be paraded as a symbol of morality for his generation when a song was circulated about him:

> England's virgin queen was Bess,
> I'll be virgin king, I guess,
> And the greatest sport in Merrie England.

The Yorks and their daughters made excellent alternates. Never since his marriage had Bertie failed his father, who wrote to him then, "You have always been so sensible & easy to work with & you have always been ready to listen to any advice & agree with my opinions about people & things that I feel we have always got on very well together. Very different with dear David."

Discreet publicity arrangements were put in hand by the Buckingham Palace staff. Gray-locked Marcus Adams, photographer by appointment, paid regular calls on the Yorks from the time Margaret was two. His gauzy, sentimental pictures were snapped up by the editors of glossy magazines, then reissued as coffee-table volumes and souvenir postcards. The chubby little princess was captured in a dozen poses—in her mother's arms, smiling and wearing her best necklace of coral and pearls, made from an old string of the duchess'; riding in an open landau with grim-faced grandparents; sitting sulkily next to Elizabeth, who clutched a handbag embroidered with her personal cipher, "E" surmounted by a crown.

Press photographers caught the two sisters whenever permission for coverage was granted by the palace. The prints were a valuable commodity on Fleet Street, where Lord Beaverbrook's *Daily Express,* Lord Rothermere's *Daily Mail,* and Labor's now-commercialized *Daily Herald* were joined in battle for circulation, luring readers with free insurance policies, cut-rate sets of the complete works of Charles Dickens—and scoop shots, if they could lay hold of them, of Margaret and Elizabeth.

It was a rare week that newsreel cameramen failed to deliver footage of somebody in the family, the children for preference, for inclusion in the film that rounded out the movie shows. They were a staple of the programs, like the big-name features from Hollywood played three in a row, cartoons, and free dishes offered to bring in the customers to escape into dreamland for four and five hours at a sitting. In better-class neighborhoods, audiences applauded the sight of George or others of his family on the screen and rose in silent respect at the close of each performance to the scratchy, recorded strains of "God Save the King!"

Alah rarely had her way in dressing up the girls unless a photographer was due to call. Then she could achieve her heart's desire and deck them out in ribbons and organdy as though they were off to a party. Their mother preferred them in matching sweaters and tartan skirts, strap-over walking shoes, wool coats, and an assortment of berets. Alah thought those outfits were far too plain. Princesses, in her opinion, ought to look like princesses every day. She was happy when her Margaret's hair grew long enough to be parted and tied with a bow.

A covey of men and women earned their living on the royal news beat. They ranged from veterans in morning coats, whose gravity matched any courtier's, to shabby hustlers who lingered in the pubs around Victoria Station, hoping to find a garrulous off-duty footman. Together, they fed tidbits of gossip to Fleet Street, articles to the magazines, and manuscripts of uniform blandness to book publishers. The trivia of Margaret's early childhood were recorded, at a price, to accompany the endless pictures.

Batches of them featured the girls' special toy, a complete house sized down to their scale and built in the garden when Royal Lodge was made habitable at last. It had diamond-paned casement windows with blue chintz curtains, real plumbing, and electric light. The working kitchen was equipped with miniature pots and pans, the beds with linen bearing the inevitable ciphered "E."

When a visit to Royal Lodge was over, Elizabeth, mistress of the Tom Thumb home, stored away the sheets and blankets and wrapped the silverware in newspapers to save it from tarnishing, then enrolled her dawdling sister to help cover the furniture with dust sheets. The plaything and everything in it cost Bertie nothing. It was a gift from the people of Wales, where coal mines were shut and poverty haunted the valleys. *Y Bwthyn Bach* said the sign on the gate, Welsh for "the little thatched house."

The duchess, whose grandfather had been a country clergyman, had a strong religious bent as well as a sure touch with a billiard cue. She said her personal bedtime prayers and taught her daughters to do the same. Margaret, the inquisitive one, wanted to know who was God and what were angels.

Alah, not the duchess, took her to church for the first time, when she was three, with what was to be a weekly shilling for the collection plate. They sat together in a pew in the family's private chapel in Windsor Great Park until Margaret's voice piped up during a prayerful pause. "Are they all asking God for things out loud?" Nanny whisked her out before the sermon began. "Oh, must we go? I wanted to hear another song."

Margaret's day invariably started with both children paying a wake-up call in their parents' bedroom, but most of her hours were spent with Alah. Elizabeth had lunch with her father and mother, Margaret upstairs in the day nursery, contesting Alah's right to feed her the brown mash of minced-up meat, gravy, and potato that she called "hoosh-mi." When the meal was finished, she was allowed to go downstairs. She would push open the door of the dining room to climb up onto Bertie's knee, hungry for attention, and regale him with a round-eyed description of what had been served on her plate. He rewarded her with a spoonful of pale brown coffee sugar, which she promptly crammed into her fat cheeks. "Windy water," otherwise soda water, was another treat. "It crackles in my nose."

Bath time brought the day to its end after supper. Papa and

Mummy went up to watch and say goodnight, then down again for dinner, served under Ainslie's supervision at eight-fifteen. The two bourgeois homebodies finished out most evenings in an easy chair apiece on either side of the fireplace. Bertie and David were both, like their mother, experts with a needle. The duke could handle petit point more deftly than his brother, but the prince knitted better scarves.

The queen was disappointed that neither of her grand-daughters promised to be anything but fumble-fingered as a needlewoman. She was distressed, too, when the Yorks made no effort to follow the example of George and herself and conduct family prayers as a daily practice. It seemed to her to be the least one could do to add substance to "God Save the King!"

Though Bertie disliked publicity with all the passion his reticent nature could generate, he reconciled himself to his daughters' popularity with the crowds. When they played under careful supervision in Hamilton Gardens, spectators pressed against the railings. They congregated outside the house on Piccadilly to wait for a carriage to arrive with liveried coachman and footman on the box and take the girls, Alah, and Bobo for an afternoon jaunt around Hyde Park. Mothers copied Margaret's clothes for their own three-year-olds, which was not hard when the duchess liked her in simple blue cottons. School-girls were encouraged to clip out pictures of the sisters for pasting into scrapbooks or pinning up on classroom bulletin boards; a portrait of George hung in every school hall. Margaret sprawled on the rug at home with newspapers spread around her, picking out photographs of the grandparents she seldom saw.

Royalty was being vended with a kind of sedate salesman-ship unknown before. The two children at first were too wrapped up in each other to be affected by the attention they received. Afterward, they grew hardened to the presence of staring faces. "Right from the beginning," Margaret said when she was grown, "I don't seem to remember noticing."

The sight and sound of her waddling after Elizabeth in Hamilton Gardens quashed one rumor. Onlookers hearing her wail, "Wait for me, Lilibet, wait for me!" could report first-hand that she definitely was not a mute.

Up to her fourth year, the princesses had no competition as the most lionized pair of their age in sight. Their fame had reached beyond their own country. Two human dolls living in a shop window in Neverland were just what most of the world's population wanted to relieve present gloom and recapture the rose-tinted joys of yesterday.

Then, in a bare plank farmhouse on the other side of the Atlantic, Elzire Dionne gave birth to five identical daughters on a morning in May, 1934. A crush of newscasters, photographers, and reporters descended on the remote village of Corbeil, Ontario, to relate hour by hour the story—how a diabetic country doctor, Alan Defoe, fought to keep the hearts beating in Annette, Cécile, Emilie, Marie, and Yvonne as they lay swaddled in a basket borrowed from the local butcher. When he succeeded, another nursery kingdom came into being for the world's delight.

Droves of American tourists made the trip north to watch the quintuplets in the hospital observatory the government erected for them. Its windows were supposedly of one-way glass so that the five girls would be unaware that they were on exhibition. They made a peerless attraction, bringing prosperity to the poverty-stricken community, where small fortunes were picked up in the souvenir trade, endorsements for baby products, and Hollywood movie contracts. Pictures of the princesses hung in their nursery, but the quintuplets were different from Margaret in their two-year-old awareness of being scrutinized by strangers on the other side of the glass. In their case, they acknowledged that it scarred their future.

They were to grow up as timid as deer at the blast of hunters' buckshot.

Hollywood caught on fast to what people everywhere were pining for. The studios had already furnished a doll of their own named Shirley Temple, whose head of blonde curls looked uncommonly like Elizabeth's.

Bertie and his wife did not worry unduly about their girls' education. He had painful memories of boyhood, when tutors drilled him in accordance with rigid Victorian rules on the command of his parents, who wanted as little as possible to do with their young and could envisage no more humane method of tackling the problem. It was enough for Bertie's daughters to be happy. A governess could take care of teaching them all they needed to know.

Miss Marion Crawford planned on becoming a child psychologist, not a governess. She was twenty-two, a Scot, and just out of teacher's college in Edinburgh with her hair Eton-cropped when she was recommended to the duchess by her sister, Lady Rose Leveson-Gower, for whom Margaret had been named. Miss Crawford was giving part-time lessons to Lady Rose's fragile daughter, Mary. Bertie and his wife went up to inspect the young teacher over an 11 A.M. bun and a cup of coffee.

Two weeks passed before she was invited to go to work on Margaret and Elizabeth for a trial month. She was none too mature, of course, and she had a crusading streak after seeing how hardship deadened the brains of children in Edinburgh slums. But she *was* lively, as Bertie noted, so she would enjoy running about and playing with the girls. She gathered the impression that George and Mary frowned on her appointment. In the course of the month, when they descended on Royal Lodge to cast an eye on her, her wobbling curtsy won a stiff smile from the queen. "Crawfie," which was another name supplied by Elizabeth, stayed on until her marriage fifteen years later.

Crawfie caught her first sight of the princess when Elizabeth was sitting up in bed with her dressing-gown cord tied to the bed knobs, encouraging an imaginary team in a turn around Hyde Park. Crawfie thereafter often found herself harnessed with a set of jingling reins, patted, and fed from a make-believe nosebag. The psychologist in her was puzzled by this obsession with horses. Bertie had a simple explanation. "It is a family idiosyncrasy. My sister Mary was the horse in my young days." Margaret, at least, was not smitten to the same degree.

Crawfie was dismayed to discover that at No. 145 Piccadilly what the girls liked best was to sit at the day nursery window, gazing out as dusk fell and the street lights gleamed beneath them. They were so secluded that she felt impelled to tell them something about life as she knew it, which included tenements as well as palaces and the little thatched house.

As soon as she had found her feet and Margaret hers, the governess opened the gates wider. Until then, Alah had not condoned her darlings' getting dirty or straying from the paths in Hamilton Gardens. Now with Crawfie they skipped out to explore Hyde Park. They peered in wonderment at more liberated children throwing bread to the ducks on the Serpentine and sailing model boats on the Round Pond close by Kensington Palace, where an assortment of aged royal relatives resided.

Alah fretted endlessly about the excursions beyond the cloister. Neither Bertie nor the duchess said a word about them, but Crawfie was getting used to what she called "royalty's economy with words." She thought it a pity that the unwritten law stipulated that the princesses should not be allowed to make friends with the fascinating young strangers they saw, only to answer a smile by smiling back.

There was no known instance of their disobeying. Margaret would have been the more likely to try. She was lovable, and she played on it. She was spoiled by her father and her sister, too, to the point where the older girl would complain, "She always wants everything I want." Then a sudden slap from Elizabeth brought a furious bite in return.

Margaret's temperament was a matter of sunshine and rain. Defiance flared in her eyes before a storm broke. When calm was restored, a warm kiss would endear her once more. Or she would ward off rebukes for being naughty by batting her eyes and breaking into a song from a cartoon designed by Walt Disney to lighten international gloom, *Who's Afraid of the Big Bad Wolf?*

One of Grandma Strathmore's reminiscences, possibly of dubious accuracy, had Margaret getting off the opening bars of "The Merry Widow" waltz before she could walk. An equally biased witness, Alah, claimed that her petite pet could pick up every tune she heard and sing it in perfect pitch not long after her second birthday.

Her father was especially susceptible to her charms. She bounced up onto his knee to be cuddled, singing to him, whispering secrets in his ear, tickling him into fits of laughter—anything that could be devised to gain more attention than staid Elizabeth. No one had his snuggly little daughter's ability to put a smile on his increasingly careworn face.

Crawfie decided to expand her experiment in giving the girls a inkling of how ordinary people lived. She asked Bertie whether she might take them to tea one afternoon at the Young Women's Christian Association and go there on the Underground instead of in a royal Daimler. Yes, he had no objection so long as the plainclothes man who watched over the household went with them, but he could stay out of sight. And the duchess' lady-in-waiting should accompany them, too.

Margaret had never before bought a train ticket or negotiated an escalator, and Crawfie was a total stranger to London's Underground with its seven interlinked systems and multitude of interchanges. She started the party off at St. James's Park station, a few minutes' drive from the house. Margaret was even slower than her sister in fumbling with her purse and counting out the coins with Grandpapa's profile stamped on them. She clutched the governess' hand as they made their brave descent down the concrete steps. She sat goggle-eyed for the brief ride to Charing Cross, where they had to tackle an escalator to the depths of the Northern Line to travel through three more stops to Tottenham Court Road. Cameramen lay in wait there, but Crawfie urged her charges into a trot to reach the YWCA. The next time Margaret ventured on a similar subterranean journey, she would be a married woman.

A mug of YWCA tea and a slice of bread and butter had to be stood in line for, bought with more money, and carried off on a tray. All was going smoothly, though Elizabeth forgot the teapot, until they were spotted. A crowd of white-coated helpers and fellow customers swarmed around the group. The fun was over. Crawfie led a retreat into the office to call for a car to collect them.

The last breakout from confinement took them for a trip on top of a double-decker bus—"a funny bus with a hat," in Margaret's description—so that the girls could peer down at people the way top-deck passengers sometimes peered down at them. After that taste of common living, the expeditions came to an abrupt end. Word from the palace said they were too dangerous. Britain's rich did not share the fears that placed American heirs and heiresses under guard after Charles A. Lindbergh's son was kidnapped and murdered. What alarmed London were bombs planted in mail boxes by the Irish Republican Army to avenge the dead shot by the Black and Tans a generation ago. Risk of being assassinated had not weakened George's resolve then to open the first Northern Ireland parliament. These days, his granddaughters must not be exposed to the chance of being grabbed and held hostage by terrorists.

Crawfie was urged to take the children to play behind the towering brick walls that enclosed the palace gardens. They did not care much for that. It would mean dressing up and minding their manners in an encounter with Grandpapa and Grandmama. They reverted to games of hide-and-seek in Hamilton Gardens, where Margaret had the fun of seeing her studious sister, in search of a mallard's nest one day, fall into the pond and emerge green with algae.

The queen maintained supervision of the children's lessons at long range. The governess was hard pressed to cram every academic course into the morning session in the boudoir opening off the drawing room, which was the only classroom. Bertie had a habit of dropping in at recess and taking them for a quick game of hopscotch on the walks of the grimy garden. After lunch at one-fifteen, four afternoons were taken up with dancing and singing classes, drawing and music. On Fridays, they set off for Royal Lodge.

Grandmama insisted that the thoughts she passed along by way of a lady-in-waiting were not to be considered as criticism. But perhaps arithmetic should be sacrificed in favor of history when it seemed unlikely that her granddaughters would ever have to balance household budgets and "that vulgar, old-fashioned thing called dates" came in useful, particularly in conversation with foreigners. Awareness of the family tree was important for them, too.

Surely thirty minutes of literature a week was far too skimpy, and should they not be committing poems to heart? The queen was aware of their passion for racing demon, a frantic card game that resulted in hands being scratched by the opponent's fingernails when it was played after tea; wouldn't they sometimes prefer a more *intellectual* pastime?

As for the mere half hour devoted to Bible reading, this

must make the entire effort appear insignificant to them. "But perhaps they do it with their Mother, too, at other times," Mary added hopefully.

Crawfie amended the schedule. There was no time for a minute of geography, and the Bible was paid no more attention than before. History, however, appeared on the curriculum four days a week, and so did arithmetic. They *might* be faced with household accounts one day. It was just as well to be prepared.

Margaret's favorite among the relatives was Uncle David without question, and happily he was the most regular visitor. He joined in when she dealt the cards for a game after tea before Alah would arrive to whisk her upstairs to bath and bed. He recognized in his brother a man dedicated to his family, "a quality," he wrote afterward, "that goes a long way in a constitutional monarchy." Uncle David brought presents, too, not "don't touch" things like the Fabergé animals that Grandmama sent, which had to be kept locked up in a glass-fronted cabinet, but books like *Winnie the Pooh* and *When We Were Very Young.* As soon as she could, she took to reciting one particular poem that struck a chord:

> They're changing guard at Buckingham Palace—
> Christopher Robin went down with Alice.
> Alice is marrying one of the guard.
> "A soldier's life is terribly hard ... "

She repaid him by painting homemade greeting cards. He kept them as mementos of a household whose style was alien to his. For a while, her taste in reading ran to something gaudier than A. A. Milne. Rummaging through a dusty box in Glamis Castle, she found her first comic book. She had no spending allowance to buy her own. The only money in her embroidered purse, which was stored with her handkerchiefs, was usually a half-crown piece given her by Alah, to be doled out penny by penny.

The tale of blood and mayhem told in the faded pages was exactly right for poring over in a place where ghosts reputedly walked the halls and one deserted tower was the lair of a monster who emerged to petrify every first-born son on his twenty-first birthday.

She straightened out her tattered find and made certain the pages were in sequence. No one was allowed to see this treasure or be present as she thumbed through it time and again. It was her secret, hers alone. Grandmama would have been appalled, but she knew nothing about it.

More than the guard was being changed at the palace. David was edging into an emotional entanglement that would upend his life.

For more than a decade, the country, like his parents, had speculated about when, whom, and if he would ever marry. The subject bobbed up continually in the newspapers, which magnified any driblet of information into a spate of headlines. "Gentlemen," he told waiting cameramen one day, "here I am—the raw material of your industry."

Britain was kept posted on his tailoring and his haberdashery, which was as innovative as his disdain for red tape. Everybody knew that he liked to strum a banjo and take a whack at the drums in a nightclub jazz band. A more serious side to his nature took him into the hovels of the unemployed in hard-hit Wales and Lancashire and into mission halls for the homeless who drifted south to London in a hopeless search for jobs. He left the impression that once he was king, a better deal would be in the making, and his popularity increased.

Readers learned about that, too, along with his problems when he went steeplechasing. "How are you falling, prince?" asked Will Rogers, the cowboy sage, during one of David's trips to the United States. "All over the place," he replied.

On one trip, he brought back a jingle he had heard in prohibition America, which he fancied might be something to amuse his father. "My father doesn't like me," he repeated to his friends. "Not at all sure I particularly like him." But George on this occasion was delighted by:

> Four and twenty Yankees, feeling very dry,
> Went across the border to get a drink of rye.
> When the rye was opened, the Yanks began to sing,
> "God bless America, but God save the king!"

David had often persuaded himself that he was in love, though no editor broke the code of lese majesty that barred publication of such stories. Gossip endemic in high society named a Kensington schoolmistress, a bewitching lady from Ireland, and an actress, among others.

His first liaison lasted for ten years, long enough for Bertie to be well aware of it. David adored the wife of the Right Honorable Dudley Ward, a Member of Parliament who had been a fellow officer of the prince's in the Grenadier Guards during the past war. Some versions of the affair said that David's attachment to Winifred Birkin, who called herself "Freda," dated back to his two student years at Magdalen College, Oxford.

Freda, "a pretty little fluff," was petite, pretty, and in awe of no one. A cottage the Dudley Wards kept at Le Touquet made a convenient haven for Freda and David, whose friendship with her obliging husband remained intact. The difficulty was that the prince had to leave her so often as First Salesman of the Empire. He wept at their partings and deluged her while he was away with letters and cablegrams, confiding how much she was missed by himself and the little dog she gave him as a traveling keepsake. He received very few letters in return.

He begged her to divorce her husband and become his wife. She turned him down, wise enough to know his father would never sanction his son's marrying a divorcée. Eventually, she dropped David in favor of a well-to-do bachelor, Michael Herbert, on whose behalf she did obtain a divorce. She went off out of range to Canada as Mrs. Herbert.

The next long-term alliance was with a woman who would make an even more impossible bride than Frieda. Elegant, witless, tawny-skinned Thelma was a twin of Gloria Morgan, whose husband was the American Reggie Vanderbilt. Thelma was in the throes of her second marriage, to a lecherous shipowner, the Viscount Marmaduke Furness. David asked her to dance after they were introduced at a weekend house party, then asked her to keep him company in his private compartment when he discovered her on the same train homeward bound for London. Her house at No. 21 Grosvenor Square accommodated the two of them from time to time when David felt that he was in love again, though marriage to Thelma, a Catholic, was prohibited.

She had an older sister, Constance, wife of Benjamin Thaw, first secretary at the United States embassy, which also stood in Grosvenor Square. Constance brought into their circle a Baltimore-born American who was finding herself lonesome in the city. Wallis Simpson was on her second marriage, too. Ernest Aldrich Simpson was an Anglo-American product, Harvard graduate, and Coldstream Guardsman during the war, whose British father owned a shipping business. Ernest ran the London office and with his wife rented an apartment in Bryanston Court.

In November, 1930, the Simpsons, man and wife for the past two years, were asked down by Connie Thaw to Thelma's place in Melton Mowbray. David was another guest. On the evening he first met Wallis, when fog hid the empty fields and still coverts outside, he disappointed her. She had anticipated being overwhelmed by the future king, the most exciting bachelor in England if what she read in the newspapers over breakfast every morning was to be believed. But he opened their brief conversation with a lackluster line of small talk: on a day like this, didn't she yearn for central heating?

"I'd hoped," she said pertly, "for something more original from the Prince of Wales." When he came to write his memoirs, he recalled that "the echoes of the passage lingered."

Friendship thickened between Mrs. Simpson and Thelma Furness. The following summer, Wallis was ambitious to be presented at court to the king and queen, as Thelma had been in an earlier season. To save expense, Thelma was willing to lend her train and the obligatory plumes she had worn in her hair and Connie would provide the necessary long white gown. A formidable handicap remained. George and Mary did not countenance divorcées at these gatherings, where they sat on their thrones in the gold-and-crimson State Room of the palace to receive the deep curtsies of the line of ladies while a string orchestra performed out of sight among the banks of flowers and potted palms.

Somewhere along the chain of command, David interceded. The usual engraved invitation from the Lord Chamberlain's office went out to Wallis. After making her bow at the palace on June 10, 1931, she went on to a party at Thelma's. David was on hand to give the Simpsons a lift home, but he suggested he make it some other time when he was asked up for a drink.

The fire generated by the sparking between David and Wallis did not ignite for almost four more years. When Uncle David was calling at No. 145 Piccadilly to play cards with his nieces, Thelma's hold on him as his mistress was secure. Bertie had no cause for alarm. His brother occasionally dined with the Simpsons and had them down in return to Fort Belvedere, a toy castle built in eighteenth-century Gothic and set on the fringe of Windsor Great Park that was his private, Bohemian retreat.

In January, 1934, Thelma sailed for New York to lend whatever moral support she was capable of to her twin, Gloria, engaged in a court contest for custody of Gloria Vanderbilt, Jr., her daughter. She would be gone for six weeks, she told Wallis. "The little man is going to be so lonely," Mrs. Simpson remarked.

"Well, dear," Thelma answered, "you look after him for me while I'm away." Wallis was willing, but David was not ready yet to break with Thelma. She heard from him most days by coded telegram or trans-Atlantic telephone.

Before she returned, she contributed to her own doom by allowing herself to be captivated by Prince Aly Khan, heir to one of the greatest fortunes in the Moslem world; his fleshy father, the Aga Khan, was ritualistically weighed in gold bars by his Ismaili followers. The son raced cars as a hobby and as a pastime conquered women, including Rita Hayworth, whom he married at a later date. David's mistress made an irresistible trophy. They sailed together from New York to Southampton in the middle of March.

A message from David was waiting there for her. Would she please interrupt her journey up to London to have tea with him in Fort Belvedere? Press reports had disclosed her relationship with Aly Khan so far as propriety would permit. She dreaded the inevitable confrontation, but she could not refuse the request.

David's manner was chilly, but he asked her back for the weekend. Those two days and nights at The Fort were the most miserable she had known, with no one else there to defrost the atmosphere except a nominal chaperon in Brig-adier-General Trotter, aide-de-camp of more than twenty years' service, whom the court called David's wet nurse.

Thelma swore she would not expose herself to such

treatment again. The next weekend she was asked down, she had the prince's permission to bring the Simpsons. At The Fort, she pleaded a cold and put herself early to bed, leaving Wallis to entertain David while her husband chatted with Trotter. The four of them dropped into the kitchens for a snack before retiring. Mrs. Simpson scrambled the eggs. It was the last time Thelma was seen on the premises. The following day, she set off with Aly Khan to drive to Spain.

Afterward, the woman spurned exacted her own brand of revenge. She let her friends know that David had been a failure as a lover, too nervous and hasty for sexual success. The tittle-tattle from the top filtered downward through the social pyramid, gaining in piquancy in the process. A considerable number of Britons came to take it for granted that he was impotent. The fact that no child was ever born to him was cited as confirmation.

If he postponed getting married, his youngest brother did not; George, the thirty-one-year old Duke of Kent, went through two ceremonies on the same November day, a highlight of the pageantry that year. He made a creditable choice in dark-eyed Marina, a refugee Greek princess, and she made a graceful appearance at his side, first in Westminster Abbey and then for Orthodox rites in the chapel of the palace. When his niece Elizabeth was invited to be a bridesmaid, Margaret asserted herself. She demanded to be taken to the abbey, too. Over Elizabeth's protests, the duchess let her have her wish.

In a pink coat and hat, she sat on a stool at her mother's feet near the altar. Margaret beamed at the sight of the sister whom she simultaneously loved and rivalled advancing in procession down the aisle. Then as she passed, Margaret in embarrassment studied her patent-leather shoes. Lunch was served for her in the palace during the second exchange of vows in the chapel.

Afterward, the wedding party emerged on the second-floor

balcony to acknowledge the applause of the crowd of thousands squeezed against the railings below. George hoisted her up onto the balustrade to wave to them. Margaret was on public display, cheered and cheered again, four years and three months old.

She was too young for Uncle David to fetch her to meet Mrs. Simpson; he had insisted that Wallis come to the abbey ceremony. Pushing his way through the guests to greet her, he introduced her around as "an American—she's wonderful." In her uneasiness, she seldom stopped talking. He took her up to his father and mother, saying that she was "a great friend of mine." They never met her again.

By now, he had taken Wallis for a spell of summer sunshine à deux in a rented villa named Mer de Monte at the Basque resort of Biarritz, sailing there in a yacht thoughtfully provided by Lord Moyne, a Tory stalwart without position in MacDonald's national government. Mr. Simpson raised no demur. News agency reporters filed accounts of David and Wallis dancing the night out. Though the stories were automatically spiked by every editor in Fleet Street, the rumblings sounded among senior courtiers at the palace and inevitably reached Bertie. The lines in his face deepened. David's flaunting of his latest love would have to continue to be concealed from the British public or the pageant could be ruined. Bertie needed more than ever the attentions of his lively little daughter to lighten the gloom.

The British Constitution—established by precedent instead of being set down on paper like the American—contained no provision for George to disinherit David, no matter how appealing the idea was to him. He took one step as a Christian to offset the unruliness of his heir. "I pray to God," George said, "that my eldest son will never marry and have children, and that nothing will come between Bertie and Lilibet and the throne."

In his view, Mrs. Simpson had nothing to recommend her
as a companion for David. The fact that she was an American
was of no consequence. Before their son left on one of his
earlier journeys to the United States, a hint from George and
Mary was relayed to a member of his entourage: "If David
found a suitable wife in America, they would be delighted."
But Wallis was an overly ambitious, middle-class commoner;
a divorcée whose first husband, Commander Earl Winfield
Spencer of the United States Navy, was alive and well in San
Diego; and she was still a married woman.

There was a graver flaw in her relationship with their son,
which led to some necessary investigating by the British Secret
Service. Herr Joachim von Ribbentrop, once a champagne
salesman and now special Nazi envoy to the Court of St.
James's, focussed his practiced charm on her and sent her
flowers after their hostess sat them side by side at a London
dinner party. His flattery of Wallis carried him into her circle
of friends who gathered in the kitschy apartment at Bryanston
Court, from which Ernest Simpson had either retreated or
been excluded.

David liked to air his German in front of von Ribbentrop
and a fellow diplomat from Berlin, Ambassador Leopold von
Hoesch. Both men filed jubilant reports back to Adolf Hitler,
who had proclaimed himself Fuehrer at the time David and
Wallis were romancing in Biarritz. The prince, von Hoesch
affirmed, "showed his complete understanding of Germany's
position and aspirations."

A succession of distinguished Britons had already been
Hitler's guests at his mountain sanctum of Berchtesgaden, his
Munich apartment, or his headquarters in Berlin. Sir Oswald
Mosley had paid his respects. So had the first Lord Rother-
mere, born Harold Harmsworth, proprietor of the *Daily Mail;*
his son Esmond; and milord's editorial major domo, George
Ward Price. Sir John Simon, British foreign secretary, had

been to and fro in the course of negotiating a treaty which ultimately sanctioned the buildup of a brand new Nazi navy.

The Fuehrer, intent on rearming the Reich, wanted all the support his emissaries could drum up among men of influence in England. David and Wallis were "most friendly" to the cause, von Ribbentrop assured his master. One of David's gambits in appreciative company was to point out that his Hanoverian descent made him seventy-five percent German himself.

Lung trouble returned to plague George in the dreary February of 1935. Hindsight convinced some of his subjects that anxiety over his son had lowered his stamina, but he was growing frail and profoundly disturbed by the emerging threat of another war in Europe, which he was determined to do everything within his power to avoid. A hedonist would have sought some Mediterranean sunlight to bake in during convalescence. George elected to go to blustery Eastbourne on the Channel coast, where he was bundled in blankets and pushed in a wheelchair along the promenade overlooking the choppy green sea. After his previous illness, he had chosen Bognor, a similar resort popular with the bourgeoisie, and had Elizabeth join him, to play on the sand while he watched.

By June, David was prepared to declare himself openly as pro-German. Speaking at a convocation of British Legion ex-servicemen, he recommended that they visit Berlin and there, in the spirit of fair play, make contact with the men they had faced on the battlefields of France seventeen years ago.

His father quickly reprimanded him. "How often have I told you, my dear boy, never to mix in politics, especially where foreign matters are concerned? The views you expressed yesterday, however sensible, are, I happen to know, contrary to those of the Foreign Office." He must not again be drawn into controversy without first consulting the ministers of the crown. David was unrepentant.

David's speech, headlined throughout the world, was accepted by Hitler as fresh evidence that British sympathy for his dreams of expansion was now so strong that no obstacles would be raised in his path. In some closed circles of London society, anti-Semites sniggered. Hitler, the Jew-baiter, was wooing a prince who probably had a dash of Jewish blood. One generation passed on to the next the discounted rumor which insisted that Prince Albert, Victoria's husband, had introduced the strain into the House of Windsor. He was sired, so it was said, not by his reputed father, Duke Ernest of Saxe-Coburg-Gotha, but by the court chamberlain, Baron von Meyern, a part-Jew.

IV

King in Brief

The old king's nature changed toward the close of his life. He was as deaf as ever, but his voice softened, and Mary no longer had to urge him to keep it down. The quarter-deck manner vanished under a gentle vagueness. Brooding over the respective futures of David and Bertie led him to spare more time for his granddaughters. Margaret set out to captivate him as she had her father. Letting Grandpapa see the pirouettes and bobs she was learning at Madame Vacani's frilly dance classes was one way of showing off.

He favored her sister, and not only because of the dynastic fact that she stood closer in line for the throne. Elizabeth was respectful, docile, but suitably intimidated by Grandpapa. He found her company less irksome than that of Margaret, with her inability to take even Grandpapa too seriously. On occasion, Margaret was excluded from such treats as a carriage ride, and Elizabeth seemed to be given better Christmas and birthday presents than those that arrived for her sister.

From listening sometimes to the radio and often to the

gramophone, she knew at least as many songs as Elizabeth. She joined her in a carolling duet that Bertie felt was good enough to be made into records to hand out to relatives one Christmas. Though her hands were too small to span four keys, Margaret was trying to teach herself to play the piano, while Miss Mabel Lander came in to give lessons to Elizabeth, who detested practicing. Margaret's sessions with Miss Lander would start later.

But the virtue of being born first and the dictates of royal inheritance made Elizabeth the superior being. Margaret's place was always one step behind her. There was nothing she could do to catch up, but she kept trying for attention. One technique developed early—use of a sharp tongue and a vivid imagination. Turning the pages of the family album, she wondered, "Why do all these pictures make Lilibet look like a stuffed pig?" And she invented dreams.

"I must tell you an amazing dream I had last night," she would tell Crawfie and her sister as an introduction to a serial story that might last over two or three days, involving cats that talked like the Cheshire specimen in *Alice in Wonderland,* wild elephants on the rampage, and horses of any number of different colors.

She was given co-billing with her sister for the final act of organized pageantry in George's reign. The quavering Mac-Donald government was on its last legs, losing ground week by week with its concessions to Hitler and Mussolini, while the Fuehrer gulled the West into believing that Germany rearmed only to save Europe from Communism and Il Duce prepared to invade Ethiopia. MacDonald's team decided on an effort to reunite opinion in Britain around the figure of George.

May 6, the twenty-fifth anniversary of his accession as king, was designated as the opening of a national jubilee, a golden opportunity to stir remembrances of Victoria's glory and celebrate his improved state of health with a thanksgiving service in St. Paul's Cathedral. Most of his family would be included in a week of pageantry. Unemployment stayed firm at a million five hundred thousand.

Alah was in her element, getting her princesses dressed in identical pink frocks and hats secured under their chins with the elastic bands that Margaret hated. The sun blazed down on the open carriage in which the two girls sat with Bertie and the duchess as it rattled out through the main gates of Buckingham Palace with an escort of Horse Guards. The holiday that had been declared filled the streets along the route of the procession with rich and poor, factory hands and tourists hauled in by excursion trains, peddlers hawking Union Jacks and assorted souvenirs, schoolchildren in hundreds of thousands lining the curbs to chorus a welcome. George had never seen such crowds; "most touching," he noted in his diary that night.

Margaret needed no telling what to do; Alah had been drilling her for years. In the decorous prose that Geoffrey Dawson deemed necessary for these occasions, *The Times* recorded that "Princess Margaret delighted all with the enthusiasm and daintiness of her hand-waving." Back in the palace, she emerged with her grandparents onto the balcony. A footman brought a stool for her to stand on to watch the shouting swarm below. After her relatives had retired inside, she stayed on for an extra moment to bask in the adulation alone.

Six-thirty bedtime was put off that evening so that she could hear Grandpapa over the radio. David's affair with Wallis was a secret from all but a handful of the audience. Between the lines of George's prepared text there was a hint of suspicion that the country might be subject to future strain.

"I am speaking to the children above all," he rasped. "Remember, children, the king is speaking to you ... As you grow up, be ready and proud to give to your country the service of your work, your mind, and your heart."

Streets in every city were strung with bunting, banners, flags, and glamorized portraits of the king, who in actual appearance seemed strangely shrunken. In the following days, he and Mary were driven in state to inspect the sight in London. The reception he received from slum-dwellers in the East End amazed the old man, who had been reluctant to court popularity. "I'd no idea they felt like that about me," he said. "I am beginning to think they must like me for myself."

Next month, he would be seventy, but a touch of vanity surfaced in him. He took his granddaughters along one day in his carriage to see the scene in the streets. "I suppose," he smiled, "you think these flags are hung out for you. Let me tell you they are for me."

A ball at the palace was part of the festivities. David asked Wallis there as his partner, but steered her away from his parents. She may have imagined the hostility gleaming in George's clouded eyes.

One more of his sons was married that autumn. Henry, Duke of Gloucester, was due to take Lady Alice Montagu-Douglas-Scott as his approved bride in rites conducted in Westminster Abbey. She did not discriminate between Elizabeth and Margaret in selecting her eight bridesmaids; she asked for both of them. Norman Hartnell, the duchess' studiedly languid couturier, designed their pink satin dresses. While her mother clasped her feet to keep her still, Margaret, poking five-year-old fun, told him, "I don't suppose that you often have to kneel to fit the necks of your customers." She had a taste of another kind of reverence when she left his salon. Every assistant knelt in a curtsy.

The wedding itself was unexpectedly subdued, performed in the palace chapel and not the abbey, because of the death of the bride's father. Eight days later, Britain turned out in a general election that made Stanley Baldwin Prime Minister of a revamped National Government. Only one more turn of the mandala was needed to set in motion the devastation of Bertie and the Yorks.

Two more months elapsed before it happened. By the end of 1935, George was in such poor physical shape that engagements for him had to be cancelled. He spent Christmas as usual at Sandringham, the draughty monstrosity of a house set among seven thousand desolate Norfolk acres; he enjoyed the place because his father, who bought it, had enjoyed it. His father had the clocks there set half an hour fast to stretch the day's shooting; George kept them that way. His granddaughters had completed their rounds of Woolworth's with Crawfie, buying the customary figurines, candy, and trinkets, when Bertie and the duchess went up to join the grandparents.

The Yorks were back at Royal Lodge, where the duchess was confined to bed with a not surprising attack of pneumonia, when Mary sent for Bertie, the most dependable of her sons. His father was failing fast. The day after Bertie arrived, George scrawled his last diary entry: "I feel rotten." He was too weak to write his signature on state documents requiring it. The time had come to summon David. On January 20, in the presence of his doctors, his family, and Archbishop Lang, George V died in the house he loved.

His last reported words were "How is the empire?" which would be in keeping with this man of model rectitude. London's social underground spread a different version. It told how his physicians tried to rally him by picturing him well again and recuperating by the sea at Bognor. He supposedly groaned, "Bugger Bognor!" then said no more. That, too, would have been in character.

At the moment of his passing, his widow stooped in the ritual of homage to kiss the hand of the new king, David.

There was no precedent for a monarch of that name in England, so he would style himself Edward VIII. Before the day ended, he ordered the clocks set back to standard time. "I wonder what other customs will be put back also," the uneasy archbishop wrote that night.

Bertie rejoined his ailing wife in Royal Lodge while arrangements for the funeral, to be held eight days later, got under way. He wanted Elizabeth to see final respects paid to his father, but Margaret was too small. Instructions given to their governess said, "Don't let all this depress them more than is absolutely necessary, Crawfie. They are so young."

Margaret jounced around the nursery with no conception of his grief; Elizabeth mourned with him. Though Margaret had not seen much of him until lately, she knew where her grandfather had gone. "Grandpapa is in heaven now, and I'm sure God finds him very useful." She relied on him to make sure that her prayers were answered. "Grandpapa is up there, and he will see to it."

Buckingham Palace with its staff of upwards of four hundred maids, footmen, cleaners, chefs, pages, grooms, chauffeurs, upholsterers, gardeners, and ratcatchers soon resembled a five-floor mausoleum more than anybody's home. Mary moved with forty-seven servants into Marlborough House, the big, square-cut mansion behind high garden walls which had sheltered George's parents before they became king and queen. David loathed living in the palace. He made Fort Belvedere his pied-à-terre and Wallis his hostess.

The presence of the unmentionable Mrs. Simpson only a few minutes' drive from Royal Lodge added to Bertie's tension at weekends. David had said nothing to him yet about desiring to marry her. But what if he did? To the family, the court, and the Cabinet, the monarchy seemed shakier than at any time since Queen Anne died. The spirit of the Silver

Jubilee was vanishing along with the man it had honored. Bertie's nervousness infected his household. Both his daughters fell into his habit of gnawing fingernails.

Their grandmother came to Royal Lodge in the spring to stay for the best part of a month, an unheard-of event until now. Behavior had to be watched to satisfy the old lady, who would not dream of sitting down to breakfast without being fully dressed for the morning ahead. Elizabeth bore the brunt of her instruction, but both girls were lectured on lines of "Proper poise begins with your feet" and "There is no substitute for good manners."

The duchess invented her own method of. teaching them the niceties of etiquette. They played "Let's pretend." "Now I'm the Prime Minister," she would say. Margaret would respond with, "Good morning, Mr. Baldwin."

"I'm the Archbishop of Canterbury." "Good morning, Your Grace."

"I'm Granny." "Good morning, Your Majesty."

Anxiety over what David might turn to next drove his courtiers into fetal attitudes of self-protection. They were disturbed on the first morning he was king when he flew in his private plane from Sandringham to London—George had never taken to the air, though he was nominally Marshal of the Royal Air Force. They were alarmed to see David in full regalia at a Westminster Abbey ceremony before Easter, gazing so fixedly at Wallis, who was sitting among the guests, that she blushed and looked away. When in March he asked Parliament to provide, among other grants, a fixed income of £50,000 a year for his unnamed future queen, politicians grew restive, too.

It was also in March that Hitler ordered his troops to reoccupy the Rhineland, stripped by the Allies of its arms factories when the First World War ended. He wondered whether Britain and France might intervene. According to one henchman, Albert Speer, he imagined that David had promised there would be no countermove by His Majesty's armies, though in fact David had no such authority. But only protests came from London and Paris. Two months later, a British cruiser rescued Emperor Haile Selassie from an Italian advance in Ethiopia. When he reached London, David refused to receive him lest Mussolini should feel offended.

If Mrs. Simpson had already asked David what his intentions were, his ministers did not dare. They would have to bide their time until he confided in Stanley Baldwin. At present, they could only resent him for being feckless, as he resented them for being fuddy-duddies. They grumbled because he was lax about going to church, wore a rakish bowler instead of a more seemly top hat, and carried his own opened umbrella when it rained. Beak-nosed Neville Chamberlain, Chancellor of the Exchequer, drew up a formal complaint. The king, the memorandum said, ought to settle down; dress more conservatively; pay more attention to the locked, leather-covered boxes that brought him a daily flow of Foreign Office cablegrams and Cabinet meeting minutes; stop talking in public about slum clearance and jobs for the unemployed. Baldwin withheld the document. He was waiting to see what developed.

Crawfie looked for some way to ease the strain on the children. Perhaps it would be good for them to learn to swim. They could not, and they wanted to. Ignoring objections from older relatives, Bertie and the duchess gave their consent. Alah's fussing over the risk of another cold had limited Margaret's acquaintanceship with anything more hazardous than bath water to an occasional paddle in the sea on a summer vacation at Eastbourne.

Arrangements were concluded with the Bath Club, a serviceable establishment with an indoor pool, though lacking the distinction of true gentlemen's clubs like gossipy White's, the highly political Brooks's, or Boodles, where legend said that if a guest asked for "Sir John," half the members turned their heads. Ernest Simpson was about to move into a room at the Guards.

The girls were outfitted with white rubber caps and regulation one-piece swimsuits initialled "BC." Crawfie and their parents agreed that in her new costume Margaret looked like "a plump navy blue water sprite." On the first trip governess and girls made from Piccadilly to the Bath, Alah went with them, toting a zipper bag packed with towels, hairbrushes, combs, talcum powder, and a box of chocolates in case hunger overcame them after taking a dip. She also included the pair of socks she was knitting to allay her fears.

Dry-land exercises on a bench by the water soon instilled confidence in Elizabeth. Amy Daly, the instructress, made slower progress with Margaret, who dawdled timidly on the ladder leading into the pool, then refused to let go of the tiled edge once she was in. Her sister urged her on like a gym mistress. "Keep steady, Margaret . . . Don't be a limpet." Bertie brought the duchess along on some afternoons as a break in the unrest at home. He could not figure out why his daughters were not too self-conscious to appear like this, splashing about in a company of strangers. He never could have done that when he was a boy.

The last vestiges of adolescent shyness in David had disappeared under the influence of Wallis, who was also cutting down his intake of Scotch. He set out to make the country aware at least that she was a friend of his as a prelude to more momentous things. The Court Circular provided a series of clues. It recorded Mr. and Mrs. Ernest Simpson among the guests at the first formal dinner of his reign, honoring Mr. and Mrs. Stanley Baldwin on May 26 at St. James's Palace.

On July 8, the next occasion of its kind, Bertie and his wife sat in a company at York House that included Mr. and Mrs. Winston Churchill; the newly appointed First Lord of the Admiralty, Sir Samuel Hoare; and Mrs. Ernest Simpson. Her husband had been omitted, as the cognoscenti were quick to notice. The pace was picking up.

David seemed eager to have the Yorks make a friend of Wallis after Bertie and the duchess met her at dinner. Uncle David's calls at Royal Lodge had virtually ended. He promised Margaret and Elizabeth he would see more of them, then forgot what he had said. He did ask them over to tea at The Fort one afternoon when Wallis was designated to preside. The girls could not understand why their parents would not let them go. It was impossible for Margaret and Elizabeth not to gather that something was *different.* They could not explain the mystery. Talk between Bertie and the duchess about David broke off as soon as the girls came through a door.

The summer brought no improvement. After eight months of coping with the ticklish business of being king, David yearned for a vacation. He would take a cruise not aboard the antiquated royal yacht *Victoria and Albert* but in the "most beautiful yacht in the world," Lady Yule's palatial *Nahlin,* which he chartered. Eight-inch-high letters on one pile of luggage identified the owner as MRS. ERNEST A. SIMP-SON, but her name did not appear on the sailing list. Another pile was labelled DUKE OF LANCASTER, an incognito used by his grandfather and namesake on his jaunts across the Channel in search of a little continental carnality.

David joined the ship at the Dalmatian port of Sibernik, and the *Nahlin* set off to sample the pleasures of the Adriatic. Soon, press photographers were dogging him and his love every time they went ashore. Only Wallis, an ignoramus on British manners and mores, imagined that their affair was still a secret. One passenger among the dozen others was Duff

Cooper, His Majesty's Secretary for War, and two Royal Navy cruisers escorted the yacht. However, imported newspapers and magazines with pictures or stories of the accelerating romance were scrupulously scissored before they went on sale in Britain. One of them reported an evening when Wallis sported a $750,000 emerald-and-diamond necklace.

David squeezed in a few extra days to show her Budapest and Vienna, and then it was over. He left her to go on to Paris before meeting him in Balmoral Castle, where he hoped she could ingratiate herself with some of his relatives; he flew back to London. A brand-new American Buick, registered in her name, was waiting to take him to Fort Belvedere. Wallis-watchers noted another break with the past; after a tiff with the Rolls-Royce company, George had insisted on British-built Daimlers.

The Yorks were at Birkhall, an unimpressive little house with whitewash on its outside walls, built in the reign of George I, standing on its own six thousand acres of the Balmoral estate. The odor of pinewood furniture lingered in all the rooms, augmented as evening fell by the scent of oil lamps, the only means of lighting. If the nights were considered sufficiently cold, Margaret and Elizabeth went to bed to the reek of a kerosene stove.

Autumns in Scotland, when the hillsides blazed red and gold, were normally a delight for the children. Papa on horseback would ride with them on their ponies. A pony trap would trot them down to the local railroad station to watch the fish express pound past along the tracks. Margaret learned the magical art of sticking two crossed pins to a rail with chewing gum, then retrieving them transformed by the wheels into a pair of doll-size scissors.

A few miles away there was Glamis Castle to explore, with storerooms like Ali Baba's cave. She spent hours rummaging through chestsful of abandoned treasure—old clothes to dress up in and parade in to delight Papa, faded photographs of Mummy and her Scottish kinfolk, musty books studded with fascinating engravings that had not been opened in half a century. Papa usually had much more time to play with her in Scotland, but not this year.

This autumn was different. Bertie fretted more and more over his brother's refusal to confide in him. David had earmarked his parents' bedroom in Balmoral for Wallis. This especially disturbed the mild-mannered duke, but "I might say it made me rather sad" was the extent of his comment.

He had obliged David by taking on some of his duties as requested. It came as a shock when his brother drove to Aberdeen station in kilt and tam-o'-shanter to collect Wallis on the day Bertie had stood in for him, laying a cornerstone at a new city hospital. It was all Margaret could do these days to stir her father to smile.

Though David had called on his mother before he came to Scotland, he had seen no reason to talk about Wallis. Mary declined to be with him in the castle. Politeness demanded an excuse: she was too preoccupied with getting settled in Marlborough House, she said. "Everyone knows more than we do," the duchess complained. "We know nothing—nothing."

"I never saw him alone for an instant," Bertie recalled afterward.

What the Yorks and others in the family did know was that in the ancient market town of Ipswich in the rustic county of Suffolk, a long hour's drive from London, a suit for divorce was pending: "Simpson W. vs. Simpson E. A." As the solicitor for Wallis, David had found Theodore Goddard of Lincoln's Inn, London, some of whose clients were stars of the legitimate West End theater. Ipswich recommended itself as the site of the action because of its remoteness from the capital.

Goddard explained that the two-tier British legal system

meant that a bewigged, silk-robed barrister, not a humble solicitor like himself, must represent her in court. The choice fell on prestigious Norman Birkett, a King's Counsel.

The existing law also divided a divorce into two stages. First, a judge could grant a decree *nisi* (Latin for "unless"), which would become absolute six months later *unless* cause were shown why it should not. Wallis would have to leave the house owned by the crown at No. 16 Cumberland Terrace, not far from Regent's Park zoo, which David had now provided for her, in order to establish necessary residence in Suffolk.

Before she departed, David made it his business to let her meet Margaret and Elizabeth. He brought her unannounced to afternoon tea at Royal Lodge. The Yorks gave neither of them a clue to their feelings. The self-assured American stranger came close to lording it over the uncle whom the girls had been taught to greet with a bobbing curtsy. He was not "Your Majesty" or "Sir" to her, but "David." Crawfie, for one, considered that Mrs. Simpson overstepped the mark when she brought him to a window of his brother's house, saying how greatly the view would be improved if some trees were uprooted and part of a hill dug away.

The duchess' charm held firm, but the encounter was growing uncomfortable for everyone. "Crawfie," she said, "would you like to take Lilibet and Margaret into the woods for a while?" Out of sight, the governess and the girls clasped hands. The children had sensed their parents' uneasiness. Who *was* the woman with Uncle David? Crawfie did not know what to tell them.

David had greater success when he asked Lord Beaverbrook's help in making certain that his *Daily Express* and the rest of Fleet Street would print no more than a formal line or two about the divorce trial. He assured the dynamic little Canadian publisher, like everyone else he spoke with, that he had no plans to marry Wallis. The truth, as he admitted later, was that his mind had been made up two years ago.

His chauffeur drove her in the Buick to Beach House, rented in Felixstowe, a port for steamers sailing the North Sea and situated within easy distance of Ipswich. Her stay was part of a legalistic masquerade, played out on the afternoon of October 27 in the Ipswich court. An international corps of reporters had infiltrated the town, but here they were confined to thirty seats, from which they could see only the back of a witness' head. Places for the public opposite the stand were left empty. Spectators farther back in the room faced thirteen police officers and four plainclothes men, on guard against photographs being sneaked of Wallis.

Her face was half hidden under the pulled-down brim of her hat when Birkett whispered her onto the stand as the first witness. "My lord," he said, "this is an undefended case." Mr. Justice Hawke, white wig accentuating the glow in his cheeks, wondered aloud why it had been brought here. He received no answer. She was suing on grounds of adultery. Two floor waiters and the hall porter from the Hotel de Paris, on the Thames near Maidenhead, swore that Ernest Simpson had stayed overnight there on July 21 and 23, 1936, in Room No. 4 with a lady who positively was not Mrs. Simpson. (Her professional name, as it turned out, was "Buttercup" Kennedy.)

Wallis ran her tongue between dry lips as she waited. If stopping in the same hotel constituted cause for divorce, hadn't she and David done that in Vienna? She suspected hostility in the judge's glances at her, but in nineteen minutes the decree *nisi* was granted. "With costs, I am afraid," he said. "Unusual circumstances." Ernest would have to bear legal fees and expenses amounting to some thousand dollars. He had already turned down the offer of a knighthood from David.

Wallis, halfway free to marry again, slipped out of a side door opened by a velvet-jacketed bailiff. Reporters who took after her found it relocked when they got there. "Silence!" shouted the bailiffs, quelling their protests. By the time they were released, she was in a car heading back to London, with Scotland Yard clearing the road ahead.

A week before, David's private secretary, Major Alexander Hardinge, who had served George since 1920, finally persuaded Baldwin to seize the initiative and urge David to ensure that Wallis abandoned her lawsuit. As a married woman, she could safely remain his mistress without risk of further ramifications. "Must this case really go on?" the Prime Minister asked, relighting his pipe and sipping Scotch and soda one morning at The Fort. He could not think of trying to restrain her, David replied. He did not mention marriage.

But he was beginning to worry how his plans would work out. Perhaps he was too independent-minded to suit most people, too little like his father. Though he avoided talking to his brother, he spoke openly of him as a successor. "Well, there is my brother Bertie," he told his closest confidant, the wordly-wise barrister Walter Monckton. The Prime Minister, who invariably said less than he knew, had also made an enigmatic comment to friends: "The Yorks will do it very well."

Bertie refused to consider the possibility. To discuss the appalling prospect might by some turn of fate bring it to reality. He could see himself only as his brother's inferior, bashful, introverted, untrained, and handicapped by the stammer that made even saying "king" an embarrassment. He had grown up, as Margaret was doing, a fixed step behind an older child. For his own sake and for his family's, he prayed on his knees that David would never give up the throne. Yet there was no telling where his infatuation might carry him.

"I feel," Bertie said, "like the proverbial sheep being led to the slaughter, which is not a comfortable feeling."

He tried in desperation to learn what his brother had in mind to do. David invented excuses for not meeting him. "He is very difficult to see," Bertie related, "and when one does he wants to talk about other matters. It is all so worrying, and I feel we all live a life of conjecture." How he could survive without the help of the duchess was inconceivable. "Your mother," he told his daughters, "is not only wonderful—she is also very wise."

All he could extract from David, was, "I will ... tell you my decision when I have made up my mind." He wanted Wallis to move into The Fort for protection against the coming storm.

Three more weeks produced no overt move. On November 16, David summoned Baldwin to Buckingham Palace. The setting was chosen for its impressing formality. There would be no Scotch-and-soda or a congenial walk around the garden this early Monday evening. David wasted no time. "I intend to marry Mrs. Simpson as soon as she is free ... " If the government stood in his path, he was "prepared to go."

It was a curiously provocative declaration if it was intended only to introduce a subject never previously referred to between the two of them. David's tenseness indicated that he had deliberated in advance about what he would say. The threat was more than implied. He had known his Prime Minister long enough to realize that Baldwin was a stickler for morality, with a wife more puritanical than he. In the outcome, most of the country believed that David was forced to choose between his mistress and his crown. It was more than likely that he had come close already to deciding that his job held limited attraction for him, so he would let Bertie shoulder the burden.

Baldwin, reasonably enough, declined to rise to the challenge on the spot. "It is impossible for me to make any
comment on it today," he said, and drove off in his modest
black limousine. David changed into tails and white tie to go
to Marlborough House for dinner with his mother.

He delayed telling her his intentions until the meal was
over. Then he repeated the summation with which he had just
warned Baldwin: marriage or, if necessary, abdication. Would
Mary be willing to talk to Wallis? She would not, she said,
ashen-faced but dry-eyed. She implored him for the sake of
the family and the country to give up the idea. As she chided
him afterward, "You did not seem to be able to take in any
point of view but your own."

Bertie had to wait until the following day to hear directly
from his brother what he planned on doing. For the present,
that amounted to nothing in particular except retire each
night to the company of Wallis. Determined not to yield,
Baldwin wasted no time. He arrived at Marlborough House
the same morning to confer with the dowager queen about
what she called "a pretty kettle of fish."

From the top-floor landing at No. 145 Piccadilly, Margaret
peered down in wonder at the stream of dignitaries being
admitted through the front door. There had never before been
such a host of people coming to confer with Papa. He was
clearly involved in some great mystery, but there was no
guessing what it might be, and there was nobody to explain to
her. The Prime Minister arrived, followed subsequently by the
stone-faced Archbishop of Canterbury and a mixed batch of
statesmen and ecclesiastics. Each of them was closeted for long
sessions with Bertie, though he relayed not a word of what
was in the making. Baldwin and the archbishop saw eye to
eye. The Most Reverend Dr. Lang objected to divorce on
principle. He would never personally administer the rites of
matrimony to any man or woman, innocent or guilty, who

had been through the divorce mill, and his rule covered every priest of the established Church of England.

The Prime Minister added more aces to his hand by sounding out fellow premiers in the British dominions of Canada, Australia, New Zealand, and the rest. He was assured that they, too, were against the marriage. He checked with Clement Attlee and other leaders of the opposition Socialists. They promised him that in the event the National Government resigned, they would shun the attempt to form another. The Liberals echoed that pledge. Geoffrey Dawson of *The Times* stalked Whitehall and the palace, an ally eager to throw the weight of his newspaper behind Baldwin when the time was ripe.

The Prime Minister did not want that done yet. He faced David with a harsh choice: renounce Wallis or abdicate in favor of Bertie, or even Elizabeth. Some hierarchs feared that the duke's health was too delicate for the task. It was argued that his ten-year-old daughter should be sovereign, with a council of regents acting for her. If David attempted to make Wallis his queen, Baldwin would quit and the government would fall. With nothing to replace it, the country and the monarchy would totter into chaos.

The Prime Minister held a final trump card, as David knew. Until half a year had elapsed, Wallis' decree could be challenged. The taint of collusion was strong. Evidence could be produced that she had been guilty when she had gone into court.

Baldwin stipulated that the crisis must be resolved behind the scenes before Christmas—and before news of it leaked to the blinkered British public. David and Wallis had a joint plan for him to take to the radio to state his case to the nation. Baldwin vetoed the idea, just as Bertie would not permit Elizabeth to be substituted for him as a sacrificial lamb.

By November 25, a week before the dam burst, Bertie

accepted the inevitable. He had no alternative. He would have to succeed his brother. "I will do my best," he said on the point of heartbreak, "if the whole fabric does not crumble under the shock and strain of it all."

In Berlin, Hitler scoffed at the thought that David might be compelled to abdicate. He had a report from one of David's German relatives, the Duke of Coburg, who had three private talks with the king in the early months of his reign. Asked whether Baldwin might usefully consult with the Fuehrer to preserve smooth relations between their countries, David had retorted, "Who is king here? Baldwin or I? I myself wish to talk to Hitler, and will do so here or in Germany. Tell him that, please."

On Hitler's orders, German newspapers kept as quiet as the British about Wallis. "You'll see," Ambassador von Ribbentrop beamed, "the Fuehrer will be proved right, the whole affair will go up in smoke, and the king will be grateful to us for having treated the crisis with such tactful reticence."

The dam gave way on December 2. Dr. A. M. F. Blunt, Bishop of the Yorkshire city of Bradford, had been to London, meeting both the archbishop and Baldwin. On his return, Blunt spoke obliquely to a diocesan conference about the king's requiring the blessings of God. "We hope he is aware of his need. Some of us wish he gave more positive signs of his awareness."

That evening, the frustrated proprietors and editors of Fleet Street agreed that those words justified breaking their silence and unfolding the story of David and Wallis as they had been itching to do for months. Dawson, who had been confident that *The Times* would be first, got lost in the rush. Margaret and her sister were engrossed with their success as swimmers. Both of them were the possessors of life-saving certificates, presented to reward their achievements at the Bath Club, but nothing could save them from a dousing in the torrent that flooded Britain as soon as the morning papers were out.

THE KING AND MRS. SIMPSON: CRISIS said the bright red letters on the placards of the newsvendors that the girls passed on a walk with Crawfie. "Down with the American whore" was a sample of the graffiti scrawled elsewhere. Outside every royal residence, the crowds swarmed, waiting expectantly for signs of action.

A "king's party" took vague shape with Churchill on its flank, begging Parliament not to be hasty in its decisions, and Mosley as its most visible leader, egging on his audiences by asking, "How would you like a Cabinet of our busybodies to choose your girl for you?" Communists and Mosley's black-shirted Fascists marched together for the first and last time in the demonstration that formed in front of Buckingham Palace, chanting, "Down with Baldwin, we want the king." The hostility of the throng at the railings of No. 145 Piccadilly frightened the family inside. "Mrs. Simpson" came the yell, and the booing blotted out the sounds of passing traffic.

Bertie was horrified. His daughters deserved some kind of explanation. He was too deeply involved in the turmoil himself to feel capable of answering their questions, and the duchess had been put to bed with influenza. It fell to the governess to tell the girls that their uncle was in love with a woman he yearned to make his wife in spite of the fact that he could not make her his queen. The distinction was too much for Margaret to fathom. Elizabeth came closer to understanding. Neither of them grasped the point that their lives, like David's and their parents', were being overturned.

Wallis took the Buick to flee Fort Belvedere in panic that evening, afraid to remain in England another day when stones were shattering windows at No. 16 Cumberland Terrace.

David was so impatient to join her at the Villa Lou Viei in Cannes that only formalities remained to be settled before Bertie was king. In Marlborough House, Bertie broke down and wept on his mother's shoulder for an hour as she sat at his side, trying to console him. "It is a terrible blow to all of us," she said. She did not add her tears to his then, but when she called on the duchess, they cried together.

David commissioned Walter Monckton to negotiate the terms of the bargain that was to be struck. David's private income, once he was dethroned, would be augmented by an extra £25,000 a year under an arrangement with his brother. He would be created Duke of Windsor and entitled to be addressed as "Your Royal Highness"; to his chagrin, a similar privilege was denied Wallis when he married her in France the following spring. The actual Bill of Abdication was pushed through Parliament in a single day. Another bill was promised him, making her divorce final so that he could immediately make her his wife. That part of the deal was cancelled at the last moment when the Cabinet belatedly detected a scent of corruption.

"We must take what is coming to us and make the best of it," the duchess said with the sound common sense that Bertie respected. She could not leave her bed, so Crawfie was deputized to let the children know that Buckingham Palace was to be their new home. They were as aghast as their father had been. "You mean forever?" Elizabeth asked.

Margaret's history lessons dealt principally with the lives of former kings and queens. She did not want her beleaguered uncle to suffer the fate of Charles I of the House of Stuart, who in the name of the divine right of kings governed England with a Parliament for eleven years, using the infamous courts of the Star Chamber and the High Commission to make his means of raising money seem legal, until he was tried as a public enemy in 1649.

"Will they behead him?" she wondered.

She saw him once more at dinner in Royal Lodge, seated there with the rest of the Yorks, uncles, and aunts. He looked tense, remote, and unhappy. Conversation, sporadic at its best, died whenever the servants came to clear away one course and bring in another. She was not clear in her mind about exactly what was going on. Mrs. Simpson wanted to be queen of England, but that was impossible. Uncle David loved her, so he was going to marry her anyway and leave the country in the hands of Papa, who would be king in his place. On the face of it, that ought to be exciting. It was hard to understand why everybody was so down on Uncle David. Margaret wasn't; if she ever married, she thought David would be a splendid name for a son.

On December 10, with Bertie and their two younger brothers signing as witnesses, David formally renounced the throne. The next day, he raced to France and Wallis. In the judgment of most of his former subjects, no woman in the world was more detestable.

V

Goodbye, Piccadilly . . .

The simplest way to repair the damage was to turn back the clocks and erase the memory of the three-hundred-thirty-five-day reign of Edward VIII, which had ended in disillusionment and murmurs that possibly Britain should be made over as a republic. As a token of his intentions, Bertie invoked the name of his father and elected to be known as George VI. Like George, he set out to work in harmony with his ministers, not battle with them. There would be no more impromptu remarks about the national need for more jobs and better housing, no more snipping at red tape.

His brother had tried half-heartedly to heave the pyramid of royalty upside down and balance it on its tip. Bertie would do his part with Baldwin in restoring it to a solid base. He was far too shy to want to be glamorized like David and too fond of his family to be tempted by any woman except his wife, who was now Queen Elizabeth. Necessity had driven him to give up the life he wanted. Now he planned on setting an example as a faithful husband and a caring father, disturbing his daughters' happiness as little as possible, even if it did mean spoiling them.

He had qualms about his physical ability to stand up to the strain. "I am new to the job, but I hope that time will be allowed to me to make amends for what has happened," he told Baldwin anxiously.

Neither of them knew that one source of infection in the country had been removed. Hitler telephoned von Ribbentrop in London and advised him that he might as well start packing. "Now that the king has been dethroned, there is certainly no other person in England who is ready to play with us. Report to me on what you've been able to do. I shan't blame you if it amounts to nothing."

The new queen was more optimistic than her husband. "The curious thing," she told the archbishop, "is that we are not afraid. I feel that God has enabled us to face the situation calmly."

Influenza still kept her at home on Saturday morning, December 12, when Bertie, looking like a hero of grand opera in the full dress uniform of admiral of the fleet with cocked hat and ceremonial sword, went off to St. James's Palace to meet his Privy Councillors. Margaret scampered with her sister to send him off with a hug. Pale and haggard, he was too preoccupied to return more than a fleeting grin.

Crawfie did what she could to fill the girls in on the significance of the day. After he came back for one o'clock luncheon, he would be formally proclaimed His Majesty George VI and entitled to a curtsy.

"Margaret, too?" Elizabeth asked.

"Margaret also," the governess confirmed, "and try not to topple over."

The children met him in the hall, knees bending in the gesture of respectfulness. It startled him, and his eyes filled before he stooped to embrace them. The change struck him hardest in trivial things like this. Margaret felt it in another way when her mother cancelled the next swimming lesson, afraid that the crowd of spectators would be too overwhelming.

The move from the house on Piccadilly was slow and wrenching. The girls felt it was a poor bargain to exchange their comfortable home for the vast and dismal palace. Margaret brooded over the mystery of how her own identity was at stake. Her father had changed his name along with his habits, and hers had gone, too. "I have only just learned to write York," she grumbled.

Her universe had been turned upside down. There were strange rooms to live in and a strange bed to sleep in, strange faces on every side. Nothing was the way it had been, and it never could be the same again. Everything surrounding her now was so *old* it was like being whisked away under a witch's spell from the familiar present into ancient times when Victoria wrote the rules for living. When she grew up, *she* would have her house furnished in a fashion that echoed the home she had been wrested from.

In her loss of the sense of security that only familiar things could give her, she missed access to her father most of all. He was hard pressed for time to spare from the burdens of being king, striving to heal his country's wounds. She was haunted by the thought of how within a year Grandpapa had died and Uncle David disappeared. Did that mean that Papa was due to go next, vanishing as if in a puff of smoke? And after that, Elizabeth? Margaret was not so rare a child that she never speculated on the effect of the unthinkable happening, which would force the crown onto her fearful head.

At Sunday-morning service in the little chapel at Royal Lodge, the congregation prayed on its knees for the king's majesty, its most gracious sovereign lord King George. Mar-

garet's voice murmured with the rest; no one was more
devout in prayer. God *must* save Papa. At every church of the
established faith in the land, the same supplications were said:
for its gracious Queen Elizabeth, the Princess Elizabeth, the
royal family. But Margaret heard no mention of herself by
name. She was apparently excluded from the list. The impact
of the omission was shattering at a time when she was groping
to supply a new answer to the confounding question, "Who
am I?"

The mail brought letters addressed to Her Majesty the
Queen. "That's Mummy now," the girls assured each other.
Bertie joked with them. "Supposing someone telephones.
Whom shall I say I am?"

Margaret twitted him to even the score. "Papa, do you sing
'God Save Thy Gracious Me'?"

"You mustn't be so cheeky," he would say, pretending to
scold, but she was one of the few joys left in the business that
cut down the time they could spend together. He had received
no training for it under the regimen that took only David
into account. Bertie had to learn on the job and pray for the
best. "Margaret," he was delighted to say, "can charm the
pearl out of an oyster."

He worked more determinedly than ever to overcome his
stammering. He was the only member of his generation in the
family to be afflicted. His daughters did not refer to it, since it
was an essential part of Papa. Margaret would no more dream
of mimicking him than of setting fire to the palace. Self-help
techniques were taught him by an Australian-born "healer"
who was in no way a qualified doctor. Lionel Logue of Harley
Street practiced the belief that the root of the defect lay in a
patient's fear of seeming different from people not affected. His
initial success had been in convincing Bertie that he was a
normal being with a curable speech defect. Deep, steady

breathing and exercises to expand the lungs were the prescription. One hardship in being king was that it made him and his family abnormal no matter what he did.

On the first Sunday of his reign, confidence in himself was put under fresh strain by a radio address delivered by the archbishop after Margaret and Elizabeth had gone to bed. "When his people listen to him," Dr. Lang intoned patronizingly, "they will note an occasional and momentary hesitation in his speech. But he has brought it into full control, and to those who hear it need cause no embarrassment, for it causes none to him who speaks."

On the Monday, his daughters heard cannon fired by shako-wearing gunners of the Royal Horse Artillery booming in Hyde Park to salute Bertie's forty-first birthday. Margaret was pleased to find that there was an extra advantage he could enjoy. He did what George had once done for Mary on *his* June birthday by appointing his wife Elizabeth to the most ancient order of chivalry and bestowing on her the Order of the Garter.

Moving out filled the house with boxes, crates, and barrels in the New Year. The two corgis, Jane and Dookie, presented a problem. Ought they to go to the palace with Bertie and the queen or be left behind with the girls, who would follow later? There were the budgerigars and canaries to be carried in their cages to the new nursery, wherever that was to be. A perpetually squawking parrot would be out of place, so the bird was sent off to the Regent Park zoo.

Crawfie used to take the girls over to see their father and mother and play in the garden. The routines of starting each day in their parents' bedroom and joining them for lunch and tea had gone forever. Once they joined them for tea in the huge Belgian Suite, a museum piece in pink and gold. That was a giggly occasion, highlighted when the governess subsided through a chair that had not been recaned since it supported guests of Victoria.

Their mother had them pack their own toys and ruled that half of them must be given away to a children's hospital. "It's impossible to decide," Margaret protested. She and Elizabeth refused to part with a single horse in the stud. They contemplated wheeling the entire collection across Green Park to their new quarters, until authority prevailed and the precious animals were bedded down in a wicker basket, ready for the movers' van.

The brightest part of the palace was the suite of rooms making up the nursery, which had all been freshly painted. A corridor there made ideal stabling for the herd. The windows looked down on the tree-lined Mall, leading straight to a corner of Trafalgar Square. Margaret found two new pastimes—watching Guardsmen march up to the thump of a band every morning, and gawking through the lace curtains at the crowd that haunted the palace at all hours of the day.

Otherwise, the new home had nothing to recommend it. It was as cold and cheerless as a vault, as easy to lose oneself in as a maze. Footsteps were hushed on miles of red carpeting, then echoed on stone where the carpeting ended. Voices were kept to a murmur, as if this were a cathedral where services never stopped. The size of the rooms and the height of the frescoed ceilings instilled the feeling that somehow she had shrunk.

She was separated from her parents and Crawfie by mountainous flights of stairs and endless corridors stretching toward every compass point. She experimented with lurking behind the towering marble columns to jump out and startle one or other of the uniformed attendants passing by on their interminable rounds.

She shared her bedroom with Alah, who sat there knitting until her princess fell asleep. Sharing was a comfort when the night wind whistled in the chimneys and mice scurried within the walls. But Alah made a poor companion when the girl wanted to talk to someone. The old nanny still pampered her like a baby, but she was at a loss to answer the questions that flooded Margaret's brain. Being tucked into bed was frustrating when there was so much to ask—about God, the world outside, and herself. Serving hot meals to her in the nursery retreat created problems, too; the footman had to traverse the width of the building from the kitchens five or six hundred yards upstairs and down.

"I do wish we could all go home," Margaret sighed. This place was not home. She had a persistent dream. A magical underground passage had been dug between the palace and Piccadilly, dark at one end, bright at the other. Through it, as she slept, she escaped from mysterious forces that threatened her into sanctuary in No. 145. Most child psychologists, had they been consulted, would have read deeper significance into it: Margaret had the desire to be reborn in another guise.

She also said prayers, to no avail, that her mother would bear another baby, a son this time, to save Elizabeth and perhaps herself at some future date from inheriting their father's plight.

He was being rushed like no monarch in memory toward his coronation to meet the same deadline that had been set for David: May 12. In ordinary circumstances, Bertie would have had eighteen months to prepare, but the program demanded a pageant to restore public faith in the continuity of kings. Delay was unthinkable.

The girls' schoolroom was Bertie's choosing, a sunny little room with a view of the gardens, five minutes' away down three flights of stairs and through the halls. They wished they had bicycles to shorten the trip. The first thought had been to use the dreary retreat in which Bertie, legs in splints, had been tutored as a boy, acquiring a limited education and worse trouble with his speech. "That won't do," he said firmly after taking a look through the doorway.

Lessons were constantly interrupted that spring. Preparations for the coronation meant fitting the children for their first long dresses. Their mother decided on ivory lace over satin and little silver bows, to be worn with cloaks of purple velvet trimmed with ermine. Elizabeth was tall enough, the queen thought, for a train, but Margaret was not.

"I must have a train, too," stormed her jealous daughter, who had taken to complaining, "Now that Papa is king, I am nothing." She was given her way. Bertie made sure that the feather-weight silver-gilt coronets ordered for his daughters were a matching pair.

As the queen's free time grew scarcer, Elizabeth began mothering her sister. Margaret's moods worried her.

"I really don't know what we are going to do with Margaret," Elizabeth would say, taking on the responsibility, while she reported the latest harassment to their governess.

Margaret missed the companionship of her parents with a six-year-old's intensity. They usually started the day with the girls and lunched with them if nothing formal was on the calendar. Bertie had too much to do to see much more of his daughters, but their mother tried to slip out into the garden when they played there with the dogs in the afternoons. Regular bedtimes were impossible to keep, to Alah's dismay. Margaret hung about, hoping to catch a glimpse of her father and mother before they left for some nightly function, then willed herself to stay awake in case they came back in time to give her a goodnight kiss.

She raced, laughing and whooping, through the corridors and up and down the stairs, bent on being noticed. Mr. Baldwin and his colleagues, Privy Councillors, divines of the church, and the mailman, ran equal risk of collision as she panted along, calling, "Wait for me!"

"So vivacious!" they would nod to each other. "Such a happy little thing!"

A walk to the palace's indoor riding school, where carriage horses were in training for the ceremonies ahead, was a pleasure, though she had not learned every one of their names like her sister. The grooms conditioned the immaculate animals to the uproar of crowds by dangling dummy figures in front of their nostrils, flourishing handkerchiefs, flags, and umbrellas, and yelling in chorus to the blare of a trumpet blown by a bandsman detailed for the exercise.

Margaret claimed first place on the builder's ladder left outside. From the top rungs, she could peer through a window at the commotion and contest any attempt to give Elizabeth or Crawfie a turn. Eventually, the three of them were invited inside to lend their cheers to the make-believe throng.

She rehearsed for her appearance in Westminster Abbey by putting on the long dress and coronet as soon as they were delivered. She had caught mid-morning glimpses of her mother in tiara and dazzling evening gown on her way to a sitting for an artist engaged on one of the portraits which were an indispensable side-order to a new reign. "I put on my coronet and walked about like Johnnie Walker," she told the queen in relating the events of one day.

Margaret and the rest of the household got no sleep after 3 A.M. on May 12, when sound engineers started testing the loudspeakers installed for the ceremony on Constitution Hill to the north of the palace. The first contingents of troops tramped in to the drumbeat of regimental bands not long after. There was too much to attend to for the princesses to breakfast with their parents today. Bertie, in any event, admitted that he could not force down a bite.

Alah got Margaret ready in the awesome long dress and silver slippers, worn over a pair of wool knee-socks. Then

Crawfie took the girls to see their mother, looking more regal than joyful in her finery, and father, who was sinking inside at the thought of spending the most trying day of his life to date.

Elizabeth was in a stew about her sister. "I do hope she won't disgrace us by falling asleep in the middle, Crawfie. After all, she is very young for a coronation, isn't she?"

Glittering with insignia, weighted down by embroidered robes, their parents left for the abbey in the four-ton state coach, drawn by a team of eight burnished Windsor Grays. The ornately carved, gilded relic of George IV rocked on its leather braces like a rowboat in a choppy sea.

At half past ten, the children hoisted their trains and clambered up into a following glass-windowed carriage. Alah was thankful that her princess was spared a dawdling ride in a stuffy, closed Daimler, an experience known to upset her stomach. A green face would not do at all today. With her sister watching anxiously beside her, she was perched on a raised seat to see and be seen.

Grandmama, cheeks made up like porcelain, sat with them, together with Great-Aunt Maud, queen of Norway and George's youngest sister, who was one of the drove of royal guests in town for the celebration. Grandmama thought the girls "looked too sweet in their lace dresses and robes."

Margaret saw the route awash with spectators. She winced as the chatter of the crowds exploded into cheers as loud as thunder and as piercing as a steam whistle when the procession approached. Old-timers on the palace staff exposed to the tumult stuffed cotton in their ears to ward off headaches on these occasions, a practice that she followed at a later date.

Postilions on foot and postilions on horseback. Floured wigs and mirror-bright jackboots. Gleaming cuirasses and plumed helmets. Men marching and men reining-in uneasy mounts. Jingle of swords and harness, shrilling of silver trumpets.

Fairy-tale costumes cleaned and pressed: scarlet, gold, white, and imperial purple. Pealing bells and hammering drums. All for Papa.

The two old ladies and the two children sat together in the abbey gallery, surveying the multitude beneath them. Bertie, his wife, and the archbishop shared the belief that the occasion should reestablish the king as the "head of our morality." Movie cameras stood high above the heads below. The archbishop had been hostile to radio until he discovered how well he sounded over a microphone. Now he had agreed that the proceedings should be broadcast in toto by the BBC.

Between the convoluted gray stone columns, the red robes of the peerage and the gold-and-white copes of the clergy spread like a versicolored carpet, scented with the odor of incense and moth balls. Coronets were tucked away, ready for the climax of hosannas toward the end of the afternoon. They would be brandished and worn in fealty to Papa after the archbishop anointed him with sacramental oil and placed on his head St. Edward's crown of England, fashioned for Charles II in 1660. Alah hovered out of sight, carrying a brush and comb apiece for the girls to keep them trim for the hours-long spectacle.

Margaret perched on the edge of her cushion, craning to see everything in the sea of movement below. The first hitch occurred out of her sight. The queen and her attendants were due to lead the way down the aisle toward the altar when one of the chaplains fainted. No one had foreseen such casualties. The procession made a belated start when he was carried off at last. Margaret had no need for either Grandmama or Great-Aunt Maud to point out the appearance of Mummy and then Papa followed by anxious pages holding up his trailing robes.

From above, the rites conducted down there looked like the working out of an elaborate gavotte, but it took so long before Papa knelt at the altar to take the oath. She fiddled in boredom with a prayer book. Then she saw something was amiss, and her fingers tightened. Neither of the bishops on either side of him had the text of the service. When the archbishop held down his copy for Papa to read, an ecclesiastical thumb obscured the key words. She could sense the tension in Papa, but he managed to overcome the situation.

He paced slowly to the massive coronation chair to be clad in more vestments. It was an appropriate moment for Grandmama to whisper an explanation. In the nick of time, the Dean of Westminster was constrained from lowering one surplice over his monarch's head inside out. The Lord Great Chamberlain did duty as another dresser. Margaret watched in fascination as his shaky fingers fumbled to fix a jewelled sword belt around Papa, who was so alarmed that he took over the job himself to save being hit under the chin with the sword hilt.

Then the supreme moment. She was intensely proud and immensely scared of what the future might bring to Papa and herself. She saw the archbishop falter as he lifted the crown, seven pounds of gold and precious stones. She held her breath when, instead of lowering it onto Papa's head, he turned it slowly around in his bony hands as though checking it for flaws in workmanship. Papa told later what had happened: the archbishop was looking for a thread of red cotton that marked its front. Somebody in the wings, mistaking the tag for a sign of slipshod housekeeping, had flicked it away.

At last, the task was completed. Papa's next move was to head for his throne. She noticed that he was pulled up short. A bishop was treading on his robe. "I had to tell him to get off it pretty sharply," Papa said, "as I nearly fell down."

Elizabeth gave a good account of her sleepy sister when they arrived home. "I only had to nudge her once or twice when she played with the prayer books too loudly." Frank Salisbury, commissioned to record the scene on canvas, had sat sketching furiously as the archbishop raised his hand in benediction over Bertie's crowned head. The painter noticed that everyone's eyes focussed on the king, except Margaret's. She was staring in awe at the Most Reverend Dr. Lang for reasons which should have surprised nobody.

Sixteen days after the coronation, Bertie had a new Prime Minister and a reshuffled Cabinet, though the coloration of the National Government remained Conservative blue. Baldwin, the impresario responsible for making Bertie king, retired in glory, created an earl and Knight of the Garter by way of recognition. Bertie continued to seek his advice and go to his house for dinner. His successor, austere Mr. Chamberlain, would stay in office, struggling to pacify Hitler, for the next three years.

A curious calm descended on the land. David's popularity was turning out to be as flimsy as a silent movie star's. Bertie, his mother, and especially his daughters were the new idols, well thought of by everyone but a tiny minority who clamored for British arms to be shipped without restriction to the loyalists of Spain, where Generalissimo Francisco Franco with Mussolini's help was in rebellion against the elected leftist government.

No king put more energy into the job than Bertie. In justifying himself, the sixth George seemed likely to be the best of the lot, the only other contender being his father. Victoria had scorned the rest of them as "my wicked Hanoverian uncles." Even in death, she could not tolerate them; she had herself buried in her own mausoleum near Windsor Castle.

The first, George Guelph of Hanover, Germany, had a just but remote claim to the English throne. His grandmother Elizabeth, queen of Bohemia, was the daughter of James I and sister of the decapitated Charles I. The Bohemian queen's daughter Sophia was married to the Elector of the principality of Hanover, Ernst August Guelph. When Sophia's cousin,

Queen Anne Stuart, died in 1714, leaving no heir, George Guelph was duly imported as king of England.

He hated the country and its people, whose language was a mystery to him. For companionship, he brought over his German Jezebels. His wife was in prison, locked up by George when he found that, in her misery with his wenching, she had taken Count Königsmark to her bed. George did not pretend to rule. He saw no point in attending meetings of his Cabinet when he could not understand a word that was said. Hanover was his homeland, and he spent most of his time there.

Nothing short of revolution could prevent his equally obnoxious eldest son and namesake from succeeding him. The second George did have a smattering of English. He, too, loved Hanover and whoring, but he was open to listening to his ministers, notably Horace Walpole and William Pitt. They served him well by laying the foundations of an empire in India and wresting Canada from the French. George was only mildly interested. What fascinated him was his fortune in gold, which he counted coin by coin, hour by hour.

"Farmer George," the next, was his grandson, heir of Frederick, the eldest of George II's offspring, who died before his father. The third George, a drowsy, moody child, needed constant prompting from his mother to "be a king." He turned a new leaf on his wedding day when he assigned his mistress, Lady Sarah Lennox, to be a bridesmaid to Charlotte of Mecklenburg. Charlotte was kept occupied bearing him fifteen children. He set out to recapture the power and influence of the crown, which his predecessors had let slip from their grasp.

As the self-styled "patriot king," he was delighted to take personal responsibility for direction of the war against his "ungrateful children" in the thirteen American colonies. After the defeat of his outnumbered Redcoats at Yorktown, Virginia, he twice toyed with the thought of abdication, but went no further than writing out dignified statements of intent.

By that time of Cornwallis' surrender at Yorktown—October, 1781—George had already shown symptoms of what his doctors could only term insanity. His greeting to John Adams on his arrival in London as the first United States envoy at the Court of St. James's could scarcely have been more lucid. "I will be very frank with you," George told him. "I was the last to consent to the separation; but the separation having been made and having become inevitable, I have always said, as I say now, that I would be the first to meet the friendship of the United States as an independent power." He might have added, "What? what?" as he was in the habit of doing to conclude every sentence. American casualties in the fighting had been modest: four thousand dead, six thousand wounded.

Farmer George lost the colonies but left a legacy in the Royal Marriages Act that enchained his descendants seven generations later, notably Bertie's daughter Margaret. The law was a result of the scandalous conduct of most of Farmer George's twelve surviving children and his total inability to control them.

Three of his daughters strayed from the paths of virtue set for them by George in his contented marriage to Charlotte, which in itself was a rarity in the bawdy circles of the eighteenth-century court.

Augusta fell in love with a royal physician—her father was beset by them.

Sophia was wed in secret to one of George's equerries. She was "afflicted with the dropsy," her father was told when she became noticeably pregnant.

Amelia, his favorite, had a desperate romance with another aging courtier but was frustrated in her desire to elope with him. Her death in 1811 was believed by George's doctors to be the final push that drove him permanently over the brink of insanity. He lived for nine years more in seclusion.

Meningitis was blamed for killing two of his sons, *Octavius* and *Alfred*, in infancy. Of the seven remaining, at least four were recognizable profligates.

William Henry, the third born, who later reigned as William IV, kept an actress as his light of love. As a young naval officer serving on the Hudson River in the War of Independence, he came close to being kidnapped by a band of colonist commandos and carried off as a prize to Philadelphia.

Edward, son number four, took advantage of the new imperialism by enjoying the favors of a Canadian fancy woman, Madame St. Laurent, for twenty-seven years, over-lapping his marriage to Victoria of Saxe-Coburg, who bore him a daughter named for herself the year before his death.

Ernest's marriage to Frederica of Mecklenburg-Strelitz broke up within a year of its consummation.

Farmer George's firstborn son, another *George*, was the most dubious member of the brood. "Prinny" made his mark on England in a number of ways. He invented a fancy shoe buckle. He ordered an Arabian Nights palace built at a cost of £500,000 in Brighton, a watering place which he made his holiday headquarters. He ran up tailors' bills of £10,000 a year on his coats alone to stay secure on fashion's pinnacle, priding himself on being recognized as "the first gentleman of Europe," while the British despised him. He staggered Scotland by dressing in a kilt of Stuart tartan to which he had no claim, starting a tradition that endured in the House of Windsor.

With Prinny and his taste for strumpets in mind, Farmer George ushered the Marriages Act through Parliament. Prinny ignored it by entering into a secret and illegal marriage with Mrs. Maria Fitzherbert, a Catholic endowed with a handsome face and a private fortune. She had more respect for the law than he did. It took hysterical tears and a threat to kill himself to persuade her to become engaged.

The newly married prince swore to his friends in and out of Parliament that he was still single, and he kept up the pretense for two more years. By a quirk of the law, he probably was. Under the 1701 Act of Settlement, he forfeited his right to the crown by marrying a Catholic. But the stringent terms of the Royal Marriages Act made the alliance null and void.

Maria exhausted her fortune, and Prinny had to pawn his jewelry to augment his, though his father was· continually badgered to squeeze more money out of Parliament to pay off Prinny's debts. Finally Farmer George drove him into what purists argued was bigamy. Prinny was so drunk that a duo of dukes had to brace him up as he exchanged vows of fidelity with the unfortunate Princess Caroline Amelia of Brunswick-Wolfenbüttel.

He lived with her for a year, then began a campaign to divorce her that devastated his father. When Farmer George was declared incurably mad, Prinny was appointed Prince Regent. His own hold on reality was flimsy. He persuaded himself that as regent he had led a cavalry charge of his regiment, the 10th Hussars, against Napoleon and the French at Waterloo.

At the age of fifty-seven, bloated with gluttony, Prinny became George IV and rewarded himself with the gaudiest, most expensive coronation the country had been saddled with so far, a £500,000 extravaganza. The fourth George emulated his father in only one respect. Rather than assent to a bill ensuring a better deal for British Catholics, Prinny, too, gave warning that he would abdicate. In the end, of course, he signed it, and subsided into a fit of weeping as he laid down the pen.

He died in 1830, unmourned, half blind, and without

descendants. The kingdom regarded his placid brother William, who succeeded him, as a decided improvement. William endeared himself to his Whig ministers by promising to help them force through a reform bill despite opposition in the Tory-dominated House of Lords. If necessary, he said, he would destroy the upper house of the legislature by creating eighty new Whig peers at the stroke of a pen. The threat in itself was enough to bring the peerage to heel.

After seven years as king, William went the way of the other "wicked Hanoverian uncles," leaving no one in the direct line of descent. Disease and dissipation had nearly demolished the family. His eighteen-year-old niece, Victoria, dead Edward's child, inherited the crown in 1837. Victoria, whose reign lasted into the twentieth century, made respectability a patriotic duty for herself, her offspring, and the country. Some aristocrats judged her to be a dreary little woman.

There was no escape for Bertie from her deathless influence. The imprint she had left on the habits of the court was indelible. After he and his wife reconciled themselves to the disappointment of having no son, he saw no alternative to tightening the standards set for Elizabeth. The gap between the heir to the throne and her sister widened.

When her parents were ceremoniously rowed down the Thames from Westminster in the archaic royal barge, less florid but more seaworthy than Cleopatra's, Elizabeth went with them; Margaret stayed with Alah. Bertie sailed aboard the *Victoria and Albert* to review his fleet of warships at Spithead, off the Isle of Wight. Elizabeth stood by his side; Margaret was out of sight below decks, possibly feeling queasy.

Coronation celebrations lasted into the fall. Mary regretted being "priggish," but she sounded the alarm about all the late nights her granddaughters were enduring. "Yawns in the morning certainly seem all wrong," she commented. "And apart from the question of health, one does feel that a punctual regular life is so essential for children."

Some things they could do together. Dressed like twins in identical frocks of hand-smocked silk, knickers to match, short white gloves, and flowery straw bonnets, they joined in the spectator sport of garden parties, which brought three thousand people through the palace gates on summer afternoons. Crawfie watched how they behaved themselves, sitting up in her room with a pair of binoculars.

The challenge was to stick close enough to a parent to proceed without pushing through the clusters of gentlemen in gray toppers and tailcoats and ladies enveloped in yards of organdy with floral fantasies for hats, who swarmed around to pay their respects. More sisterly instruction was lavished on Margaret. "If you see someone with a funny hat, you must *not* point at it and laugh, and you must *not* be in too much of a hurry to get through the crowds to the tea table."

Margaret sighed with relief when they reached sanctuary in the private enclosure where the royal tea tent was pitched. Admission there was by more exclusive special ticket. The lines stretched a hundred yards long across the trampled lawn under the gaze of Beefeaters in medieval red who edged the site like a border of geraniums. Bandsmen of the Guards played a potpourri of hit songs from the current crop of musical comedies to the beat of their captain conductor, baton in hand, ceremonial sword at his waist.

Politeness required the girl to stay until the strains of "God Save the King!" signalled that the performance was coming to a close. Guests took the cue to move in toward the garden gate at the north entrance, where Margaret, filled with tea and cake, made her exit with her family.

She was on equal footing with Elizabeth in being prepared for bed before court was held on those evenings when Bertie and his queen welcomed the season's debutantes along with a sprinkling of suitable older women of Wallis' vintage. For comfort's sake, Bertie wore a crown less ponderous than St. Edward's when he took to his throne, placed side by side on the dais with another for the queen.

In nightgowns and rosebud-patterned robes, the sisters were treated to a preview of their parents in their splendor, with a goodnight kiss apiece before father and mother made their entrance into the throne room to more gentle music from a regimental band. Then the two girls would retreat to a strategic window to goggle at the incoming limousines, stopping one by one to deliver the players in the tableau, gentlemen in prescribed silk hose, knee breeches, and medals, the ladies with five-foot-long trains and bearing three ostrich plumes in their freshly waved hair.

When Margaret complained about being left out of the frolic, Elizabeth consoled her. "Never mind. One day, you and I will be down there, sharing all the fun. And I shall have a perfectly enormous train, yards long." Margaret without a doubt would want one to match, just like their dressing gowns. If she was sent to bed before the last guests' cars had pulled away in the early morning, it was under protest. Morning-after yawns would have to be smothered if Grandmama was around.

Bertie kept alive the hope that somehow his children could sample more of the everyday world than he had been allowed as a boy. How to do it flummoxed him, since he had no personal experience to draw on. It was for Crawfie to come up with suggestions, which he rarely turned down. A company of Girl Scouts meeting in the palace? Sound idea. But he set his foot down about their wearing long stockings of regulation black. He had been forced to wear those horrors in his knickerbockered younger days.

The local Girl Scout leader foresaw only problems when the plan was broached to her. How could the princesses possibly

mingle with girls of a different class who were taught on
principle to regard each other as equals and sisters? Miss Violet
Synge, the Scout leader, was converted after she arrived for tea
to meet Elizabeth and Margaret. There was, however, another
difficulty. One eager recruit was too young to qualify under
the rule that set ten as the minimum age.

Tears from Margaret usually stirred her sister to action.
Couldn't something be done for Margaret? The solution was
to enroll her as a Brownie and assign two others from a
nearby pack to keep her contented. Only one other puzzle
needed to be resolved: how to stop mothers sending all the
other girls to the palace not in uniform but in party frills,
white gloves, and patent-leather shoes, aspiring junior debs
chaperoned by governesses and clucking nannies?

VI

... Farewell, Leicester Square!

The pattern of the London social season was an Edwardian heirloom. It called for the king's presence in Buckingham Palace each May to begin presiding over an immutable program of courts, grand balls, tea parties, banquets, galas, shows of flowers and horses, cricket matches, horse racing, and displays of military grandeur as intrinsic to the calendar as Easter or Christmas.

On horseback, he also celebrated his birthday, not on December 14, the actual date, but on the second Thursday in June, in hope of better weather to swell the crowd. The clock was pushed a few minutes backward or forward if necessary so that the affair began on the stroke of eleven, come what may. His two senior regiments of cavalry—the Lifeguards, and the Blues and Royals—escorted him to the scene in Whitehall, where infantry brigades of Guardsmen awaited him. If the day was warm, one or two of them invariably fainted, leaving a momentary gap in the lines of scarlet tunics, black bearskins, and bayonetted rifles.

The same month saw thoroughbreds competing at Royal Ascot, Berkshire, in the Derby, and the Oaks at Epsom Down, Surrey. In July, oarsmen skulled racing shells in the Royal Regatta on the placid Thames at Henley; prize horseflesh was put through its paces at Wembley, Middlesex; and enthusiastic gardeners made a bee-line for Windsor Castle for the Royal Rose Show.

Bertie appeared on schedule, always met by the hurrahs of audiences dressed in their best for the honor of catching sight of him if only over rows of bobbing heads and fluttering Union Jacks. In 1938, the second summer of his reign, his understudies had to stand in for him more and more often. Hitler had taken Austria that spring and now he was demanding a slice of Czechoslovakia. For days at a time, Bertie dared not risk leaving the palace while Chamberlain hurried to divert the approach of war.

A London season like this would never be repeated. Actors and spectators went through with it as usual like figurines driven by clockwork, but in September the music stopped. The government expected German bombs to kill fifty thousand Britons in the first few days of attack. Soldiers and civilians worked side by side to dig slit trenches in London parks to provide primitive protection. Every citizen was ordered to be fitted for a gas mask. Anti-aircraft guns were trundled out on Westminster Bridge and the Horse Guards Parade. Cellars and basements were commandeered as air-raid shelters, and the wail of warning sirens was heard for the first time in a radio rehearsal. Four of every five London parents applied for their children to be evacuated to safety outside the sprawling city.

Margaret and Elizabeth left, but only for a day. They went with their mother to the Clydeside shipyard where she was to launch the liner *Queen Elizabeth*. She read a message from her husband to the onlookers: "He bids the people of this country to be of good cheer . . . He knows well that, as ever before in critical times, they will keep cool heads and brave hearts."

His younger daughter supplied a touch of entertainment just before her mother swung the champagne against the ship's bow. Margaret skipped up onto a chair to stand taller than her grave-looking sister. As the wood props were knocked away and the steel hull started its slide into the grimy water, the chorus of salutes blasting from other ships' horns startled her to the point of tumbling over.

In her father's creed, "The highest of distinctions is service to others." He applied the rule to Elizabeth, but not to Margaret. He taught her sister that duty came first in everything. He expected nothing of his baffled younger daughter except her love. For lack of a son, he had to forfeit Elizabeth to the claims of history. To ease the pain it caused him, he made a pet of Margaret, who had many more talents than the ability to love. None of them was allowed to be developed, but if she realized the reason, she laid no blame on Papa. He was the idol whose memory must not be tarnished. She did what was expected of her.

He decided that she could get along on lessons from the governess, though Crawfie would have liked to see her more substantially educated, to encourage the growth of personality. She was constantly teasing, coaxing her with "Laugh, Crawfie!" when she ran into trouble for willfulness. Meantime, Elizabeth was put to work taking sessions in constitutional history with Sir Henry Marten in his study at Eton College, Windsor, where he was the cherubic vice-provost. The distinction between the girls was underlined again: What Elizabeth did was important, but Margaret's deeds were of little consequence.

She went on her own way. If she offended anyone, it was

not her fault; the culprit was always a convenient "Cousin Halifax," a creation of her fancy, and she looked for fresh targets for her mockery.

Elizabeth's sober-sided habits fell within range. She was as set in her ways as a spinster aunt, and Margaret was merciless in mocking her. Elizabeth's nighttime routine was a ritual followed as faithfully as a church service. The stable of toy horses must be inspected first. Then in her room she would undress and fold every garment that would be worn again as neatly as a laundress. In nightgown and robe, she brushed her hair, counting the strokes, and then her teeth, precisely as the dentist advised.

Margaret had the whole performance down pat; it gave her the chance to assert that her superior, sloppier method of doing things was more intelligent than her sister's. "She was a perfect little horror," one witness of her act remembered. "She made everything her sister did look absurd, patting the clothes into place, jeering all the time. 'A place for everything, and everything in its place' and 'We must not forget, cleanliness is next to godliness.'" I suppose it was vicious in a way, but it was indescribably funny."

She had quick ears as well as sharp eyes. She could rattle off songs on the newly acquired miniature piano—dance tunes, classics, music-hall ditties dating back to the last war, like "Keep the Home Fires Burning" and "It's a Long Way to Tipperary," which her father was fond of hearing. For different reasons, he sometimes felt as sorry for her as for Elizabeth. "She has so much talent," he used to sigh, "and it must go to waste."

Though her health was more precarious than her sister's, losing weight was a pleasure for Margaret. "Look, Mummy, I am quite a good shape now, not like a football as I used to be." Crawfie put the pared-down look to Margaret's being what was usually called "highly strung," caused by an overactive imagination. One question on the child's mind some-times popped out. "Supposing Papa should ever die, like Grandpapa?" If that should happen, she would be like luckless Elizabeth, a single life away from the crown that had been imposed on their father.

The scare eased when Chamberlain flew back from Munich waving a sheet of paper signed by Hitler and himself. "Peace for our time," the Prime Minister called it. Alarm flared again when the Fuehrer partitioned Czechoslovakia and listed Poland as the next object of attention. Chamberlain rejected one proposal that he should call a general election and another that he ought to find a place in the government for one of his harshest critics, Winston Churchill, who was decrying the leisurely pace of British rearmament.

Chamberlain had another critic across the Atlantic in Franklin Delano Roosevelt, who thought that the Prime Minister was all too eager to appease the Germans. FDR had intervened to no effect in the Czechoslovakian emergency by appealing to Hitler for a peaceful settlement. Now the President was out to forge some stronger links with Bertie; England would be the first American defense line in the event of war.

"I need not assure you," said the letter from the White House, "that it would give my wife and me the greatest pleasure to see you ... If you bring either or both of the children with you they will also be very welcome, and I shall try to have one or two Roosevelts of approximately the same age to play with them!"

Bertie's timetable was not yet clear. A trip to Canada would have to precede a visit to the United States. But one of the President's fancies had to be brought to earth immediately. "I am afraid that we shall not be taking the children with us if we go to Canada, as they are much too young for such a strenuous tour." The idea of their going was not discussed with either of them. He protected his young with the devotion of a male stickleback. Later, when the family travelled by air, he took the precaution of splitting up the four of them, Margaret and himself in one plane, Elizabeth and her mother in another.

He would not allow the British fleet to be stripped in a time of emergency of the battleship *Repulse*, scheduled for his use when the dates for the Atlantic crossing were finally settled. In its place, the Admiralty chartered the liner *Empress of Australia*, which would be sailing from Southampton on May 5. Grandmama took the girls down by train to see their parents off. She had rather thought her granddaughters might be sent to stay with her in Marlborough House while Bertie was away. It was decided that they would be more comfortable—and less restrained—in familiar surroundings in the palace.

Bertie and the queen were saddened by the parting. No tears were shed by the girls. The outing and the sight of ships of all sizes berthed in the maze of docks in the pale sunshine were too rare to be spoiled by sobbing. As soon as they got home again, Grandmama set to work drawing up a schedule of excursions to places she personally found more fascinating— art galleries, the British Museum, the Tower of London, and the Royal Mint among them.

Crawfie had almost seven uninterrupted weeks in which to catch up on the girls' lessons. Long letters from their parents kept them posted on the progress of the tour. An account of the Sunday picnic on the lawn at Roosevelt's country home in Hyde Park, New York, bewildered Margaret. "But that's just around the corner!" said the child whose grandmother thought half-an-hour's geography a week was sufficient. And what in the world was a *hot dog*? Margaret had never heard of anyone eating such a thing.

But over the hot dogs served at Hyde Park, Bertie and his

wife had left a deep impression on their host. "They are very delightful and understanding people," he reflected, "and, incidentally, know a great deal not only about foreign affairs in general but also about social legislation." He joked that they would both qualify for inclusion in *The Red Network,* a book accepted as gospel by rabid rightwingers. Preaching guilt by association, it named Roosevelt and his wife, Eleanor, as Communists.

Margaret went back to Southampton with Elizabeth, Crawfie, and Alah to greet her father and mother at the end of June. A destroyer, gleaming with fresh gray paint, ferried them out to meet the incoming liner. She temporarily lost the services of Alah, who retired below with an incipient attack of *mal de mer.* Meanwhile, Margaret managed to get her wool coat and shoes smudged with gray, which required hasty dabbing from a bottle of cleaning fluid.

She had news for her parents when a round of hugs and kisses had been exchanged. She had lost some teeth, and she was growing thinner. With her ninth birthday not far off, she was old enough to recognize a distinct change in her father when the family of four stepped out on the balcony of the palace that evening to acknowledge the tumult of Londoners welcoming Bertie home.

He had gained confidence in himself on his travels. He was more certain in his judgments of people, less reluctant to face what he called the "hell" of opening his mouth in public. He was feeling his way toward his own concept of being king. "There must be no more high-hat business," he ruled, "the sort of thing that my father and those of his day regarded as essential as the correct attitude—the feeling that certain things could not be done."

He took his wife and daughters with him when he set out to lay some ghosts of his childhood. He had not returned to the Royal Naval College at Dartmouth since he left there as

an undistinguished cadet, slow in his studies, over-anxious to
please. On a wet July afternoon, the gold and white *Victoria
and Albert* anchored in the River Dart. Bertie and his party
were landed on the steps leading up the steep hill to the
sprawling red-brick building where nine hundred boys, trot-
ting everywhere on the double, were in training as naval
officers.

One of Bertie's close companions was Louis Mountbatten,
son of Prince Louis of Battenberg, who as the German-born
First Sea Lord of the British Admiralty followed his king's
example and anglicized his name in 1917. Lord Louis' mother
was one of Victoria's bevy of grandchildren. A nephew of his
was at Dartmouth—Philip, a tow-headed eighteen-year-old
prince whose parents had been forced into exile from Greece.
Almost casually, Lord Louis suggested that Cadet Captain
Philip should be the princesses' escort during their weekend
stay.

Some of Bertie's party found him rambunctious and
"somewhat tiresome." He seemed to concentrate on teasing
Margaret, possibly because he had already met her once, but
not her sister. Three days before the *Empress of Australia* sailed
from Southampton, he had been to tea at the palace with his
mother, Princess Alice, deaf from birth, who dressed in a nun's
gray habit and whose mind was sometimes clouded.

So far as both the girls were concerned, a boy was a being
from another planet. This one was far from servile. He was a
show-off who did not disguise his boredom at being drawn
into playing trains with them on the model railroad laid out
on the nursery floor of the house tenanted by the Captain of
the College, Admiral Sir Frederick Dalrymple-Hamilton.

After a snack of ginger biscuits and lemonade, he ushered
them to the tennis courts, where he impressed Elizabeth in
particular by leaping over the nets. "How high he can jump!"
gasped the adolescent who would be fourteen next year. At a

farewell meal aboard Bertie's yacht the following afternoon, it was Margaret's turn to be overawed by Philip. She hadn't seen anyone eat so many platefuls of shrimp, polished off with a banana split.

He took out a rowboat to join in the flotilla of more than a hundred craft of every description, propelled by wind, steam, or gasoline, that trailed the *Victoria and Albert* as she headed for the harbor mouth, where the sea ran high. "You must signal them to go back," said Bertie in alarm. After a command over the loudspeaker, they fell away one by one.

Philip rowed on alone, and Elizabeth asked for her father's binoculars to watch him. Bertie was less susceptible. "The damned young fool! He must go back. Otherwise we will have to heave to and send him back." Eventually, the loudspeaker convinced him to obey.

Six weeks later, the country was at war with Germany. Elizabeth was already bemused with Philip, "so tall, blond, and good-looking," as she told Bobo. An aunt of his, the oddly named Princess Nicholas of Greece, would soon begin to talk about his qualifications as a husband for Bertie's elder daughter.

On Sunday, September 3, when Neville Chamberlain announced his failure to keep peace in Europe, Bertie and the queen were in London, the girls at Birkhall with the customary accompaniment of staff, ponies, and dogs. "Why had Mummy and Papa to go back?" Margaret asked the governess. "Do you think the Germans will come and get them?" Her sister thought that nobody ought to talk about battles in front of her sister. "We don't want to upset her."

"Who is this Hitler, spoiling everything?" Margaret wanted to know—current affairs, like politics, had no place in the classroom.

Elizabeth had a partial answer to give. "The Germans are brutes." She had picked up something of the sort from her father. He was out of sympathy with those Conservative peers and businessmen who, when weeks went by without a battle fought in France or a bomb dropped on Britain, waited hopefully for peace feelers from Berlin which might enable the war in which only Poland bled to be converted into an anti-Soviet campaign.

In the new diary he had just started, with a Hanoverian weakness for capital letters, he wrote, "The country is calm, firm and united behind its leaders, resolved to fight until Liberty & Justice are once again safe in the World." On that first Sunday evening of the war, he went on the air to repeat the thought and add, "War can no longer be confined to the battlefield. But we can only do the right as we see the right, and reverently commit our cause to God."

The broadcast was made at six o'clock. From now on, he and their mother would try to telephone the girls every evening at that time. "Carry on as long as possible, just as usual" was the standing instruction to Crawfie and the rest of the Birkhall staff. Bertie and the queen were tempted to bring their daughters home, but decided against it. He could not make out why the Germans did not force the fighting. "We must wait and see," he concluded, and was still saying so when the year ended. Elizabeth was crushed to discover he had not sent Philip a Christmas card.

Life in the Scottish Highlands was tranquil, empty, and increasingly chilly when frost whitened heather and window panes. Logs crackling in the fireplaces could not cope with Birkhall's chill. Margaret was intrigued to find that water froze overnight in the carafe in her bedroom and the facecloth in the bathroom was stiff with ice. Alah wondered whether her princess' attacks of sniffles would ever end. Grandmama, cooped up at Badminton, the Gloucestershire retreat of her nephew, the Duke of Beaufort, was afraid that colds were "a family liability."

For one brief spell, there was a swarm of other children around, but they were not to be made friends of. The government arranged for them to be evacuated in the millions along with their schoolteachers and mothers from supposed target cities. Bertie opened up a house on the Balmoral estate for a party of migrants from Glasgow.

The two sisters had only Crawfie's word to tell them how such people lived. There had never been a time like this when society, rich and poor, was put through a Mixmaster. Bewildered mothers from the slums hesitated to come to the Thursday-afternoon sewing parties organized in the Birkhall schoolroom chiefly to provide the princesses with something to do. Alah presided over the teapot, Margaret and Elizabeth passed round the cups, sandwiches, fruitcake, and jam-covered scones.

Margaret was also assigned to crank the antediluvian phonograph and set the needle on the records, which blared tinny music from the massive horn. The schoolroom was an addition to the house, its plank walls heated only by a cast-iron stove. To suit the circumstances, she kept *Che gelida manina,* a recording of Gigli singing *La Bohème*'s aria to Mimi, spinning on the turntable—"Thy tiny hand is frozen, Let me warm it into life."

It did not matter that only Crawfie caught the joke. Playing records was easier than trying to exchange a few words with complete unknowns like the women from Glasgow with accents so thick it was a feat to understand them. Margaret could stand aside and smile to herself when she saw Elizabeth forging ahead with the right sort of polite questions. "Where do you come from? . . . How long have you been here?" And the inevitable "How interesting!" Margaret hadn't yet picked up the knack for making royal small talk. There was no reason to try. All she ever had to do was to be herself. She would choose the people she mixed with, and if she didn't care to mix, she might exercise her prerogative and be independent.

Nobody was safe from her mockery. The foibles of old men were especially tempting. Some of the family friends who dropped in to pass the time of day with Elizabeth steered clear of her sister, convinced that she would laugh at them when their backs were turned.

She was "poor little Margaret" in her governess' opinion. "She is far too individual, far too quick-witted," Crawfie concluded piously, "for the state of life to which it has pleased God to call her."

The modest experiment in socializing with the poor ended in disappointment as it did in most evacuation areas. Too many city children were short of warm clothes or rubber boots to adapt to country living. The remoteness of the Highlands and the silence of the woods scared them. In the village, the usual stories spread: Evacuees brought in fleas and bedbugs, and some of them wet their beds. More and more of them took the next bus home. Across the country, a million more had done much the same.

Filling the endless days was a problem at Birkhall. The radio helped to break the monotony. So did rides on George, the pony, and even visits with Alah to the dentist in Aberdeen who checked Margaret's teeth for cavities and fitted wires and rubber bands on Elizabeth's. Rather than let the children study the newspapers, Crawfie read to them, censoring the "horrible details."

Chamberlain, who had admitted a temporarily docile Winston Churchill into his Cabinet of nine as First Lord of the Admiralty, concluded that the war had settled down into a contest of attrition, which Britain could win with a minimum of casualties and trouble. One item in short supply was timber. Crews of Canadian lumberjacks set up camp close to Birkhall, and bulldozers began gouging out the pines for their sawmill.

Margaret watched in fascination. Papa had brought back some miniature Indian totem poles from his North American tour. She kept hers on a shelf in her room. One or two of these woodsmen looked like Indians to her. Could it be that they knew how to carve and color such souvenirs?

She went down with Elizabeth to Girl Scout meetings in the village hall when the first snows covered the stubbled fields. No one at Birkhall knew where Bertie's daughters would be spending Christmas. They could not be passed by when the farm bailiff's wife decided to put on a play for the holidays with the Scouts making up its cast. Margaret was satisfied to be given the role of *The Christmas Child,* rocking a doll Jesus in a cradle. Her gawky sister was to be one of the Three Kings.

They knew their lines, and Margaret and Crawfie had made crowns of painted cardboard and cellophane when the Christmas child came down with another cold. Before an understudy could take over, mumps broke out in the village. The production died aborning.

In the palace, the queen's uneasiness over the long separation increased when she was told how the bitter weather was affecting Margaret. When Bertie came back from six days with the British Expeditionary Force in France, he was persuaded that the uncanny calm there made it safe enough for the family to be together at Sandringham for Christmas, even though the house was near enough to the Suffolk coast to come within easy range of sneak attack. Elizabeth's best present was a new pony, Pussyfoot. She was relieved that the little mare passed inspection by Owen, the groom, who was something of a demigod since it was he who taught her to ride. Bertie recognized that in the matter of horses, his opinions ran second to Owen's in her esteem.

Calm lasted into the spring. "Hitler has missed the bus," Chamberlain crowed. Bertie installed his daughters in the more comfortable temperatures of Royal Lodge. There they brushed up against a second set of evacuees, thirty or so Cockney children from the poverty-ridden East End of London who were billeted on the Windsor estate. Their accents were equally outlandish but less impenetrable than Glasgow's.

They were also rated "more intelligent" and "considerably cleaner" than the previous batch, so girls among them were invited to join the select company of Girl Guides and go hiking in the woods and picnicking with the princesses. Golly made sure they were all well fed, and Margaret added some more impersonations to her private repertoire.

The guard was still up against boys. "Girls only" was the rule at the dancing classes for which the intrepid Miss Vacani was brought down from London once a week. War or no war, her pupils turned up frilled and furbelowed as before. Pussyfoot and the other pets did not absorb as much of Elizabeth's devotion as they were intended to do. Turning fourteen, she continued to be treated like a little girl, but once in a long while she spotted a boy she thought was "very nice." Margaret could only wonder what would happen when adolescence caught up with *her*.

The government's bland assumption that Britain could win an almost bloodless victory fell apart in April when Hitler's Wehrmacht took over Denmark unopposed and within a matter of weeks crushed the British forces shipped over to fight for Norway. His own outraged Conservatives helped drive Chamberlain out of office. Bertie would have preferred to see him succeeded by lanky Lord Halifax, a man of similar pliability in his dealings with Hitler, but he finally agreed with Chamberlain that a firmer choice would be Churchill, whose Victorian flamboyance had rapidly made him a public hero.

On Friday, May 10, the day of his appointment, the Wehrmacht swept relentlessly through Belgium, the Netherlands, and northern France. "I have nothing to offer," said the romantic new Prime Minister, "but blood, toil, tears, and sweat." On the Sunday morning, Crawfie heard from the queen. Would she please move the girls into Windsor Castle "anyway for the rest of the week?" The governess broke the news to them. Alah took the instruction literally and packed only enough clothes to take Margaret through to the following Saturday. She and her sister, in fact, lived at the castle for the next five years, in a state of isolation paralleled in some ways by the captives who once scratched their names on the dungeon stones deep below.

The girls, nanny, and governess made their entrance at nightfall. Every window was shrouded in blackout curtains as security against expected air raids. Watchmen patrolled the stone corridors, where dim lamp bulbs glowed in the sockets. On the walls, faded patches showed where a fortune in paintings had hung. A distant vault housed the crown jewels, wrapped in old newspapers and locked in leather hatboxes. Dust sheets hid the furniture in the state apartments, and glass-fronted cabinets had been turned about to face the walls for fear of bomb-shattered fragments flying like darts. Every chandelier had been dismantled for the same reason.

Margaret clung to Crawfie. On a night like this, her imagination was likely to gallop away. The Romans had been at Windsor in Julius Caesar's days. On Windsor Hill, so legend said, King Arthur held court with his knights. William the Conqueror built the encircling walls, Edward IV the Chapel of St. George, where Henry VIII lay buried. The tomb of Charles I was here, as well as the silk shirt he wore to meet the headsman's axe.

Footsteps echoing, the refugees were led to their quarters. Margaret would share a room with Alah in the Lancaster Tower, another work of Henry VIII, whose walls were thick enough to accommodate a bathroom cut into them. Elizabeth

had Bobo as her roommate next door. Crawfie was spirited
away up a spiral stairway to the Victoria Tower.

In the bedrooms, there were only electric fires to give fitful
heat; power was rationed to keep arms factories working at
desperate tilt. The workings of the alarm system were
carefully explained to the new guests. One set of bells would
sound whenever sirens wailed, another when rooftop spotters
sighted enemy planes approaching—a "red alert," signalling the
need to hurry down to one of the dungeons, equipped as a
bunker with reinforced walls, beds, and chemical toilets.
Dinner, said the resident Master of the Household, was served
sharp at eight in the oak-paneled Octagon Room. In the spirit
of the men who adhered to the code in every corner of
Victoria's empire, he added solemnly, "We dress." Long
dresses or black ties and dinner jackets were de rigueur.

Two days later, the Germans broke through the Allied lines
at Sedan. In less than a week, the decision had to be taken to
pull out of battle the maximum possible number of men in
the ten divisions of the British Expeditionary Force; the
Germans had a hundred and thirty-four divisions rampaging
on the western front.

On their parents' instruction, the two princesses were
shielded from news of the disaster that appeared inevitable.
They were outside the castle, playing in the sunlight with
Crawfie, when Margaret's ears caught the rumble of distant
gunfire and exploding shells. Her immediate thought was for
Papa. Was he in danger? The anxiety could not be purely
altruistic. If anything happened to him, Elizabeth would be
queen of an embattled England, with Margaret next in the
event of catastrophe.

"Crawfie, whatever is it?" Fighter planes streaked through
the blue sky, heading for the Channel. The sounds, like
faraway thunder, kept the two girls on edge. The governess
warranted that what they heard came from somewhere farther

off than London. Later in the day, they listened to the radio. The evacuation of the British Expeditionary Force was under way at Dunkirk. Navy destroyers were picking up most of the routed soldiers from the beaches. Pleasure boats, fishing smacks, and ferries brought off the rest.

Margaret could scarcely wait for the evening telephone call. She had to take her turn after her sister. "Are you all right, Papa, and Mummy, too?" Yes, they were. The King did not mention to either of his daughters that he thought Hitler's next move would be to leapfrog the Channel for instantaneous invasion of England.

Civil servants in Whitehall devised elaborate plans to evacuate Bertie and his family. Margaret and Elizabeth, they urged, ought to be flown to Canada. The king and queen should flee to the west country, as far as possible from London. The dogged little queen had the conclusive say about that: "The children will not leave unless I do. I shall not leave unless their father does, and the king will not leave the country in any circumstances whatever."

Other children, less exposed and more anonymous, were sent overseas to escape. Eleven thousand wives, sons, and daughters of families with money to spare for the passage scrambled out posthaste. Bertie had one shooting range laid down in the palace gardens and another at Windsor; he practiced with handguns and rifles, intending to die fighting, if he had to.

Hitler's takeover plans in Holland had envisaged seizing Queen Wilhelmina as a hostage and in Norway, King Haakon. The British high command saw imminent danger of German paratroops trying to capture Bertie and his family. Armored cars stood ready day and night in London to whisk him and the queen out of harm's way. At Windsor Castle, a tank waited to collect the princesses in an emergency.

Flights of Luftwaffe bombers droned overhead in the first

half of July, as the lull ended and preparations for invasion
were pushed ahead. On the nineteenth of the month, Hitler
made a final offer of peace. He would permit Britain to hold
on to all its empire except Egypt and Iraq, which he wanted
for the Reich. He contemplated dethroning Bertie and
reinstalling David. Some of the Fuehrer's British admirers,
including Mosley, had already been interned together with
every German national in the country. Lord Halifax was given
the job of dismissing Hitler's impertinence in a radio speech.
Churchill defined Britain's war aims: total victory.

The Luftwaffe opened its full-scale attack on south-coast
ports on August 13, under orders to drive the nation down by
bombs alone. The toll exacted by Royal Air Force fighters
brought about an early switch in strategy: the Germans set out
to destroy the fighter bases. Then Hitler changed his mind.
Britain's will to resist must be broken immediately, before the
approach of autumn gales hampered cross-Channel landings.
On September 7, his air force turned aside to blitz London by
day and night.

Bells dinning through the castle one night sent Crawfie
scurrying underground. Neither Margaret nor Elizabeth was
in sight, nor was Alah. The immaculate Master of the
Household, Sir Hill Child, was fuming, "They simply must
come." The governess raced upstairs to find them.

With elderly deliberation, Alah was putting on her white
uniform and cap. Elizabeth, too, with nightgown off, was
busily dressing herself, while Margaret hunted for underwear
to match her dress because Bobo's choice was the wrong color.
Crawfie rounded them all up and sped them down to the
shelter. By midnight, when the red alert clanged, Margaret
was asleep. The Master of the Household decided to make
some tea. Two hours later, the clamor of sirens sounded the all
clear.

Arrangements had to be improved for next time. Each girl

packed a small traveling case with personal belongings, a book
or two, and the locked diary which their mother insisted they
write up every night before bed. They were fitted out with
steel helmets, romper suits like Mr. Churchill's, and gas masks,
which Elizabeth and only Elizabeth wore without complaining for ten minutes' practice every day. At the height of the
blitz, they spent every night down in the dungeon, starting at
seven o'clock.

If daylight alerts caught them outdoors, they ran to one of
Great-great-grandmother Victoria's imitation temples that
dotted the grounds or to the hillside caves dug to the order of
the third George. The designated tank rumbled out to collect
them. Squeezing the dogs and then the girls in through the
turret took time. Margaret maneuvered to be last one in,
hoping to see puffs of shellbursts in the sky or even an RAF
fighter hounding a Focke-Wulf.

As the nights lengthened, they could stand on the battlements, hearing the faraway thud of high explosives and crack
of anti-aircraft batteries, watching the steady glow of East End
London burning into shimmering incandescence as more
bombs showered down. Bertie and the queen checked into the
palace every weekday. Its first bomb lodged itself under stone
steps by his study, then shattered windows when it exploded
the next morning. Seventy-two hours later, aim and effect
were deadlier. Bertie was in his sitting room. The only shelter
was a maids' room in the basement, shored up with wooden
beams of lumber and partitioned with wallboard; building a
reinforced concrete hideaway had to wait until 1941. From his
window, he saw two bombs falling, to wreck the chapel and a
nearby workshop.

It took him a week to recover from the shaking. "One must
be careful," he told himself, "not to become 'dugout
minded.'" His wife was more resilient. "I'm glad we've been
bombed," she said. "It makes me feel I can look the East End

in the face." The children were not told how narrow the escape had been. Neither was Winston Churchill.

Their daughters saw more of them after that. They drove out to the castle every night, Bertie beginning to look as old as his own father; the queen had circles underlining her blue eyes. An old servant climbed to the top of the Round Tower to watch for them. At first sight of the car, he raised the Royal Standard to its mast top in greeting.

One November night, Air Ministry detectors picked up the Luftwaffe's director "X" beam aimed straight for the castle. It appeared that Hitler had ordered another attempt to get Bertie, and this time his family, too. Watchers saw the planes heading in, lit by a full moon in a clear sky. The red warning sounded, but the fleet flew on. In the cathedral town of Coventry, more than two thousand buildings were demolished, and nearly six hundred people killed.

Margaret was enjoying male company at breakfast and lunch; officers of the Grenadier Guards were stationed there. She took a permanent place at table opposite her sister so that she, too, could pick who would sit on either side of her. Gossip spiced the meals; she liked to pass along every tidbit that came her way. If she could not get them laughing any other way, she would cross her eyes and giggle. Her parents frowned on the habit in old-fashioned fear that she would end up with a permanent squint.

Reports of her carrying-on reached Badminton and Grandmama, who had her assiduous attendant, Lady Cynthia Colville, write a firm note about it. "Her Majesty is rather sorry to hear that Princess Margaret is so spoilt, though perhaps it is hardly surprising. I daresay, too, she has a more complicated and difficult nature, and one that will require a great deal of skill and insight in dealing with."

Margaret grabbed whatever opportunity that came along to amuse herself; Elizabeth's conscience bothered her if she found herself having fun when the country stood alone against Germany and now Italy. Both the girls had their same roles again when *The Christmas Child* was dusted off and staged without interruption in December, 1940. As a theatrical warehouse, the castle was much better supplied than Birkhall had been. The governess led expeditions to borrow costumes and props out of storage. Real boys were enlisted among the evacuees to play the scarf-wrapped shepherds and two of the Three Kings. Elizabeth with a golden crown on her head dressed up as the third.

Bertie and the queen came to watch the performance in St. George's Hall. He contained himself at the sight of his older daughter solemnly leading the procession of young actors up through the audience, bearing make-believe frankincense and myrrh. Then Margaret, in white, knelt by the cradle. Clear as a bell, she sang "Gentle Jesus, meek and mild, Look upon this little child," and Bertie's eyes streamed with tears. Emotion always did run high in the Hanoverians. "We cry rather a lot in this family" was a later comment from Margaret, who was prone to weeping herself.

The reception given to *The Christmas Child*—£30 in the collection plate was solid evidence of success—sparked an idea for next year. Margaret badgered Crawfie into agreeing to put on a pantomime, one of the mishmash concoctions of musical comedy, slapstick, and fairy tale that were a standard treat for children before the lights went out.

A master at the school in the park wrote the script, and Margaret sketched the costumes for *Aladdin and His Wonderful Lamp.* She had to produce another set of drawings when she found that his libretto was for *Cinderella.* She held out for the starring role and argued the governess into charging admission.

"No one will pay to look at us," Elizabeth protested.

"Nonsense!" snapped Margaret. "They'll pay anything to see us, and it's for the queen's wool fund." Unimaginable

numbers of socks for servicemen could be knitted from the
proceeds.

For weeks, her life centered on *Cinderella*. Nothing else
matched this for importance. She wanted real scenery; two
painters went to work on it. Her crinoline dress had to be a
real theatrical costume; it was rented along with wigs and the
rest from Raynes of London. She would have liked a real
coach to ride in, but she settled for having wheels attached to
an old sedan chair, originally used by the third George's wife,
Charlotte. Aunt Marina lent her a fan; Margaret purred to
discover it had been Marie Antoinette's.

"I don't think Princess Margaret was quite so merry this
year," noted one of the faithful photographers who arrived to
record the production's progress. "She is taking herself a little
seriously." Seriousness was out in a girl who was never written
about in a newspaper or magazine except as a happy little
madcap. "I'm sure that won't last," added the compliant
camerawoman.

Cinderella needed publicizing. Posters were painted to take
care of that, scenes from the show and others of its kind—
Mother Goose, Dick Whittington, The Sleeping Beauty, and so
on. The stage that Victoria had ordered built in the Waterloo
Chamber was set, and four hundred seats were made ready.
Margaret contributed one more touch. Portraits of the
ancestors which used to grace the room had been stored away,
leaving the imposing labelled frames empty. She applied the
posters to fill them. "Charles I", for instance, was now Dick
Whittington, thrice Lord Mayor of London, and his remarkable cat. Bertie was so fond of the transformation that he took
guests around to show them his daughter's handiwork.

On the day of the performance, stage fright struck so hard
that she skipped breakfast and stayed in bed. Alah did not
know what to make of it. Her poor child looked as if she were
coming down with something again, though she kept insisting,

"It's quite all right." Even Crawfie, no alarmist, doubted whether Margaret could pull herself together to play Cinderella, starting at two o-clock.

Ten minutes before show time, she came out of her room. Having makeup applied to her cheeks, mascara to eyelashes, lipstick on mouth, and a beauty patch by her chin was the only treatment. Onstage, as one member of the inevitably enraptured audience remarked, she looked "so lovely that she brought down the house."

Another pantomime was produced every Christmas until the war ended. So was her morning performance in bed on opening day as panic coincided with the prospect of playing the principal girl, not a permanent, everyday understudy. By VE Day, the wool fund had made nearly £900.

For the rest of the year, Elizabeth came first. There was a ready-made opportunity for the national propaganda machine to picture her as just like the girl next door when she reached sixteen. The law required her age group to register for war work. She signed on at the Windsor Labor Exchange, then pestered her father into giving permission for her to join the Auxiliary Territorial Service. Margaret was furious that age had euchred her once more. She consoled herself by noting how wretched the khaki cap, tunic, and skirt looked on her sister. "I was born too late," she stormed, alone in the schoolroom one day with Crawfie, as "Lil" steered a Red Cross truck off down the roadway.

Though "Lil" was only a junior lieutenant in the ATS, she was already Colonel-in-Chief of the Grenadiers. The appointment was an early present from Bertie. On her birthday, she made her first inspection. At a march past in the castle's Great Quadrangle, she took the salute and afterward gave a party for the six hundred officers and men who had been on spit-and-polish parade. She was old enough now under the terms of the latest Regency Act, 1937 version, to be appointed a Counsellor of State if her father should leave the country or be certified infirm in mind or body.

Crawfie filled in some background for her sole remaining pupil. The first law of this kind dated back to King Hal, who set sixteen as the qualifying age for princesses, eighteen for princes. George III's days of apparent insanity produced three similar sets of legislation, making a total of nine to date.

"I see," Margaret said. "A regent is in lieu of the king?" Crawfie credited her with full marks for a nimble definition. Margaret, she explained, would qualify as a counsellor eventually. But four years was a lifetime to wait. "Now I'm floored. I'll be put in my place," the girl said.

The wound got rubbed raw when she went "supporting Lil" on some public outing, then found herself scissored out of the photographs in the newspapers. They were down to four pages these days because of the shortage of newsprint. "I've been censored again," she would say, ruefully. Her reaction was taken by a majority of people within the court as a mark of egotism, of seeking to share the limelight on equal terms. At least one other had a conflicting interpretation. "Being constantly left out of those pictures was a real psychic blow. She took it to signify that in the newspapers' opinion she was nobody. It explained a lot about her determination to gain attention."

Finally, her hurt became so plain that a Ministry of Information bulletin circulated to editors asked, "Please do not cut Princess Margaret out of pictures unless unavoidable." Pressure on space usually made the request impossible to fulfill when British and United States men at arms were routing the Afrika Corps and preparing to invade Italy.

As hard as anything else to be borne with was Elizabeth's adolescence. Philip was carrying on something like a courtship. He wrote to her regularly from the ships of the battle squadron in which he served. He spent part of his leaves at the castle. He exchanged photographs with her. He watched her play *Aladdin* in 1943, and Bertie watched them both, intrigued to see his daughter's confusion when he made jokes about Philip.

Margaret tagged along with the two of them when he came to Windsor, determined not to be left out. Going on fourteen, she was grasping at straws to be noticed. A handsome officer who came into view, particularly an air force pilot, might find himself treated as a hero or an equal, depending on her mood. She must be accepted as a grownup, not a child, and she did not care much if she created a nuisance of herself. She let Crawfie, who was on vacation, know what happened by letter one Christmas:

"The Bofors officers came. Quite nice. Then we rolled back the carpet and we danced to the gramaphone [sic] as it has been mended. Danced till 1 o'clock. Then on the next evening ... Philip went mad. We played charades, clumps, and then we danced and danced and danced ... Lilibet has a cold. Bother. We danced 4 night running ... With heaps, piles, mounds, mountains of love from Margaret."

VII

Questions of Inheritance

Before he went to bed, Bertie made a final entry in his diary. "Poor darlings, they have never had any fun yet." The date was Tuesday, May 8, 1945. His daughters had just spent what Margaret thought of as the most beautiful evening of her life.

Floodlights glared against the palace walls. Street lamps glowed for the first time in more than five years. Music blasted out from hurriedly installed loudspeakers. Church bells pealed, and pubs ran dry. The war in Europe had trickled to an end, and to Bertie it seemed "a terrible anti-climax." News of victory had leaked out in driblets. Midnight had been set for the formal surrender. But the German people had been told of their defeat twenty-four hours ago. So at three o'clock this afternoon, Churchill had ignored the arrangement worked out in wrangling with Washington and Moscow and hastened to pronounce this as VE Day. Bertie, so meticulous that he could instantly spot a medal ribbon out of place on any uniform, wished that the whole situation could have been handled more smoothly.

Londoners did not care. The Russians had found Hitler dead and charred outside his Berlin bunker. His supersonic rockets, which had done more to demoralize England—and the two princesses at Windsor—than any other weapon of war, would never fall again. Margaret had tossed out her German textbooks and warned Crawfie that she had learned more of Hitler's language than she had ever intended to.

It seemed as though conquering the Japanese would take the better part of two years more, but few thought about that tonight. Eight times already, Margaret and Elizabeth had walked out beside their parents on the palace balcony in response to the clamor down below. Then a fantastic idea entered Margaret's head. She would like to celebrate in a way no other princess had ever attempted; she wanted to mix with the crowds that carpeted every inch of the roadway outside and join them in chanting for still another chance to cheer Papa and Mummy.

She was not sure that it would not be hazardous. All she had been taught by old Alah emphasized that a princess must maintain dignity and distance between herself and common people. She was afraid that if she were recognized she might be mobbed. But if she wore an old wool coat and kept a scarf tied tight under her chin, she would pass for any other girl.

She pleaded her case with Bertie. He was agreeable if she was certain it would be fun for her. Elizabeth would go with her, and a Guards officer would be provided for each of them as an escort. The little group emerged into the world from a side gate onto a street shadowed by trees where the crowd was thinner. Margaret had grown into adolescence since the last time she had been out like this to sample the joys of ordinary people.

The four of them edged their path into the throng. "The

king! The king! The king!" The chant vibrated deep into the bones. When he appeared once more with his wife, Margaret came close to yelling her head off. She stayed close to her escort as the quartet was jostled down the Mall toward Trafalgar Square, shouting out the songs everyone around them was singing: "Roll Out the Barrel" . . . "Run, Rabbit, Run" . . . and the classical Cockney hosanna "Knees Up, Mother Brown."

Anonymous and ecstatic, she linked arms in the chains of strangers who kicked up their heels and danced. When hats began to get knocked off heads, she bubbled, "Oh, I must try that!" and out went her hands in the general melee. Princesses and protectors joined the surge off the roadway to the grass verges in the park, where bonfires blazed. Her apprehension had vanished. She could only gasp. "Such *fun!*"

Yard by yard, they got as far as Piccadilly, where the crowds thickened into another wall-to-wall gala before the night was over. "It was absolutely wonderful," she reported back to Papa. "Everyone was absolutely marvelous."

Her father did not share her exhilaration. Victory in itself was no solution to the country's present problems. There was no knowing what the cost of defeating Japan would be in men or money. And the British were clearly restless under Churchill. "I have found it difficult to rejoice or relax as there is still so much hard work ahead to deal with," Bertie confessed.

By the end of July, he was amazed that he had a new Prime Minister in Clement Attlee, as scrupulous and colorless as himself and of course a Socialist. A general election had swept the Labor Party into power and Churchill out. There was barely time to brief Attlee on the secret of the atomic bomb, which Bertie knew about but Attlee did not, before it was dropped twice on Japan to resolve one of the problems that had plagued the king.

On August 15, VJ Day, he took Margaret and the rest of his family with him to open his first peacetime Parliament since 1938. Six days short of her fifteenth birthday, Margaret sat in a chair of state on the left of the two thrones as though she had been comporting herself in the House of Lords all her life.

Bertie's speech from the throne, written by his new ministers, announced plans for a different kind of kingdom. Social security; cradle-to-grave health services; government takeover of the coal mines and the Bank of England. The previous day, the Treasury had given warning that without American help the country would be "virtually bankrupt." Twenty-four hours after Bertie's speech, American aid—lend-lease—was cut off.

A social revolution was under way without the means in sight to pay for it, fought every step by the Tories without loss of a drop of blood. Houses, food, clothing, furniture, automobiles, liquor, refrigerators, and cigarettes were all in desperately short supply or else unobtainable. Buying a pair of curtains meant giving up clothes-ration coupons. The bill for waging the war had run up to roughly $17 billion.

At the close of the month, Margaret and the rest of them escaped to Balmoral, where for a while her resentment of Elizabeth disturbed the autumn calm. It was time, Bertie decided, to teach his older daughter how to handle a gun. He had laid down a rule that all of them must make do on a standard issue of clothing coupons for their personal use. That made it impossible to buy her a suit of sporty tweed. Instead, he lent her a pair of his own plus-fours.

Though the grouse shooting was poor—an icy spring had killed off young birds in the thousands—deer had not suffered to anything like the same extent. The head keeper took Elizabeth off to the moors day after day, careful to observe the proprieties by eating his lunch with the keepers on one side of a convenient rock while she munched alone on the other; she considered that extremely thoughtful of them. She filled every evening with her shooting talk, the stag she had stalked and the stag she had missed, the size of antlers and the kick of shotguns.

Margaret could not stand it. She felt discriminated against, and she had to take steps to protect herself. She was never going out shooting, she said, because it was not a fit sport for women. And didn't Lilibet look silly, wearing Papa's trousers? Margaret swore *she* would not stoop to anything so ridiculous.

She fell ill before Christmas. Pain struck her one night when she was back in the palace. Doctors hurried in through the fog that shrouded the capital. Appendicitis was her problem, and surgery was advisable to avoid the risk of peritonitis. The question of her being taken into a hospital did not arise. A princess' privacy was sacrosanct. Her bedroom was converted into an operating theater by staff of the Great Ormond Street Hospital for Sick Children. Surgeons and nurses from there handled the task.

She passed her convalescence listening to the radio and reading magazines. Comic books had given way to women's weeklies, those confections of romantic fiction, knitting patterns, and recipes for making the most of skimpy rations, put together in a package designed to set readers daydreaming of a future in which there were homes for everybody and shops crammed with gorgeous new clothes. Glossier products like *The Tatler* and *The Bystander* also found a place in the pile. They offered a different route to Shangri-La. Their pages of photographs of dashing young men and dauntless debutantes conjured up England in the thirties, a world that had disappeared in the blitz.

Piece by piece, the disrupted calendar of royal living was being put together again. Bertie had gone to Ascot that summer and seen his "Rising Light" capture one race by a short head. "It was thrilling for me as I had never seen one of my own horses win before," he confided in his diary. They would revert to Sandringham this Christmas.

A christening was one of the round of inconsequential affairs to be attended before then—of Wing Commander Peter Townsend's second son. Bertie had decided to introduce some new blood into his circle of courtiers by naming twenty-eight heroes of the war as "equerries of honor." Townsend, a former fighter pilot, was one of them.

This soft-spoken, even-tempered airman had been recommended for the Distinguished Flying Cross for displaying "qualities of leadership, skill, and determination of the highest order, with little regard for his own safety." In the course of downing eleven of the Luftwaffe, he had been shot down over Kent with wounds in the feet.

In Bertie's estimation, Peter was an outstanding choice— born in Rangoon, Burma, son of a British army officer; married during the war to beautiful Rosemary Pawle; eager to meet any demand made of him at the expense of his own convenience. Towsend had the baby christened Hugo George as a gesture of appreciation for the king's esteem for him. Margaret went to the ceremony; Bertie was a godfather.

At Sandringham over the holidays, she had some fresh impersonations for her father's entertainment—doctors, nurses, and the more groveling visitors who had arrived when she lay in bed, waiting for her stitches to be snipped out, afraid to laugh because it hurt. Elizabeth looked upset as usual when the fun threatened to get out of hand. It was useless to complain as she had in the past, "Stop her, Mummy! Oh, please stop her!" Margaret was too old to listen. Grandmama, too, was beginning to resign herself to her outbursts. "She is so outrageously amusing that one can't help encouraging her," the old lady confessed.

The clocks at Sandringham might have been turned back

ten years, not the thirty minutes David had once demanded. Lights gleamed in the windows, and music from the over-worked phonograph pinpointed the room where Margaret held court. "Meg, it's too loud!" was a repeated cry of her father's. "Will you please turn it down?" Guests came and left in a steady flow. Beaming, crisply pressed Guards officers, the pride of the peerage, were on tap as companions and dance partners for the girls. Bertie wanted the Brigade of Guards and his Household Cavalry out of battle dress and back into pre-war finery without wasting time about it.

There were some significant differences. Most rooms in the red-brick monster of a house were depressingly cold—coal was scarce this season. Food coupons were too precious for steaks and chops to be served for breakfast as in the old days, though game bagged on the estate helped make up for the shortage of meat. Baccarat, a nightly pastime for Bertie's grandfather, another Bertie, had disappeared; jigsaw puzzles, laid out on a hall table, were the substitute.

Among members of the king's generation, talk centered on food, fuel, and how to make do on clothes rationing. For his family, he kept up a show of gaiety when inside he felt "burned out," as he told his brother Harry. The medicine that his physician, Sir John Weir, prescribed seemed to do no good. He yearned to get away from people and the ever-present dispatch boxes, but that was impossible. "I am perfectly well really," he acknowledged, "but feel that I cannot cope competently with all the varied and many questions that come up." Margaret's laughter was a temporary tonic he could rely on.

She came into her own in the games of charades which were a favorite of her mother's. The queen chose the words which, syllable by syllable, had to be acted out by family and guests. When Eleanor Roosevelt, the President's widow, went to call on Bertie on a later weekend, she found Churchill in the company, fondling a cigar, too glum to take part in such fribble.

On the second day of the New Year, Alah retired to bed early. The strain of the war had told on her, too. Country dancing was the attraction after dinner that evening, but in a house of more than three hundred rooms, hers was out of earshot. In the morning, her breakfast tray was found untouched outside her door. She was buried from her own Hertfordshire home, which she had left to nurse the queen as a baby. Margaret needed someone else to care for her now. Ruby MacDonald, who had interrupted her service as a maid to go off on war work, would carry on the job.

Most of the clothes in her mistress' wardrobe were handed on from Elizabeth. New ones were unobtainable except a dress or two each year. Margaret took that for granted, but she spent hours sketching the outfits she would buy one fine day. Her sister's old hats were not so welcome. She was turned off those when a woman reporter detected that Margaret was wearing a hand-me-down and found two photographs to prove it.

Elizabeth, who had never really cared how she looked, started paying more attention to herself when Philip stepped up his calls. For the first time, she was given a free hand in her shopping instead of inheriting her mother's made-over gowns. But habit was strong in her. The clothes she bought would have suited the queen. Margaret remained on the end of the receiving line.

Her quarters in the palace still lay behind a door bearing the name tag NURSERY, and she still took lessons from Crawfie. Her sister had her own suite, with a footman and a housemaid attached. Furnishing it was done by rounding up a hodge-podge of items out of storage or removing an antique piece or two from an already overcrowded room. Elizabeth was content to let someone else do the selecting. Margaret enrolled herself in the rummaging detail and bore off a succession of knick-knacks to brighten up her room. Her best find was a discarded piano. Dust rose and cobwebs fluttered when she pulled up an empty crate and rattled off a few bars of Chopin.

She haunted her sister's new lodgings, to gossip, read a book, play a record, or stare toward Big Ben, booming out the time from the clock tower of the Houses of Parliament. Elizabeth went to meetings of Bertie's counsellors now that it was accepted that her mother would bear no son. A standard of her own with a personal coat of arms, a lady-in-waiting, and a secretary were extra perquisites.

Margaret could not always suppress her envy. "No wonder you are always so punctual," she told Elizabeth, hearing Big Ben chime. "You can't very well help it."

She persisted in hanging around when Philip came to call, which he did now as a matter of course. He worked at present as an instructor at a naval school for petty officers at Corsham, in Wiltshire, ninety miles away, spending weekend leaves at the Chester Street town house of Lord Louis—"Uncle Dickie"— which was a few minutes' drive from the palace in Philip's battered black-and-green MG.

He had turned twenty-five years old in June, 1946, yet he acted the schoolboy. Romping in the corridors, playing ball with both the girls, was one way to melt the older one's reserve when she knew so little about men of any age other than her father. Margaret accepted the high jinks as an invitation to join in, refusing to believe she was unwanted. Philip showed her one considerable token of sympathy by changing the sign on her door from NURSERY to MAGGIE'S ROOM.

Bertie liked him, but he found it hard to believe that his elder daughter was in love with the first eligible young man to come her way. Philip, he thought, "is intelligent, has a good sense of humor, and thinks about things in the right way." But Bertie had been stalling for two years over whether he would qualify as a husband for a future queen.

One problem was his nationality. Admiralty regulations stipulated that only a British subject could receive a permanent rank of officer in the Navy. Philip was eager to renounce Greek nationality, but Bertie was a loyal member of the fraternity of kings; he had to be careful to do nothing to diminish the hope of Philip's Uncle George of being restored to the throne in Athens.

Bertie had done his best for fellow members of the club imperiled by the war. He went in person to greet Queen Wilhelmina when she fled aboard a British destroyer from Rotterdam, bringing only the clothes she was wearing. King Haakon, in flight from Norway, was put up in Buckingham Palace. On the eve of the London blitz, King Gustav of Sweden attempted to negotiate an Anglo-German peace, but Bertie made allowances for the duress applied to the doddering old man, doyen of all Europe's monarchs. He did agree that the name of Victor Emmanuel of Italy should be stricken from the rolls of the Knights of the Garter and his banner taken down from its place in St. George's Chapel, Windsor. But even after Cousin Leopold of Belgium capitulated to Hitler, Bertie kept his name on the roll, and Leopold's banner still hung high in the chapel, undisturbed.

It took a king to understand the unique circumstances of another of his kind. They were all peculiar, tribal beings, inheritors by definition, cushioned by wealth that they had never earned, predestined for roles which were impossible to refuse without risk of stirring upheaval among people trained to revere them. The bloodlines between many of them were as intertwined as in exhibits in a pedigree show, be they Holstein cattle, Abyssinian cats, or St. Bernards. The wiser were alert to the biological hazards involved when cousins too often married each other.

The fraternity had been stripped of members in the recent fighting. Zog had been driven from Albania in 1939. Boris had died in Bulgaria in 1943, and then the Communists had thrown out his son Simeon three years later, the same year that Victor Emmanuel abdicated in Rome and his son Humbert was forced into retirement the next month by a referendum that made Italy a republic. King Peter's chances of being recalled from his London exile by Marshal Tito of Yugoslavia had to be assessed at zero. As the least damaged, most prestigious monarchy of the handful surviving, England, in Bertie's view, was obliged to do whatever was feasible for George of Greece.

Churchill came as close to believing in the divine right of kings as any politician of his age. He surpassed Bertie in his enthusiasm for a sovereign's cause. As Prime Minister, he had sent sixty thousand British troops into Greece after the Germans withdrew in 1944. The appointed mission of His Majesty's forces was to put down the guerrilla fighters of the Communist-led Greek resistance in order to smooth the path for George's return. At that same time, Uncle Dickie, serving as Supreme Allied Commander in Southeast Asia, was urging his nephew Philip to seek British citizenship. Bertie advised Mountbatten to consult the Greek king, exiled in Cairo, who raised no objection to Philip's ambition.

Now the Greeks had voted "yes" in a plebiscite to decide whether or not they wanted a king. George was back in Athens by the autumn of 1946, but Bertie still hesitated. For Philip suddenly to change his nationality might be taken as evidence that the future of the monarchy in Greece was so shaky that this prince was bowing out of the line of succession. But Elizabeth wanted him as her husband, and Bertie yielded to her. Philip's wish could be granted. The problem was what he should call himself when his family used no surname, which was scarcely surprising. The one to which they had closest ties was Schleswig-Holstein-Sonderburg-Glucksburg.

His uncertain identification bothered Margaret more than the girl who intended to be married to him. "But he's not English," Margaret told Crawfie. "Would it make a difference?" He had so much charm and energy that any sheltered young girl felt the force of his personality, whether or not she found herself in love with him.

Bertie was ready to dub him "His Royal Highness Prince Philip." Both Attlee and Uncle Dickie thought this was appropriate, but the new British subject chose something simpler: "Lieutenant Philip—Royal Navy." Bertie applauded the decision. As for a surname, "Mountbatten" would serve very nicely.

One of his supreme qualifications as the potential father of a future king was his abounding good health. In the past, the fraternity of monarchs had been only dimly aware of the hazards of disease, which were as much a part of the inheritance as pomp and privilege. Anybody who had seen members of the House of Hapsburg could recognize the pouched mouth and elongated lower lip as a mark of the family that ruled in Europe for nearly five centuries, beginning in Hungary in 1438.

Velasquez captured the pout in his portraits of the seventeenth-century kings of Spain. Franz Josef was visibly a Hapsburg when he reigned as emperor of Austria and king of Hungary before his medieval empire collapsed in the First World War. The science of genetics, developed in the twentieth century, concerned with studying how life in all its shapes and complexities was transmitted from one generation to the next. By the time genetics had established itself at the theoretical core of biology, the last Hapsburg had long since abandoned his throne. But finally the pout could be recognized for what it really was—a dominant trait, possibly passed on by the functioning of a single gene starting at the moment of conception.

Geneticists learned that when a mother's egg cell was fertilized by a father's sperm cell, an entirely new master cell was formed; it was the model for the trillions of others that built the baby's body and brain. Each parent contributed half the genes it contained. Where they were different, one set would be labelled dominant, the other recessive. Genes recessive in one sexual union might be dominant in another; the birth of a son could be followed by the birth of a daughter, a healthy child by a weakling. Every infant, and therefore every adult, was a hybrid, not an average of the characters of the mother and father, which remained the belief of most commoners and kings.

The master cell commanded every step of a baby's growth into a fetus and then into an individual from the hour of its birth. From each parent, it inherited qualities, combined by chance into a brand new arrangement. Its bones, muscles, blood, nerves, brain tissue—every cell would be identical with the master in genetic makeup with one exception. As the sex cells developed, they would carry fifty per cent of the number of genes in the rest. Only the mating of male and female would produce the whole.

No electron micrograph would enable anyone to *see* a gene any more than a physicist could observe an atom, but theory could be tested and proven by experiment, just as theory resulted in hydrogen bombs. The size of genes could be calculated as measuring something between ten and twenty millionths of an inch in diameter. Science speculated that life on earth first appeared in similar unit form. As the world aged, higher levels of life evolved through processes of

mutation and Darwinian natural selection. Primitive orga-
nisms with very few genes bred single-celled specks with many
more, until finally multi-cellular plants and animals arrived,
including mankind. Biologists identified about 267,000 species
of plants and some million species of animals inhabiting the
planet. Genetically, all life was interrelated.

They defined the gene as "the biologist's atom" and "the
elementary unit of inheritance." One gene seemingly determined whether a child's hair would be curly or straight,
another whether it would have blue eyes or brown or possibly
be color blind. In the courts of Europe, the Hapsburgs were
associated with something more genetically sinister than a tell-
tale look around the mouth. It was believed, wrongly, that the
family carried hemophilia: "the royal disease," as it was called,
which produces "bleeders"—people whose blood either fails to
clot at all after a nick or bruise or else clots dangerously
slowly.

It took the geneticists to discover that hemophiliacs probably differ from nonbleeders by a single gene, the one assumed
to be essential for synthesizing within body cells the protein
that causes blood to coagulate and harden to seal a wound.
Hemophilia was rare among women, because of its sex linkage.
The defective gene was borne in the egg cell, not the sperm.
No sons of a hemophiliac father would be bleeders, but half
his daughters would be carriers.

There was, and is as yet, no way in the world to discover in
advance of a child's birth whether or not the mother harbored
the aberrant gene apart from knowledge of what happened in
her family in the past. If she did and bore only daughters, the
probability was that one in two of them would follow her
pattern. If she bore a son, the odds were the same, but only
the baby's hemorrhaging would identify him as a bleeder.

Hemophilia could also result from a mutation occurring
like spontaneous combustion in a woman's genetic pattern.

Two scientists, James Neel in the United States and J. B. S. Haldane in Britain, calculated that in each generation, mutations produced hemophilia and some other hereditary diseases in as many as one of every hundred thousand sex cells. How that happened they did not know; the cause remains a mystery today.

Great-great-grandmother Victoria was a victim of spontaneous mutation at some stage of her life. Her youngest son, Leopold, born when she was thirty-four, inherited hemophilia from her; his brothers escaped. Leopold's most dramatic brush with bleeding to death came in his schoolroom when he accidentally scratched the palate of his mouth with the pen he was chewing. His mother treated him as a semi-invalid most of his life until, at thirty-one, he bruised his head in a fall and died of a brain hemorrhage.

Of her five daughters, two were recognizable as carriers, Alice and Beatrice. Alice became the wife of Louis, Prince of Hesse, and their daughter Alix inherited the defective gene. When Tsar Nicholas made dimpled Alix his bride in 1894, it was debatable whether he knew what had killed her Uncle Leopold ten years earlier. The medical profession was slowly recognizing the implications of a child's bleeding to death from minor injuries and in some instances recommended against marriage for members of afflicted families. But of all the fraternity of kings, the Romanovs of Russia were the least penetrable to unasked-for advice from outside the court. Alix's son Alexis was a hemophiliac.

Beatrice, Victoria's youngest child, married Prince Henry of Battenburg and bore a daughter, Ena, who was also a carrier. She in turn found a husband in twenty-year-old Alfonso, King of Spain, who was desperately anxious to marry into the British royal family. On their wedding day in Madrid, an anarchist's bomb flung at their carriage blew soldiers, horses, and spectators to pieces. The bride and groom were not hurt, but she introduced a different kind of peril into yet another dynasty—hemophilia.

Her mother, Beatrice, had a mission of destruction to perform in behalf of her own mother, Victoria, which may have had some bearing on the inner knowledge of genetic disease among the Hanoverians. Victoria confided detailed accounts of every turn of family life in her diaries, which passed on her death in 1901 into Beatrice's hands. Her mother had left her the task of transcribing the indiscreet record into blue copybooks. Beatrice copied only portions and doctored what she wrote. As she went along, she burned the original manuscript page by page.

Alix, the tsarina, had an older sister, Irene, wife of Prince Henry of Prussia, who was a brother of Germany's pompous Kaiser Wilhelm. Two of Irene's sons were suspected bleeders, though medical documentation was suppressed; the imperial German family could not permit lesser beings to learn that the pedigree was tainted.

The eldest of Alix's sisters was another Victoria, grandmother of the engaging young man who at present had no name other than Lieutenant Philip, Royal Navy, soon to be engaged to Elizabeth, future queen of England. The incidence of the mutant gene was unpredictable. By chance, his grandmother did not carry it, according to all the evidence. Her two daughters, Louisa and Philip's mother, Alice, were similarly spared. The most specific proof of his grandmother's good fortune lay in her only son, Louis, Philip's Uncle Dickie. Hemophilia bypassed this branch of the family. The compulsion, shared by nephew and uncle, to take on every kind of physical challenge could be interpreted as a kind of self-congratulation.

Both were spared the inheritance of another disorder that haunted the Hanoverians after the third George's suffering could no longer be concealed from Parliament or public. Philip and Uncle Dickie were eminently sane. They were no more likely than the average medical practitioner at this time to have more than heard the word "porphyria."

Elizabeth mooned over her devotion to Philip, while Margaret devoted herself to the cause of personal freedom on the threshold of being sixteen. The rules for Elizabeth were tight. Even the rumor that she was in love was firmly denied in an official statement from the palace, though everyone who saw how she behaved was aware of the lie.

For Margaret, rules did not exist. She was still fifteen and in rebellion against being palmed off with her sister's castoffs when she wore her own first evening gown. The full-skirted white dress needed christening. She knew precisely how and where—on the dance floor of the Savoy Hotel, where Carol Gibbons, a drawling American, led his band from the piano keyboard. She had heard many a broadcast of his, introduced by the song that identified him, *"Soft Lights and Sweet Music."*

She arrived with a party of a half-dozen or so, all of them years older than she and chosen with care—not too stodgy, not too carefree. Faces turned to watch her as she entered and stayed turned her way all evening as she danced as light as foam. It was glorious to be noticed. She had learned to waltz, foxtrot and quickstep from Miss Vacani. The rumba she spun into she had taught herself. The next morning's newspapers did not scissor her out of the pictures.

She decided that one of her life's true loves was the theater, and the ballet in particular. Nothing compared with it for blotting out present conditions of life in Britain. Existence for most people was as drab as it had been in war with something new added: doubt about the future. She was enchanted by the color, costumes, music, and dance, concocted in a world of make-believe. It was the other end of the spectrum from popping away at pheasant and stalking deer. From the royal box, she saw Margot Fonteyn in action on the stage of Covent Garden opera house one week after another, then went home to rhapsodize about her. Admiration for the arts among the rest of the family was tenuous. They joshed her by nicknaming her "Margo." She quite liked that.

Bertie felt he should interrupt Philip's wooing of Elizabeth even if she did think that was hard-hearted. She must be taken out of range and go with her parents to South Africa, where Bertie would open parliament in Cape Town, then spend two months on tour. To her delight, Margaret would be going, too. To her chagrin, Crawfie would not. It was a pity to break off her lessons, the queen said, "but it seemed too bad to separate the family just now."

After fourteen years with the princesses, the governess would soon be married. In her private opinion, Margaret should be left behind at the palace. She was too young, too delicate for the strain of travel. The adulation she would receive would probably turn her head and spoil her completely, making her impossible when she returned. "She was always willful and headstrong," Crawfie reflected.

Not every Labor member of parliament was convinced that royal privilege extended so far as to warrant issuing bookfuls of extra clothes coupons for the trip. Bickering in Westminster faded when the South African Wool Board made a present to the queen and her daughters of two outfits apiece, the choice to be their own. Margaret hurried to go shopping: a pink wool coat with a smart little hat dressed up with two feathers; a Norman Hartnell evening dress; a seafaring suit with brass buttons and a matching sailor hat.

For a moment as she left the palace, her exuberance disappeared. Tears filled her eyes when she said goodbye to Crawfie. Only the queen looked as if she might possibly enjoy herself on the tour. Elizabeth was downcast over separation from Philip. Bertie was close to exhaustion.

On the first days out of Portsmouth, the battleship *Vanguard* ran into heavy February weather. Margaret took to her cabin, which had been done over in rosebud chintz to her specifications. Elizabeth temporarily decided that she felt so ill she was willing to die. Bertie, never a good sailor, settled down to get all the rest he could. The queen resorted to playing Chinese checkers, with one hand clutching the skittering board. Ladies-in-waiting among the party of two dozen attendants drew up a crisis rotation, taking turns on call. One of the group, Peter Townsend, once again showed his ability to dispense with sleep.

Before the ship sailed into calmer latitudes, Margaret hauled herself out of bed to join her mother at the checkerboard and play the piano for her father. Radiograms from Attlee alarmed him. Britain was held in the clasp of the worst winter in sixty-six years. Blizzards blocked the roads, reservoirs froze, plumbing burst. Coalstocks were giving out, making power cuts imperative, and that meant no light, no heat, and no cooking for long spells every day.

Criticism of the family's absence rippled through every level of society. The royals ought to be where they belonged, sharing the privations of this battle with the weather. The point came where Bertie offered to cancel the trip, but Attlee advised against it. Margaret agreed. What good would it do to return? "They couldn't even send us a snowball!"

The sunbaked panorama of Africa unrolled as their fourteen-coach White Train kept a tight ten-thousand-mile schedule. Margaret accepted the ordained invitation to ride aboard the locomotive for a spell and take a turn tooting the whistle. On this first breakout from her homeland, every possible delight had to be sampled. There was no telling when a second chance would come her way.

She saw an ostrich farm, a Zulu war dance, vultures, and fireworks that singed her sister's dress. She squeezed an inspection of a gold mine into the program when she found that particular divertissement had been neglected. Where Elizabeth kept Philip's picture on view in every room she slept in and wrote him constantly, Margaret dashed off notes to Crawfie. Elizabeth shared her father's guilt about being in places where food was unlimited and the sun hot.

Margaret concentrated on enjoying herself. She paraded the few words of Afrikaans she had been tutored in aboard *Vanguard*. She went to the races and skipped with glee when she backed a winner with the first bet of her life. She was on hand for every function that studded the pages of the day-to-day programs, always striving to add a touch that would leave behind a special memory of herself. And with Elizabeth she broke away from the schedule to ride on the beaches beside the Indian Ocean with Peter Townsend.

He could think of her only as a schoolgirl, but to her he was as perfect a squire as any who served his mistress in the days of castles and dragons. This man of gentle charm seemed to be more than professionally kind as others in his circumstances were. He was invariably courteous, but he didn't fawn over her and stir her into mocking him behind his back. He made it appear that he understood her nearly as well as she knew her own nature. Precious few people were like that.

On this flight into sunlight, she behaved like a hungry child set loose in a bakeshop, cramming down experience like chocolate cake. She drove herself so hard all day that she would be too excited to catch more than a few hours of sleep. Then she would doze off minutes before her next appearance was due in front of another array of white-clad people, banners, and Union Jacks. Some of the fifty days in Africa she counted as lost. When her temperature rose to 102 degrees, under protest she obeyed doctors' orders to stay in bed.

Elizabeth celebrated her coming-of-age on April 21 in Cape Town, taking up her job as heir to the throne with a birthday speech on the radio. Her voice was clear but tremulous. "I declare before you all that my whole life, whether it be long or short, shall be devoted to your service ... I know that your support will be unfailingly given. God bless all of you who are willing to share it."

South Africa's gift for her was a casket of twenty-one diamonds. Margaret was not surprised. Minutes later, she was stunned to be handed a similar present. Elizabeth could not decide for the life of her what kind of necklace her diamonds should be set in. Her sister had a sketch ready for hers before *Vanguard* reached home waters in May.

She looked in worse shape than anyone when the family arrived back at the palace, and all of them were drooping with fatigue. Crawfie felt a surge of anxiety over Margaret that she could not attempt to explain. She was wrong, though, about the aftereffects of the admiration that had been showered on her pupil for the past four months. Margaret seemed glad to get back into the schoolroom routine. She had never been so pliable, possibly because she had found a man on the trip whose friendship she looked forward to. Elizabeth had been sending Philip photographs of herself when she was sixteen. Now Margaret was that age, and she was rather fond of Peter Townsend, who would be on hand at Balmoral that summer.

Two months after they came home, Bertie steeled himself to part with his elder daughter. Her engagement to Philip Mountbatten was announced in July. With the disasters of winter all but forgotten, the publicity machinery was cranked up in preparation for another pageant; the marriage of a model princess to a kinsman she loved. Genealogists reckoned that through the lineage of Victoria, they were third cousins, and through descendants of George III, fourth cousins once removed. The place and date for the wedding were fixed: Westminster Abbey, on November 20. Bertie had a surprise ready for his future son-in-law. He created him a Royal Highness, which was something he had refused to do for the former Mrs. Simpson.

As the day drew nearer when she would lose the challenging company of her sister, Margaret still seemed weary. Crawfie called a halt to sessions in the classroom; they were resumed only fitfully after that. Higher learning was deemed unnecessary in a princess. She was more interested in helping the governess set up house in the Christopher Wren cottage behind Kensington Palace that Bertie had granted as a home for Crawfie now that she was Mrs. George Buthlay.

Margaret's wedding present for her was a set of three bedside lamps. "I intend to continue brightening your life," she grinned. Like Snow White, housekeeping for the seven dwarfs, she sang while she worked around the cottage as though the place were her own.

Gifts for Elizabeth poured in from everywhere, and her sister helped with the chores of unwrapping. From Wales came a chunk of local gold for the wedding ring. "There is enough for two," the prospective bride exclaimed. "We can save a piece for Margaret." Another package from the same locale contained a hunk of rock, sent for good luck. It was a bit of Mount Snowdon, said the covering letter.

Handkerchiefs arrived by the gross—cotton, cambric, silk, and lace. Grandmama inspected them through her lorgnette. If there were any to spare, she said, she could use them for sale at one of her charity bazaars. For philanthropy's sake, the mounds of presents were sorted and put on view in St. James's Palace: admission after opening day, one shilling. Mile-long lines stretched down the Mall. Romance was good medicine for the relief of gloom.

Mahatma Gandhi had just succeeded in wresting a pledge of independence for India from the Attlee government. The Hindu ascetic sent Elizabeth a loincloth he had personally knitted. "What a horrible thing!" gasped Grandmama when she saw it on display at St. James's.

Philip, at her elbow, gave a hint of independence. "I don't think it's horrible. Gandhi is a wonderful man." Grandmama and her furled umbrella proceeded in silence. Margaret went by the next day to hide the offending garment from the land where Uncle Dickie was in charge of ending the rule of the British raj.

The fraternity turned out in force to see Elizabeth married. Some left their palaces and others their places of exile to parade in uniform, decorations, and court gowns, ancient and modern. They arrived from Denmark, Norway, Greece, the Netherlands, Belgium, Sweden, Luxembourg, and Iraq. They came claiming rights to the lost monarchies of Rumania, Yugoslavia, and Spain. Crowned or otherwise, a total of five kings, five queens, four princes, and three princesses, not counting the bride and her family, sat down at the wedding breakfast in the State Supper Room to eat filet of sole, partridge in casserole, and ice cream, served on the royal gold. A brand-new royal peer was there—twenty-four hours earlier, Bertie had created Philip the Duke of Edinburgh.

Margaret's face was pale after the bridal couple had been driven off through the evening drizzle in an open landau to Waterloo Station, where their honeymoon train was waiting. Elizabeth's corgi Susan lay at her feet.

Margaret still wore her bridesmaid's dress of ivory silk tulle. She could not picture what life would be like now that she had been left behind. There would be no one so close to tease and share secrets with. Nobody but her sister knew exactly what it meant having Papa the king. She was convinced that the two of them read each other's minds, as identical twins were supposed to be able to do. From now on, Philip would be closer to Lil than she, which made her a company of one, and she hated the thought of being alone unless she chose to be.

She went to Crawfie's old room in the palace to talk about her gloom.

"Never mind," Crawfie said. "You will be next."

Dejection was gone in an instant. "Don't be silly!" Margaret

Elizabeth was 8 and Margaret was 4 and their mother was still the Duchess of York when this photograph was taken in 1934. They lived in a narrow stone house on Piccadilly and played in the park and their greatest treat was a ride in Grandpapa's carriage.

In this photograph taken in one of Buckingham Palace's formal reception rooms, while the rest of the royal family, and even the Corgi, acceded to the photographer's request to look off to the side, 9-year-old Margaret determinedly kept her eye on the camera—the kind of thing that always made Elizabeth say, "I really don't know what we're going to do with her."

Everything changed when Papa became King in 1934. Elizabeth was now heir to the crown and 6-year-old Margaret soon began to mourn, "Now that Papa is king, I am nothing." The Royal Family posed after the coronation: Queen Elizabeth, Princess Elizabeth, the dowager Queen Mary, Princess Margaret and King George VI.

When war broke out, the princesses moved outside London to the relative safety of Windsor Castle. "Poor dears, they never have any fun," the King fretted, but Margaret knew how to make her own fun. She organized a Christmas pantomime for family and friends in which she starred as Cinderella—"so lovely she brought down the house." Elizabeth was relegated to a secondary role.

After the war, Margaret became the leader of the madcap, young aristocratic set of London, dancing until dawn, partying incessantly. But by day, she did her share of royal "work," including serving as Commodore of the Sea Rangers, whose uniform she wears here.

Margaret was a sad-eyed princess on the twenty-third birthday. It was to be years before the "Townsend matter" would be resolved. In the meantime, she lived with her mother at Clarence House, fulfilled her royal duties and sought consolation in religion.

Peter Townsend was the man she loved. He was a former fighter pilot, a hero of the Battle of Britain, equerry to the King—and divorced. When it was learned that this man of gentle charm was more to Margaret than a member of the Palace staff, newspapers broke out in thundering, scandalized headlines. After years of separation and soul-searching, the heartbroken princess renounced Townsend, putting the Church's teachings and her royal duty above her love.

Two lonely women posed in the Throne Room at Buckingham Palace wearing their coronation robes of velvet and ermine on the day of Elizabeth's coronation in 1953. The widowed queen and her younger daughter, who did not yet know whether she would be permitted to marry the man she loved.

Family and friends, indeed the whole nation, were delighted when the Princess married audacious and charming Anthony Armstrong-Jones on a sun-blessed May morning in Westminster Chapel. Princess Anne, her niece, was one of the bridesmaids.

One of the most touching mother-and-child photographs of our time is the one Tony Armstrong-Jones took of his wife, Her Royal Highness, the Princess Margaret, Countess of Snowdon, and his son.

When Princess Margaret and Lord Snowdon posed for this picture with their children, Lady Sarah Armstrong-Jones and Lord Linley, in 1967, there was already gossip about the marriage and criticism of Margaret's neglect of her royal duties.

The fairy tale princess had turned into a dumpy middle-aged woman and the fairy tale marriage was on the rocks when Princess Margaret and her husband enrolled their children in school. This was the last picture of them together before their separation.

At 45, Margaret, her face puffy and jowled, was the subject of increasingly sharp criticism. Her favorite refuge was Mustique, a speck of an island in the Caribbean owned by her friend Colin Tennant, where the life was easy and gay. Her favorite escort there and in London was, at least for a time, 28-year-old Roddy Llewellyn (above), a dropout from Establishment society.

smiled. "You know quite well Papa and Mummy need me to keep them in order. What would they do without me?"

A letter from her father arrived for his newly married daughter on her honeymoon. "Our family, us four, the 'Royal Family,' must remain together with additions of course at suitable moments!! . . . I can, I know, always count on you, & now Philip, to help us in our work. Your leaving us has left a great blank in our lives but do remember that your old home is still yours & do come back to it as much & as often as possible. I can see that you are sublimely happy with Philip which is right but don't forget us is the wish of Your ever loving and devoted *Papa*."

Two more months went by before the King noticed the pain of cramp in both legs. He made no mention of it to anyone for the time being, but he started jotting down notes of the symptoms against the day when he might be compelled to consult his doctors.

VIII

A Small, Cruel Sea

The country was splitting in two like a log cleft by a woodsman's wedge. Every blow of the government's sledgehammer deepened the division. Its intention to create a Socialist democracy by nationalizing industry was unchanged.

The British had survived the war largely in hope that peace would bring immediate betterment to their lives. Instead, they were in the thick of another struggle to save the kingdom from going under in a tidal wave of debt. British markets overseas had dwindled or disappeared entirely since 1940. "Export or die" was more than a chilling slogan when the overcrowded country, smaller than the state of Oregon, depended on income from sales abroad to buy enough to feed its people. The better life had to be deferred indefinitely. Spending on imports must be pared to the bone. The hammer swung again to drive down consumption of tobacco, gasoline, and newsprint. Wheat was needed for making bread, so bread was rationed, for the first time in the nation's history. Meat was limited to a few cents' worth a week for everybody.

Luxuries and fancy foods were reserved for customers in richer lands. That was the theory, anyway.

The split produced two parts of unequal size, one of the few, the other of the many. The difference in general lay in how much money was available to soften or obliterate the painful edge of austerity. Most Britons, Socialists and Tories alike, grumbled incessantly but accepted sacrifice. The government's backers, still a majority, took unprecedented taxation as the price of ushering in the welfare state to transform the kingdom. Its opponents denounced Socialism as an insane experiment and prayed for the day Labor would be thrown out.

Two nations existed side by side, as alien to each other as in the youth of Benjamin Disraeli, Victoria's pet Prime Minister, who wrote a novel, *Sybil,* on the theme. The distinction was sharpest in London. With cash in hand, a knowing shopper there could find almost anything on the black market, whose depth of color varied from charcoal dark to off-white. Steaks, gasoline, Scotch, nylon stockings, cigarettes, men suit's and women's dresses—the makings of easy living were on tap if the right spigot was turned.

Attlee had echoed Churchill in declaring, "We are engaged in another Battle of Britain. It cannot be won by the few. It demands a united effort by the whole nation." The few who could not wait to relish the pleasures of peace and comfort were not listening. One ingenuous American imagined that "the Britain of today counts only sixty people who still retain incomes of $16,800 and up a year." The truth was that fashionable London had rarely seen such wanton spending in half a century, but not by check, please.

Most Londoners put in a nine-to-five working day, then caught a bus or a train home to a skimpy meal, rounded off perhaps by an outing to the movies, a session with one of the madcap comedy shows on the BBC, or a trip to a pub where beer supplies held out. The few stirred themselves to dress for an unrationed dinner in a favorite restaurant, where the carpet was probably threadbare and the tablecloths continually re-darned but a steady customer could rely on being served almost anything he fancied except a slice of bread that was temptingly white rather than nutritiously gray.

In the clubs and cabarets that opened up on the side streets like evening primroses, the dance floors were jammed every night with escapologists, some law-abiding, others less scrupulous. The most celebrated among them was Margaret, unfettered and intent on enjoying herself. Her mother and father were at a loss about what to do. In Crawfie's estimation, "She did not seem to be settling down at·all."

Lessons passed the weekday mornings. After that, her hours were empty. She mooned through the afternoons, lonely without Elizabeth. There was not much to look forward to except another evening party or a night out. Grandmama thought some definite assignments should be arranged. Since everyone was supposed to be working harder to get the country back on its feet, her granddaughter should be taught to set an example. The old lady's complaints led to nothing but discussions about finding occupations for Margaret. Her father, worried about the unspoken-of pain in his legs, could not bear to push his second daughter off into the outside world so soon after he had surrendered the first.

He liked her to be home by midnight, which was a rule she respected no more than any other. On the floor of Ciro's club or downstairs in the Savoy Hotel, she would choose the tallest male in the party to dance with at the approach of curfew so that she could hide behind him, murmuring the lyrics of tunes she knew by heart.

Money did not matter in her case. She had none of her own apart from the £1,000 a year she drew as a legacy from her mother's departed friend, Mrs. Ronald Greville, in whose house at Polesden Lacey, Surrey, Bertie and his bride had spent part of their 1923 honeymoon. For pin money, Margaret was dependent on her father. She had to wait until she was twenty-one to qualify for an official income of £6,000. But no one in her circle expected a kinetic little princess to pay for anything. Seven nights a week, her escorts were ready to run up bank overdrafts if they must for the privilege of being in her adolescent orbit.

Margaret was fodder for Fleet Street. In the ceaseless struggle for bigger circulations, editors concluded accurately enough that readers were tired of gloom. The prescription called for glamour, news from different planets where the lights never dimmed and women wore either mink or swimsuits. The affairs of any Hollywood seductress made good copy, but chronicling the expeditions of a home-grown princess topped it. Reporters and photographers stuck to her trail. A waiter eager to earn an extra quid or two, or a management looking for publicity, tipped off the newspapers when she walked through the door. To this era belonged her advice to one dance-floor partner: "Look into my eyes! The *Express* says they're the most beautiful in the world."

Sometimes, she danced through a night with a kind of desperate determination to prove her autonomy and fend off loneliness. The governess' alarm increased during the final months of her employment. Compassion for Margaret prompted her to stay on in the palace while her husband lived in a South Kensington hotel. Otherwise, with Bertie and the queen so often away, the girl would be left by herself in one enormous wing with only servants and staff for company. Crawfie could do nothing as a teacher with a student who came to class dog-tired, but the queen made light of the problem. "We are only young once. We want her to have a good time."

She was too fragile to last as a gadabout without faltering.

Attacks of migraine had to be ignored sometimes, and so did her all-too-common colds. Measles kept her in bed, with a day and a night nurse in attendance for a month. From what they had read, they expected to find her a fretful patient. She turned out to be as hungry for kindness as a lonesome child. Bedpans occupied a customary place as the keystone of her jokes.

Fibrositis was the next diagnosis the doctors produced. Her neck was so stiff she could not turn her head—"First a child and now a cripple," in her mocking self-appraisal. Gossip said she picked up a chill on a lively country house party. The house she had gone to in fact was Windlesham Manor, between London and Windsor, which Bertie chose as emergency accommodations for Elizabeth and Philip after the house they had counted on moving into, Sunninghill Park near Ascot, burned down.

Type-casting the two sisters was well under way. Elizabeth the Good emerged in every word written about her as a young woman of solid, middle-class virtue, joyfully married and expecting a baby in November. Margaret was identified obversely as the merry, mindless minx who lived purely for pleasure. Both portraits pictured them in two dimensions like characters in a pantomime poster. Elizabeth had a violent temper. For the present, she was excessively dependent on her mother. Her father on the other hand had occasion to caution her about behaving like a martinet in her treatment of her inferiors. In her role of colonel-in-chief, she had given one hapless private on inspection parade such a dressing down for sloppiness that she sounded like a drill sergeant. This third dimension was ignored in print.

Margaret retained a softness that was being subdued in her sister. It was Margaret who would pluck a rose from a bouquet and hand it back to whoever had presented it, and

Margaret who in South Africa went over to visit a group of lepers she had noticed, isolated in a bus. She was a weaker, more sensitive creature, considerate and commanding in turn, undecided about her fit in the scheme of things. Nervousness continued to plague her. Her stomach churned whenever she woke up on a day that provided her with a public job to do. None of that got reported either.

The relationship with Elizabeth had changed when she and Philip, their honeymoon over, moved into a palace suite, waiting for their town house to be made livable. For the first time in her life, Margaret started to defer to the sister who would reign as sovereign one day. The mysterious crystallization of personality that turned heirs into monarchs had begun, working more slowly than in their father, whom emergency had forced through the process. Taunting and mimicking a future queen was unforgivable in anyone. The intangible distance stretched wider.

They went together to take a look at the unkempt mansion chosen for husband and wife. "Ghastly" was Margaret's judgment of Clarence House. Elizabeth was uncertain about what should be done; Margaret plowed through a stack of homemaking magazines for inspiration. The house, a section of St. James's Palace, had lost its windows to a German bomb, and boards covered the holes. It contained one bathroom, and all the rooms, some dating back to the fourth George, had gathered dust since the blitz.

A nursery and bathroom had to be installed without delay. Elizabeth was picking up some of Philip's spirit. Her parents urged her to return to the palace to have her baby. She insisted for once on being given her way. Her child would be delivered in her bedroom in Clarence House, with Bobo standing by to take charge.

Margaret fussed over her sister long in advance, stuffing

cushions in behind her back, scolding her if she dared break into a trot to exercise the indispensable Corgis. She was certain that the old perambulator, kept for the unborn brother, would be wheeled out of hiding. She was not disappointed.

In her fourth month of pregnancy, Elizabeth's duty calendar was cut short and her sister's gallivanting interrupted. Margaret took up the slack, christening ships, planting trees with gilded spades, snipping opening-day ribbons, inspecting hospitals—alone. On her eighteenth birthday, she acquired her first lady-in-waiting to handle mail, do the shopping, and attend her like a shadow.

Jennifer Bevan, an amiable, twenty-two-year-old brunette, would cover her yawns along with Margaret when they went night-clubbing again. The appointment, which paid nothing more than a dress allowance, was hard going sometimes. But Margaret had a gift for cultivating friendships when she cared to use it. Jennifer was enlisted as a friend as well as a companion.

At eighteen, Margaret was also equipped, Bertie thought, to cope with a September mission to Amsterdam that Elizabeth would probably have handled otherwise—the pain in his legs was progressively worse. Dauntless, dumpy Queen Wilhelmina at the age of sixty-eight was resigning the crown of the House of Orange in favor of her daughter Juliana, for eleven years the wife of Bernhard of Lippe-Biesterfeld. By tradition, there would be no coronation but a simple swearing-in ceremony at The Hague, making Juliana queen and her obscurely German husband Prince of the Netherlands. The blemish of his membership in the Hitler Youth Movement had been cancelled out by his war record as an RAF fighter pilot and leader of the resistance in occupied Holland.

Grandmama sorted through her treasures and gave Margaret a diamond-and-pearl diadem to wear at the inaugural banquet. Elizabeth supplied her more seasoned lady-in-waiting, Lady Margaret Egerton, for the trip. In the closed circuit of court life, another marriage was about to be celebrated. Margaret Egerton was due to become the wife of Jack Colville, Elizabeth's private secretary, soon after they got back, and the royal Margaret would be a bridesmaid.

Bertie again entrusted Peter Townsend with the job of escort. Margaret needed a comforting presence to bolster her courage. This first solo performance intimidated her. Some of those who watched developments thought afterward that the affinity between her and Peter quickened on the trip to the Netherlands. One of them explained: "I believe they were fond of each other almost at first sight. But in the normal course of events, they weren't exactly thrown together in the palace. Outside those walls, however, it was a different story. They had far more opportunity to get to know each other."

The welcome by the Dutch elated her, and they were delighted by the warmth that showed in Margaret. Once again, every day had to be brimfull—an evening cruise through canals glistening with floodlights; a trip to see Delft porcelains; a stop to watch tulip bulbs auctioned off at Aaslmere; a breathtaking scamper through the Rijksmuseum, hung with the legacies of Rembrandt van Rijn. She earned a good report for dignity and decorum on her return. "There was not a difficult moment," said a senior member of the party, intimating a degree of surprise.

The first doctor Bertie summoned was his seventy-year-old manipulative surgeon, Commander Sir Morton Smart, who had treated him for strains and aches in the past. The commander was alarmed when he inspected his patient's right foot, and urged him to seek additional medical opinion without wasting more time.

Bertie was left in a quandary. In his country's present condition of decline, it was essential to hold on to what remained of the empire that Disraeli had assembled for

Victoria. India was gone. Bertie had done all he could to revitalize loyalty in South Africa by showing himself and his family there. Australia and New Zealand came next on the list. He was scheduled to appear there the following spring with the queen and Margaret.

He let ten days pass before two more doctors examined him. Sir Thomas Dunhill, two years older than Smart, had served as surgeon to Bertie's father. Sir Maurice Cassidy, physician ordinary by title to both George and Bertie, was Smart's age. What they saw of the foot and leg convinced the three physicians that they ought to call in another. Meantime, they recommended that X-rays and blood tests should be made and the Australian tour postponed. To spare his daughters anxiety, Bertie told them nothing. Margaret was happily planning what to wear to justify her reputation when she arrived on the other side of the globe.

The fourth consultant, Professor James Learmonth, of Edinburgh, specialist in diseases of the blood vessels, was a comparatively youthful fifty-three. He immediately diagnosed arteriosclerosis: an obstruction in the arteries threatened to bring on gangrene. To check it, Bertie's leg might have to be amputated. First, it was worth trying to see what some undisturbed weeks in bed would do to avoid surgery.

The professor conducted his examination on Friday, November 12. Bertie kept the findings secret. Elizabeth's baby was expected within the next forty-eight hours. Margaret had been pressed into spending the weekend at Sandbeck Park in Yorkshire, some two hundred driving miles away, with the Earl and Countess of Scarborough. Her sister had tried out on her the names she had in mind: Charles for a boy, Anne for a girl, which was still the queen's preference.

Margaret dithered around the Scarboroughs' telephone through Saturday and Sunday, trying to check on Elizabeth's progress. The dilapidated state of General Post Office equipment made a tedious business of getting calls through to London. Late on Sunday evening, the news came for her. According to legend, she whooped, "Hurray! I'm Charley's Aunt" as she hung up. Had she tagged herself with the title of that deathless theatrical farce with its transvestite hero "from Brazil, where the nuts come from"? Her followers were sure she had. Personally, she was proud of the label, whether it was her doing or not.

Bertie had protested for half a week that he would be well enough to cross the Pacific in the spring. On Tuesday, he gave in to his doctors. The tour was abandoned, and his daughters were finally told why before the reasons were spelled out in a palace bulletin. Margaret felt the double blow of disappointment and fear for Bertie.

She borrowed optimism from her mother. "When Papa decided he could no longer struggle to keep going," his daughter explained, "he went to sleep for two days." He was confined to bed for weeks, as sanguine as his family about his chances. "Of course, it will take me some time to recover from it, but with rest and care I am sure I shall."

Margaret ordered her piano pushed into place outside his bedroom door. She had kept her talent for entertaining Papa. When he was allowed up for brief periods each day, she lent him her arm. "It's a blessing I'm not very tall. I make a good walking stick."

She was beside him when he limped into the music room of the palace ten days before Christmas for the christening of his first grandson, Charles Philip Arthur George. Elizabeth had served the country impeccably. "After all," she said, "it is what we are made for."

An extra surgeon, fifty-seven-year-old Professor James Ross, was added to the muster of six medical men who re-examined Bertie in March. He was enraged by what they had to confide to him. Unless he wished to live as an invalid, he must undergo a different kind of surgery from that which had originally been contemplated: cutting close to his right groin in a lumbar sympathectomy. "So all our treatment has been a waste of time," he stammered before the doctors calmed him.

They suggested that the operation be performed at the Royal Masonic Hospital. In common with most Hanoverians since 1782, Bertie was an ardent Freemason, "but I've never heard of a king going to a hospital before," he objected. So an operating room was set up in the palace for Professor Learmonth and his assistant, Professor Ross, to do their work on March 12. Hand-scrawled placards of the newspaper sellers the next morning spread the word: HE'S ALL RIGHT.

One of his first concerns in convalescence was to make up to Margaret for her letdown over the Australian expedition. Grandmama liked to reminisce about her travels in nineteenth-century Italy when she was nothing more than Princess Mary of Teck, a great-great-granddaughter of the third George. Margaret could follow in her footsteps, though of course that land was a republic now, with Luigi Einaudi its first president.

He was waiting for her with a band and a guard of honor when her father's flight touched down at Naples airport. Her mother had lent Margaret her own secretary, Tom Harvey, and his wife, Lady Mary, and there was a detective on hand to shield her from the crowds. Ruby MacDonald had never had such a wardrobe to keep pressed and clean—a dozen or so outfits for the five-week junket.

Italians took the presence of *la bella Margherita* as proof that her country had forgiven and forgotten the sins of the *Fascisti*. They pushed flowers in her hands and dinned *Santa Lucia* into her ears. They wrestled with the carabinieri to move in closer at every stop on the Cook's tour—Naples, Capri, Sorrento, Amalfi, Pompeii. If they could not get to see her in person, they turned to their newspapers, laden with photographs of her snapped by a following horde of papparazzi.

She applied dense makeup for protection against the searing sun before she stole a swim on a guarded beach, but a telephoto lens caught her at the water's edge: The prints caused a tremor on Fleet Street. It was hard to discern her pale swimsuit. "Holy God!" yelped one editor. "She's gone in wearing nothing but a damned bathing cap." Margaret the minx was considered capable of anything. Retouchers' brushes clarified the situation before the picture was published.

Another outcry arose when, in stately black with a lacy shawl covering her head, she arrived at the Vatican for a private audience with Pius XII. Her defenders searched the archives and found that best of all justifications, a precedent, admittedly hoary. Grandmama as a girl had called on an earlier Pope. Purist critics reacted as if Margaret had embarked on a campaign to undo four hundred and fifteen years of history and restore England to the authority of Rome. Henry VIII had rejected that to have his own new independent church grant an annulment of his first marriage to Catherine of Aragon. Margaret had no qualms about accepting a painting of the Virgin as a souvenir from the Holy Father.

The notion of converting to a rival faith did not cross her mind. Another seldom-reported fact of the third dimension was that she was a devout Anglican, whose constancy had grown in her father's illness. She went to take communion in the Chapel Royal of St. James's Palace early in the morning of his operation. If she had any concealed motive in visiting Pius, it was the hope of ensuring extra prayers for Bertie's recovery.

The fine print in the contract with the public which Gable talked about, spelling out the price of publicity, remained illegible to her, but her flight to May sunshine piqued some upper-class English. They thought that they deserved a break, too, but rigid currency controls made that impossible when a travel allowance was only a few miserable pound notes. The country was in deep financial trouble again, so grave that Bertie feared a repetition of the 1931 Depression. Two of his ministers, Ernest Bevin, whom he admired, and Sir Stafford Cripps, whom he did not, would have to go to Washington and Ottawa to lay on still more credit.

Margaret saw Florence, Venice, Torcello, and Stresa, then crossed the Simplon Pass into Switzerland. She paid another duty call there on Great-great Aunt Ena, who was safely beyond the age of childbearing and living in Lausanne, exiled from Madrid. She glowed over the girl, not unlike the doting duenna in Colette's *Gigi*. "She has blossomed out deliciously. What a success she will be in Paris!" A more discerning observer, a social satellite of the British royals, jotted down a chillier diary entry after Margaret came home. "There is already," he decided, "a Marie Antoinette aroma about her."

She rode overnight in a wagon-lit to Paris; had her hair done on the Rue St. Honoré; lunched at the Elysée Palace with President Vincent Auriol, who would be making a state visit to London next year; danced until three at a British Embassy ball; took in the haute couture paraded on mannequins' backs in the salons of Christian Dior and Jean Dessès; spent a day around the shops; and bought a teddy bear to take back for her baby nephew. Very soon, she would be nineteen.

The timing of the whole five weeks turned out to be providential for the family budget. If her exodus had been put off much longer, the cost would have jumped by about thirty per cent. Shortly after her birthday, the country's debts had risen past the point where its currency could any longer be defended on world money markets. Back from Washington, Sir Stafford Cripps announced that the value of a pound must be dropped from $4.03 to $2.80. The sledgehammer fell again, reducing the meat ration to fourteen cents' worth a week and the sugar allowance to eight ounces a head.

The exclusive inner nation in which Margaret enjoyed herself would not let austerity darken its spirits. More acreage of newsprint than before was given over to pictures and columns detailing how she and her coterie spent their evenings on the town at theaters, balls, supper parties, and nightclubs. Bertie condoned almost everything.

He doted on gaiety himself now that his doctors ordered him to ease up on official engagements and break if he could the habit of fretting over everything from the state of the country to the care of rhododendrons in his gardens. Margaret kept him posted on the joys he had to miss. "It's been wonderful," she would say as a night ended. "I'll tell my father about it."

He did take exception when she turned out in a Dior gown from Paris that only suspension prevented from slipping any lower off her shoulders. For the next wearing, it was reinforced with shoulder straps. The gossip columns supplied a quote from her for their readers: "I can't really be elegant, but wait until I'm thirty."

The country called her circle "the Margaret set." The set romped its way through a 1950 general election that bruised Attlee's Labor Party and returned it to power with a majority so slim as to stall further moves toward a Socialist utopia. She treated the rise and fall of political parties like a horse race. As the results filtered in, she sat hunched over the radio in her second-floor sitting room in the palace while her parents listened to another on the floor below. Tories and Labor took turns edging each other out of the lead, which sent her racing downstairs and up again in excitement to babble with Bertie.

When South Korea was invaded, London, complying with hints from Washington, earmarked nearly $10 billion for rearming. The British shuddered to hear that atomic bombs were not being ruled out to achieve victory. The Margaret set continued to make equally commanding headlines.

It was usually the men around her who received the most attention. An exception was Sharman, the bouncy blonde daughter of Lew Douglas, benevolent United States Ambassador to the Court of St. James's. To Margaret and most of a population penned up on the tight little island, the United States was Santa's workshop, source of food packages and nylon stockings, movie stars, and brotherly goodwill. As a messenger from fantasyland, Sharman won a quick place in the midst of the set.

She was two years older than Margaret, uninhibited, self-assured, and irresistible to a girl whose nature was quite the contrary. The two of them met for coffee in Sharman's room at the embassy in Grosvenor Square to make their plans for new tricks to stir up London. The ambassador's breezy daughter made friends in Fleet Street as easily as in the palace by seldom refusing a reporter's telephone call.

Danny Kaye owed his place in the clique to Sharman. She booked the seats to see his exuberant act at the London Palladium, which made him an overnight idol with the pleasure-starved British. Then, after he had finished leading a closing chorus from the edge of the orchestra pit, she whisked Margaret and her party into his dressing room. It was another case of instant admiration. Kaye was a better mimic than she could hope to be. She added an impersonation of him to her repertoire as a prelude to tantalizing her father into going to the show.

Her sister and brother-in-law were roped into a fancy-dress affair at the embassy that Sharman sparked. Philip's cousin and best man at his wedding, David Milford-Haven, was invited, too, as the porter in a fanciful trio comprising Philip as the mustached waiter and Elizabeth as the demure upstairs maid.

A line of eight young ladies, rehearsed by Danny Kaye, performed a watered-down can-can. One of them was Margaret, another Sharman Douglas. The glimpse of regal thighs was restricted, since kicks went no higher than knee height, but newspaper readers the following morning gained the impression that the party had escalated into a vintage Edwardian frolic.

Margaret, winsome and controversial beyond a doubt, was ready for love, in popular opinion. A young man noticed at her side more than once or twice would find himself added to the roster of imagined suitors. The list of them was circulated as widely in the United States as at home. Americans were assumed to be equally fascinated by her prospects for romance.

This made Billy Wallace an automatic candidate in the handicapping. With a million pounds of his own, he was the lank stepson of Herbert Agar, Pulitzer prize-winning editor from Louisville, Kentucky. Margaret visited the Agar's Sussex home. For an audience with marriage on its mind, that was enough to support the fancy that courtship was in the wind.

The field for these esoteric Gold Cup stakes appeared to be wide open. Willing to please their customers in the betting craze that developed, in a nation of reluctant Spartans, bookmakers laid odds on the outcome, with their calculations based of necessity on rumor. Staff writers for American magazines, wire services, and communication networks filed running accounts of the fabled marathon.

They cited the red-haired Earl of Dalkeith, one of Grandmama's godsons, as a prime contender, recalling as if it mattered that his father had once been tipped as a possible husband for Bertie's only sister, Mary; she confounded gossips of her generation by marrying sober-sided Henry Lascelles, sixth earl of Harewood, who combined farming in Yorkshire with amassing a collection of Italian master paintings.

Colin Tennant, a schoolboy at Eton when he met Margaret

during her wartime incarceration at Windsor, figured high on the roll. The heir of a rich industrialist, Lord Glenconner, he had the style and the means to be welcome in the set, but he did not become of consequence until later.

She made a friend of Simon Phipps whose father's place in Bertie's affection went back to his days as a naval cadet. This was a young man of uncommon complexity, the kind that held strong appeal for her. He quit the Coldstream Guards to be ordained a chaplain at Trinity College, Cambridge, then went on to serve working-class congregations in parsonages in Coventry and Huddersfield. He, too, had a significant part to play in the future, but not now.

She sat with Mark Bonham-Carter at a table in the 400 Club, which resulted in the entry of his name into the record. Tom Egerton took her to the races and Lord Ogilvy drove her to a fox hunt. At Blenheim Palace, the monumental Oxfordshire seat of the dukes of Marlborough, she appeared at house parties hosted by Sonny Blandford, who would inherit the dukedom one day. Julian Fane escorted her to the opera and Michael Tree to church. The six young bachelors found themselves being touted as other secret suppliants for her favor. Denying it did not accomplish much. Everyone knew that a primary requirement of membership in the set was flawless discretion, unless you were Sharman Douglas.

The half-dozen young men, along with three or four more whose names cropped up in the sweepstakes, had much in common. They were all passably handsome, impeccably behaved, and endowed with enough income, earned or inherited, to support a wife in high style. Together with the girls they brought with them, drawn from backgrounds similar to their own, they made up the Margaret set.

By and large, they were companionable people whom she liked to be out with, nightclubbing, at a show, trading well-spiked gossip about everybody and everything. Almost all the men were the sons or grandsons of family friends, of royal household staff, or of the most solidly established aristocracy. There was no firm evidence that any one of them envisaged himself as her husband; it was clear that she was enchanted with none of them. One by one, they were let go, to become engaged or be married or disappear from view.

She floated in a small, land-locked sea. It was as inconceivable for her to dip into other waters as for Bertie to be admitted into a public hospital.

Yet every so often she liked to experiment. Mark Bonham-Carter was due to treat her to a theater. She mentioned to her father that they would be going on to supper afterwards with a comedienne in the show at her flat on King's Road, Chelsea, a district of London on a par with Bohemia or Greenwich Village for artiness and carefree style. Joyce Grenfell, who specialized in gentle mimicry of her upper-class peers, was irreproachable as a hostess, a cousin of Simon Phipps. But Bertie was not sure about Chelsea, which he knew best for its annual spring flower show and its hospital for aged, scarlet-uniformed army pensioners.

"Will you be able to find the place?" he wondered.

Margaret could only repeat what her chauffeur had told her. "It's over a sweetshop near a bus stop." That was the joke of the day to her father. He had not heard before of a princess going hunting in the dark for an address on raffish King's Road.

One man in whose company she revelled was overlooked in the annals of her alleged attachments. The name of Peter Townsend was never mentioned. Balmoral was the place where she could spend the most time with him. Hilltops around Deeside were marked with conical piles of rock, built to Victoria's order to memorialize events in the family that met with her approval. For fun one day, Margaret set the first stone of a new cairn in place when she was out riding with

Peter. From then on, whichever of them reached the crest first accepted the obligation of adding another rock.

The man and wife who edited America's biggest-selling women's magazine decided that the time had come to probe more deeply into the personalities of Margaret and her sister. Bruce and Beatrice Gould of *Ladies' Home Journal* flew to London, looking for someone to tackle the assignment. Contacts at the palace recommended Dermot Morrah, late Fellow of All Souls College, Oxford, and a writer of polished prose who would be granted access to as much as the court considered might be disclosed.

The Goulds commissioned articles from him, and not long afterward he wrote a book, *The Royal Family*, which in its opening said of Margaret, "To have been born, and to remain, the junior member of a partnership of two necessarily leaves its mark upon character." He expected—this was 1950—that "she will pass into some eminent family among her father's people, which she will dignify by linking it essentially with the throne and so become the ancestress of a line of loyal subjects serving the King in a private station."

Then the two editors heard about Crawfie, living in retirement, saddened by the abrupt cooling of her association with her ex-students after sixteen years of royal service. Under repeated urging, she agreed to try telling her story. The manuscript produced a sensational rise in the magazine's circulation and an international best-seller in *The Little Princesses*, which provided the first sensitive insight into the making of Margaret and Elizabeth. Bought for British serialization, it set some kind of record by being run twice, originally in *Woman's Own*, then in its sister weekly, *Home Notes*.

It also rattled the foundations of the royal household. Crawfie, the court concluded, had overstepped the bounds of discretion, shared too many confidences about the two girls and their parents, let fall too many clues to Margaret's mercurial temperament and the frailty of her health. There were stories of squabbles between two sisters who were supposed to treat each other like angels, and light-hearted reference to jokes about bedpans. Margaret made a point of reading it and, according to friends, rated it more sentimental than objectionable. But she was in a minority at court. Only carefully regulated publicity about the family could be tolerated as part of the price of popularity, and it must go no further than cautious press handouts and the normal run of Fleet Street frippery.

The Little Princesses added to the scales the pebble that resulted in tighter restrictions on employees at the palace. An oath of silence would be required of them in the future. The image of Margaret and the others that was presented must be controlled by all means possible. Dermot Morrah's book allowed that there was "a dash of absinthe in her character," which went as far as prudence warranted.

The ups and downs of her health, however, could not be disguised. She made a joke of the number of times she caught colds. "We are both very prone," she told·Bertie. Influenza barred her from joining in the formalized frisking that followed the arrival of her Paris host, Vincent Auriol, at Victoria Station, where Bertie waited to greet him in front of television cameras. After Haakon of Norway had come and gone on a similar errand, she was put to bed again with German measles.

There was no harm, in palace judgment, in letting the kingdom know that for her coming of age at Balmoral, she ordered a sequined dress with a crinoline skirt—no shoulder straps—from the queen's most dependable couturier, Mr. Hartnell, who proclaimed it the prettiest he had ever designed.

From her parents, she received a new green Daimler roadster, from her sister a turquoise necklace with diamond-and-turquoise earrings, from Peter a sheepskin saddle.

She and the equerry took the horses out for a birthday ride, Margaret astride the new saddle. Like virtually all the court, Bertie took their companionship as commonplace, a squire attending his lady. Peter was solid, dependable upper middle class, inconceivable as a lover of Margaret. The servants who surveyed the couple were quick to reach different conclusions. They caught sight of them holding hands. Sometimes he would swing her off her feet in shared bursts of laughter. She maneuvered to have him sit with her at mealtimes whenever she could. They walked the hills together, out of range of everyone's eyes. Among footmen and maids, the word circulated: "She's in love with him, and him a married man."

On the evening of her twenty-first birthday, on a slope overlooking Balmoral Castle, a bonfire had been made ready. She put the torch for lighting it into Peter's hand and cheered him as he raced on long legs with it toward the pile of logs and brushwood.

The queen had looked forward to the salmon fishing, her husband to getting in some shooting, which he contrived to do by traveling as far as possible in a Land Rover, then having himself attached by a leather trace to the pony that pulled him uphill. But the weather turned cold and wet, the cough that resisted penicillin worsened, and the chill he developed made his throat sore. Called to the castle, his doctors implored him to return to London for X-rays.

A different group attended him this time. Professor Learmonth had departed with a knighthood, bestowed by Bertie in bathrobe and slippers on the day of the surgeon's final examination. "You used a knife on me." Bertie smiled. "Now I'm going to use one on you." Sir Horace Evans of the Royal

Masonic Hospital was in charge now. He already had a shrewd idea of what lay at the root of his patient's troubles.

Bertie waited to watch the Braemar games and kilted dancing to the pipers' drone early in September, then travelled south by train; he would fly back the next day. Sir Horace consulted with one more doctor, Mr. Clement Price Thomas, specialist in chest cancers. After looking at the X-rays, their advice to Bertie back at Balmoral was unanimous: a segment of lung tissue should be removed for microscopic study. He cut short his vacation to go back to the palace again for the bronchoscopy.

The microscope confirmed that his left lung was cancerous, but Price Thomas did not tell him so. The explanation given Bertie to justify the excision was that it was necessary because a bronchial tube was blocked. He reconciled himself to undergoing an operation he dreaded. "If it's going to help to get me well again I don't mind, but the very idea of the surgeon's knife again is hell.

It was always said that the truth of his condition was unknown to him, since the facts were withheld, but that fell into the realm of the ridiculous. He and the queen pored over every bulletin issued from the palace to make certain that a balance was struck between false hope and despair. There was no likelihood that their daughters were less perceptive.

Elizabeth and her mother had gone down with him on September 18, the day he heard he must lose a lung. With her husband, Elizabeth would leave to tour Canada and the United States less than three weeks from now. Margaret was asked to stay on in the castle to watch over her two-year-old nephew and Elizabeth's second baby, Anne, born in August, 1950. Bertie faced the operating table with one more burden on his conscience: stalemated by the Tory opposition, Prime Minister Attlee was calling an election for next month.

Surgery was scheduled for Sunday, September 23, in the Buhl Room of the palace. Margaret was emotionally spent. She could not endure being kept away. On the Saturday, thin and wan, she flew to London. Before her father went under the anesthetic, she slipped into Lambeth Palace chapel with her mother, sister, and Philip to pray for his survival.

The surgical team set to work in the knowledge that at any moment a heart attack could make their efforts futile. Exploratory incisions told Price Thomas that nerves of the larynx would need to be sacrificed together with the left lung. Possibly, the king could never speak again except to whisper. And there were signs that the right lung was infected, too. The task was completed, the final sutures and bandages placed, but suspense continued for days, racking his family, Margaret perhaps most of all.

On the third day, with heart and vocal chords functioning satisfactorily, he signed the warrant appointing the queen, his daughters, his brother Henry, and his sister Mary Counsellors of State. He may have sensed the slow approach of death, but he was serene about its pace. On October 8 at London Airport Margaret and her mother waved goodbye to Philip and Elizabeth. She carried with her a bulky envelope, to remain sealed unless the pace quickened and made her queen. Charles and Anne would be in the care of their aunt and their grandmother, who spelled each other in recharging Bertie's spirits.

At the end of October, Britain turned out to vote again. The Tories won seventeen more seats than before, but the Labor Party received 231,000 more votes than the government which the fifty-five-year-old king appointed Winston Churchill, aged seventy-six, to form. For the second time in eighteen months, the kingdom was off on a wavering course to no particular destination.

A letter from Harry Truman, whom they visited in the White House, followed Elizabeth and Philip home. "As one father to another, we can be very proud of our daughters. You have the better of me—because you have two!" The younger of them was in such a state of tension after five weeks of anguish that she was sent off for a few days to unwind in Paris with her Aunt Marina. For Elizabeth and Philip, another round of empire-holding was in the making. In January, they would be off once more, this time to East Africa, Australia, and New Zealand, the trip that had never come off for Bertie or Margaret.

He recorded his Christmas Day broadcast in advance, a few hoarse sentences at a time, so that his rest could be uninterrupted over the holidays at Sandringham. The dream now was that in the spring he could take his wife and younger daughter back to South Africa and soak up the sun there. They shored up each other's hopes by refusing to discuss any other possibility, but the doubts remained.

He was out walking one morning when a bleak wind blew off the North Sea. He passed a farmer, who saluted him with head bared. "Sir, you should take more care of yourself in this weather."

Bertie smiled faintly. "I may not have long to live. I want to get about while I can."

He and the others left for three or four days in London at the end of January. Margaret went through the motions of being fitted for new clothes for the South African vacation. His doctors examined him and reported that they were pleased with his progress. He took his whole family to Drury Lane Theater, set among the sights and scents of Covent Garden market, to celebrate at *South Pacific*. In the morning, Elizabeth and her husband would be leaving London on the tour programmed to include flying across that ocean itself. Hatless and windblown, Bertie was at the airport with the queen and Margaret to wave them *au revoir* before the three turned back to Sandringham.

He shot hares on the crisp, sunny afternoon of February 5 while his wife and daughter went sailing on the Norfolk Broads. After dinner, Margaret played the piano for him as he sat by the fire, thumbing the paws of Roddy, his golden retriever, in search of thorns. The nine o'clock radio news reported Elizabeth's safe arrival at Sagana Lodge in a Kenya game forest, where she would shoot home movies as mementos.

At ten-thirty, he retired to his suite on the ground floor. Margaret and her mother led a party of friends into the ballroom to watch a movie, which was still running at midnight when a watchman in the garden noticed Bertie reach out to fasten the latch on a bedroom window. At seven-thirty the next morning, his valet, James MacDonald, taking up the tea tray, found him dead.

The news was passed along the chain of command. The task of telling the queen fell to the equerry-in-charge, Sir Harold Campbell, an old sailor who had served Bertie for more than twenty years. "I never knew a woman could be so brave," he thought. She went first to Bertie's room and then into Margaret's.

"It seems," his daughter said not long afterward, "that life has stood still. Sometimes I wonder how it can go on." One of the other equerries on duty at Sandringham was Townsend. For solace in her devastation, she turned to her mother and to Peter.

IX

The Lost Ones

At one stroke, she had lost both her father and, in a different sense, her sister. Elizabeth as queen could never again be approached as an equal. Passage through the looking glass had transformed her from Lilibet into Her Majesty, to be honored, deferred to, and owed curtsy in greeting. She was head of the state, the church, and the armed forces. Her available time would have to be rationed from now on. Day-to-day intimacy was a thing of the past. Margaret could justifiably repeat what she had said when she was first taken to live in the palace: "Now that Papa is king, I am nothing."

Her situation in some ways was that of a widow's only child. At Sandringham, where Bertie's body remained, mother and daughter seldom left each other as they waited out the days before the new queen came home. When they left the house to take a walk, they went arm in arm, a haggard girl and a desolate woman. Dr. Ansell prescribed sedatives for Margaret, but she avoided taking them. Eating or sleeping came hard, but she avoided taking pills. They could not be good for her. She had to stay alert in case her mother needed her.

"To think," the girl said, "that I have to wait so long before I see Papa again."

She vowed to give up drinking so much as a glass of wine as well as the cigarettes she had taken to, copying Bertie's heavy habit. The first news pictures of Margaret flourishing a long-stemmed holder over a restaurant table had caused ripples of indignation. Women had been smoking in public for half a century, but since no precedent existed, it was rated inexcusable for a princess.

Talking for any length of time with Elizabeth before she returned was virtually impossible. A single telephone line served Sagana Lodge. A priority call from London asked what she wished to be known as, now she was queen. Her decision was clear-cut. "My own name, of course. What else?" That was certain to create some immediate problems when this was also her mother's name, until the household and the country remembered to differentiate between "the queen" and "the queen mother." The morning mail would need careful sorting.

Elizabeth wore black when she stepped from her plane at London Airport; the clothes had been packed in her luggage. Uncle Dickie stood in the group that met her and Philip. So did Prime Minister Churchill; in contrast with her, tears trickled down his plump cheeks as he stooped to kiss her hand. Grandmama rose from her wheelchair to curtsy to her twenty-five-year-old granddaughter when she saw her at Clarence House, but she could not restrain herself from remarking on the dress, "Much too short for mourning." Elizabeth received a curtsy from her mother and sister, too, when she reached Sandringham in the February dusk.

The three women followed on foot behind the estate-wagon that carried the body to the little chapel in the grounds on the first stage of the journey to the railroad station. It was taken on from there to Buckingham Palace; a lying-in-state in Westminster Hall; and finally to St. George's Chapel in Windsor Castle. According to the philosophy of monarchy, the throne had not stood empty for an instant. At the moment of her father's dying, Elizabeth reigned.

She had already peered from behind lace curtains at Clarence House as heralds in scarlet, blue, and gold blew a fanfare on silver trumpets, and the braid-encrusted Earl Marshal proclaimed that "the High and Mighty Princess Elizabeth Alexandra Mary is now, by the Death of our late Sovereign of Happy Memory, become Queen Elizabeth the Second, by the Grace of God, Queen of this Realm and all Her other Realms and Territories."

Margaret walked alone by the hour in the gardens of the palace with her Sealyhams, Johnny and Pippin. She ate most meals with her mother, whose sadness was better concealed, often with a television set turned on nearby to fill in their silences. Parliament sent its formal sympathy to Elizabeth, her mother, and grandmother. As in the prayers said at every service of the established church, Margaret's name was forgotten.

She acted as if she felt the need to reassure herself that the God she believed in was not an Old Testament figure of vengeance who had cut down three kings in her family within sixteen years. Letters exchanged with Simon Phipps brought him down from Huddersfield, where he worked as a curate. Every Monday evening in Lent, she went to a half-hour lecture on the secrets of living as a Christian, delivered at St. Paul's Knightsbridge. She took herself to Lambeth Palace to talk to the Most Reverend Geoffrey Fisher, a more congenial soul who had succeeded the icy Dr. Lang as Archbishop of Canterbury.

Not everything he told her could be accepted on trust. She had to work out the implications for herself of "the Lord giveth and the Lord taketh away." Dread could not be entirely dismissed. The thought of evil striking Elizabeth and her family was enough to bring on panic. The archbishop found, as he said, "every meeting with her was a sort of friendly argument. She was always friendly, always intelligent, but would state her views and would let me state my views, which we would discuss and argue ... "

She paid at least equal attention to what Peter Townsend had to say. She used to go to Bertie when she had a problem she wanted help with. Now she turned to Peter, tall, slender, and eighteen years older than herself, of a generation wiser and less challenging than that of the young bucks of her gadabout days. Religion meant as much to him as to her. He quoted the Bible to help heal her wounds. There was no question that she was in love with this man with the thick dark hair and reflective gray eyes as he began to restore a feeling of security in her.

He minimized his troubles for her sake. His marriage had broken down under the pressures of his work. He had filled his original three-year appointment as an equerry of honor ably enough to be promoted to Deputy Master of the Household in 1950. Spending much time with his family had been difficult before that. He might be on duty at the palace until midnight, waiting until Bertie went to bed.

After a few hours' sleep in his cubbyhole there, Peter would be up, bathed and shaved to catch the first train to Windsor soon after five o'clock to see his wife and children for half an hour or so in the grace-and-favor cottage which Bertie provided for him. A return trip brought Peter back on duty by nine o'clock. Sometimes over a weekend, he would slip away from his post to snatch half a day at home.

A footman, Ralphe White, who flouted regulations and sold his reminiscences for publication, overheard Bertie dress his equerry down for one absence without leave. "Beautiful weather at Windsor over the weekend, Sir," he said off guard one Monday morning.

Bertie, who had not hesitated to reprimand an admiral who omitted to wear the requisite sword at his coronation, glared. "How do you know? You're not supposed to have been there."

Peter's family saw less of him when he was promoted. The deputy master was away for weeks on end when the court travelled away from London. His wife, Rosemary, blamed their long separations, first in the war and now in his job, for the difficulties that festered between them. They had known each other only six weeks when they were married. "Ridiculous, wasn't it?" Peter said sadly. His attorneys recommended action for divorce. Bertie had been aware of what was ahead during his last Christmas at Sandringham.

Margaret would claim years afterward that her taste in men was for "rugged outdoor types." Peter did not come in that category. There was a delicacy in him that made him a polar opposite of Philip, who exhibited an air of breezy arrogance mixed with discontent over the limitations under which he operated as husband of the queen, an ex-navy officer with no specific work to do, barred from seeing what his wife's dispatch boxes contained, excluded from her Tuesday meetings with her Prime Minister.

The hand of Winston Churchill, who held monarchy to be sacred, was visible in a decision she made when her reign was two months old to change her married name. Legally she had been Elizabeth Mountbatten. By order in Council, she declared now that "I and My children shall be styled and known as the House and Family of Windsor and that My descendants, other than female descendants who marry and their descendants, shall bear the name of Windsor." Charles and

Anne became changelings so far as names went. Uncle Dickie, who claimed lineage equal with the Hanovers, would never again look forward to Mountbattens inheriting the English crown.

Peter disliked being dragooned for shooting parties at Balmoral as much as Margaret. He preferred to stay behind with the women, adding a bright word to their conversation. If he was tempted to try putting down a stag, he went off with a gun alone. Philip gave him a lower rating than had Bertie. The gentle ex-fighter pilot, still an RAF reservist, could irritate him. On one day's shooting, Philip, put off his mark, commanded him, "Be quiet!"

The grace-and-favor cottage at Windsor was surrendered after the suit for divorce from Rosemary was filed. Peter moved into Buckingham Palace to be on permanent call.

Margaret gave up her den in the old nursery suite on the third floor after Elizabeth brought her family to live in the palace in May. Charles and Anne would occupy the rooms, along with Nanny Lightbody and Nanny Anderson. Aunt Margo took up new quarters at the front of the palace, while her mother stayed on undisturbed in the second-floor royal suite until Clarence House, empty now, was made over for her and her unmarried daughter. For the time being, Elizabeth and her husband made do with the Belgian Suite on the ground floor.

Her instructions to the staff were as specific as her choice of royal name. "I want everything to continue exactly as it did for my father." She worked at his desk with the same dispatch boxes that had haunted him. He kept racing pigeons and collected stamps, and so would she. He had a ticker tape installed; like him, she wanted to see horse-racing results as soon as they came clicking in. Her parents had put lovebirds and canaries in cages in the nursery when she was a child; she followed the example for her son and daughter. She brought Bobo over with a resplendent new title as Queen's Dresser and an assistant, Elizabeth MacGregor, formerly housekeeper at Clarence House.

Philip took on James MacDonald, discoverer of the death of his previous master, as an additional valet, who started the day by drawing the bath and laying out the clothes, though Philip shaved himself and sat in a bathrobe to breakfast with his wife—they served themselves—to fifteen minutes of bagpipe music; Victoria launched that melodious tradition. His opinion of the six-hundred-room monstrosity of a home to which the state, not his wife, held title grew more supercilious with the passage of time.

"This isn't ours—it's a tied cottage," he decided, which was a kindlier description than Bertie's; he called it "an icebox" before central heating was put in. His grandfather had envisioned having the whole sepulcher demolished.

The divorce action ran its course. Ten months after Bertie's end, Peter was free to remarry. The judge found him the innocent party and awarded him custody of his two sons. Rosemary proceeded to take a second husband in John de Laszlo, son of the society portrait painter, Philip, for whom Bertie had sat some twenty years earlier.

The idea of marriage to Peter became more than a wishful dream for Margaret. She wanted him and needed him, and he was in love with her. That was obvious to everyone who saw them together. One contemporary of hers said: "It was impossible to recognize the truth of the situation at first. I suppose most of us had taken it for granted that she would fall for someone—well, flashier. He seemed to be such a gentle, sober sort. I would guess that she made the pace. How they admitted their feelings to each other, I suppose we shall never know. Neither one of them has ever talked about it except to each other so far as I'm aware, but Peter came out so sadly in the end that I suspect he might want to tell his side of it all one day."

In his last year of life, Bertie had recognized the closeness between them, and like his wife done nothing to frustrate them. Footman White detected the prevailing climate when they set off from Balmoral on a picnic at Loch Muich. Two hampers had been packed, and two estate wagons were waiting.

He picked up one of them to put in the back of the second car. "Why aren't both baskets going in my car?" Bertie asked sharply.

"Margaret and Peter are going for a picnic of their own," his wife answered.

"Oh, no, they're not. We're all going together."

He and his wife drove off with both hampers. Margaret and Peter glanced at each other. She shrugged her shoulders, and they climbed into the second car, following the first.

The incident was cited later as a hint that Bertie would not have approved of his daughter's marrying Peter. That had to be considered as the flimsiest speculation. Her father had rarely denied his daughter anything she set her mind to and heart on. He had promoted Peter and overlooked his rare lapses. If the deputy master had thought of resigning at the outset of filing for divorce, he had been discouraged from leaving. The probability, if not the certainty, was that Margaret expected to meet no obstacles on the road toward becoming Peter's wife. She evidently said as much to her sister and mother.

Peter introduced *his* mother to Margaret one palace teatime, still addressing her according to protocol as "Ma'am," while both women called him "Peter" with equal affection. Gladys Townsend was flattered to discover that Margaret was well briefed on life among the Townsends. Toward the end of her stay under her sister's roof, Margaret exhibited symptoms of anxiety in her: doctors ascribed the pangs to gastritis.

By Eastertime in 1953, Clarence House was ready for its new tenants. At her insistence, Margaret's personal suite with pink-walled sitting room and chaste Thomas Sheraton furniture had its own front door. She would spend her next seven years living there. Marlborough House stood vacant. A few minutes before five o'clock struck on the evening of March 24, she said farewell to Grandmama in her bedroom there. Before the day was past, the fantastic old lady's life was over, but her unbending influence on the family remained.

Three principals made up the establishment at Clarence House—Margaret, her mother, and Peter in his latest appointment as Comptroller of the Household. The two women wanted him to be almost a member of their fragment of the family. His days would be theirs, while he slept and kept his office in a miniature house next door, which stood between this one of theirs and St. James's Palace proper. Margaret could interpret his obtaining official approval for a job that put him into intimate contact with her as a further sign that he would pass scrutiny as a prospective husband.

Fresh moves toward the goal had to be postponed for the present. This was the year of Elizabeth's coronation, and no other event in the family could be allowed to conflict with it. The question of Margaret's marriage must wait its turn. The country was smitten with coronation fever. Elizabeth's enthronement, set for June 2, was scheduled to provide the longest television spectacular ever screened in the kingdom, seven hours and fifteen minutes of it; the fifty-day trial of Joseph McCarthy of Wisconsin by his peers in the United States waited over next year's horizon. Courtiers ruled at first that TV cameras would add to the strain imposed on her. She intervened to correct that impression in the same fashion as she had the ceremony itself abridged. "Did my father do it?"

"Yes, Your Majesty," nodded the archbishop.

"Then I will, too."

The day was scripted to be a mélange of holy rite and straight show business, with elements of opéra bouffe, rose tournament, and Thanksgiving parade thrown in for good measure. The archbishop prepared a little primer, consisting of a daily theme for meditation and a prayer or two to be pondered over in the course of the preceding month. Elizabeth, her mother, and Philip each received a bound copy, and Dr. Fisher, remembering their earnest arguments, also dispatched one for Margaret. She was moved to such gratitude that he counted his gift to her "the most precious thing that I ever did." The invitation the Earl Marshal sent her for the ceremony stood on the mantel over the ormulu fireplace in her ground-floor sitting room. Again, each week in Lent found her in class at St. Paul's, attempting to decipher the will of God.

In the basement of the palace, the pre-war finery was pulled out of storage—scarlet breeches, pink silk stockings, velvet caps, and gold-and-scarlet coats on which gold epaulets embroidered with Elizabeth's new cipher must be sewn. The corps of footmen broke in new black pumps which, for the parade, would carry blister-raising gold buckles. Elizabeth practiced wearing each of the two crowns fundamental to the ritual, brought over from the Tower of London to be fitted for size.

Patriotism swept the land like the first warm winds of spring after a long, harsh winter. The British by and large were convinced that the crowning of this slim young matron whose excitement matched theirs would work wonders for everyone. A new golden age was assumed to be in the making to restore the splendors of the first Elizabeth, "Good Queen Bess," adored while she lived as almost more than mortal.

Evoking the Elizabethan Age of three hundred and fifty

years ago became a minor obsession. "Though God hath raised me high," Elizabeth I declared, "yet this I count the glory of my crown—that I have reigned with your loves." In loving Elizabeth II, her people looked for miracles. The arts would flourish again as in the time of William Shakespeare, Francis Bacon, and Edmund Spenser. Like sixteenth-century mariners, scientists would seek new shores, even on the moon, and Britain would catch up as a superpower by building its own hydrogen bombs. Industry, it was hoped, had already set the pace when the world's first jetliner service opened the previous year with DeHavilland Comets whisking passengers between London and Johannesburg in less than twenty-four hours.

The month before the coronation, Margaret went up with Peter and her mother for a Comet flip over the Alps. She still wore mourning, but black was no match for her exhilaration. She felt too skittish to try a hand at the controls, so she sat in the air crew's cabin while her mother, too timid to drive a car, nudged the plane toward the speed of sound.

Some aspects of life under the first Elizabeth were thoughtfully underplayed. The ginger-haired queen was given credit for starting a colonial empire and so improving conditions at home that England was like a new country as it shed its somber medieval past. The victory that Sir Francis Drake plus Channel storms scored over the galleons of her former suitor, Philip of Spain, was a popular theme. His reason for ordering out his armada was not: he was determined to punish her for consenting to the beheading in 1587 of her cousin, Mary Stuart, star-crossed queen of Scots, and the repression of her fellow Catholics that followed the execution.

The men Elizabeth took on as favorites, her vanity, her double-dealing ("she lived and lied for her country," according to one assessment), the violent temper which she did not hesitate to show by striking and spitting at her courtiers—these were usually omitted from the record in its 1953 edition. One thing counterbalanced all her faults in the eyes of the second Elizabeth's subjects: good queen Bess loved England.

Coronation season brought out the navy in magisterial might before budget cuts put warships in mothballs or reduced them to scrap. One hundred and sixty ships reaching all the way to Cowes were arrayed for Elizabeth's review. In the high Himalayas, a New Zealander, Edmund Hillary, and his Nepalese guide, Tensing Norkay, fought snow and ice to conquer Mount Everest in honor of her.

Londoners danced in the streets, in church halls, and hotel ballrooms. The Dorchester was the site for a civic-minded Red, White, and Blue Ball. Margaret, who had emerged from black by then, was encircled by young men who had once been judged her beaux. Johnny Dalkeith, married now to Jane McNeill, was there, together with Billy Wallace, Lord Hambleden, and Tom Egerton. David Naylor-Leyland, Lord Patrick Plunket, and exiled Prince Nicholas of Yugoslavia hovered over her. "I must come dancing more often," she concluded. No one was certain what had put the sparkle back in her eyes.

After the dinner party her mother gave on Monday, June 1, Margaret changed into street clothes to leave Clarence House behind for a while and repeat a bit of private ritual, wandering as a commoner through the gathering swarm of people camping out on the sidewalks to be sure of front-row places in the morning. When morning came, she put on the white satin embroidered with pearls, diamanté, and silver thread in the workrooms of Mr. Hartnell, where her sister's gown had also been designed and stitched. A coronet on her head, a trailing robe of ermine-trimmed purple velvet over her shoulders, and she was ready to ride in a glass coach beside her mother to Westminster Abbey.

Rain fell in a steady drizzle that grew heavier as the day progressed, seeping into marchers' buckled shoes and ammunition boots, sending the soupy mixture of flour and starch that whitened their hair trickling down the cheeks of liveried footmen and postilions. The rain ceased for a minute or so when the coachman reined the swaying state coach to a halt outside the abbey. Philip, in admiral's uniform, leaped down to help out his wife in her crimson velvet robe and Victoria's diamond-and-pearl diadem.

Heralds had preceded Margaret into her seat by her mother in the raised gallery and more followed behind, after her page and lady-in-waiting. In place among the lesser guests, Mr. Hartnell was enraptured. "She moved in white beauty like a snowdrop," he reported, with her eyes "steadily fixed upon the high altar." Others thought that her gaze focussed principally on her sister, as much in question as in reverence.

She repeated every response in a fervor of devotion as the rites began and Elizabeth, slowly stripped of the clothes she had arrived in, stood in a virginal white linen shift. Then after sacraments, the new Queen was anointed, the golden orb (symbol of royal power) placed in her left hand, and the scepter with its 530-carat diamond (emblem of sovereignty) into the right. As the imperial crown was lowered onto her sister's tranquil head, Margaret burst into tears. It was a moment of extirpation; the jealousy that had always lurked there had vanished from her heart. The slim young woman weighted down by the accouterments of the ceremony was no longer Lilibet, the rival, but Her Majesty. Margaret's feeling about her began to be recrystallized. "I get enormously impressed when she walks into a room," she said at a later date. "It's a kind of magic."

On that June day in 1953, she had no cause to envy the attention showered on the new queen. Margaret was totally satisfied with her own life. She was gloriously in love, a person of supreme importance to the one who loved her.

In the late evening, when floodlight glared on the palace

balcony, she slipped out with a few friends through a side gate in the railings. Unnoticed among the thousands who packed tight around the tall iron bars, she piped out a cheer for Elizabeth, then edged her way down the Mall under arches installed like rainbows overseeing this day of hope and glory.

The glow of national satisfaction with the royals lasted no longer than through one weekend and into the next. On Sunday morning, June 14, thunderous headlines broke the calm. Reports that Peter meant more than a member of the staff to Margaret had been picked up as they filtered through the upper levels of London society and circulated in the United States and Europe. The fiery little editor of *The People,* a full-size newspaper that outdid most tabloids in its zest for sensation-mongering, decided that personally he wanted no part of another coverup on Mrs. Simpson lines. He resorted to one of Fleet Street's hoariest tricks to circumvent palace privilege and Britain's punitive laws against libel and defamation of character.

To get the story safely into print, he listed the known details and denounced them as "utterly untrue." He concluded the front-page account by calling for an official denial from the palace to "stop the scandalous rumors."

A fox was loose among the geese. Margaret's first response was anger. She had pitied her sister when she was being courted by Philip, because the whole world learned about that romance. "Poor Lil," she had said. "Nothing of your own. Not even your love affair." For the moment, she felt no pity for herself. The sequence as she had planned it was not to be disturbed by editorial sleight of hand contorting the affair into something "scandalous." Perhaps next year her engagement would be announced.

Next to Peter, the man most affronted was Elizabeth's press secretary, Commander Richard Colville, who had worked for her father. Schooling at Harrow and service in the navy were among his professional qualifications. Reporters complained that he valued discretion above public relations and silence above discretion. "He seemed to think" said one of them, "most people, particularly the press, were tradesmen." Elizabeth dubbed him "poor Richard" on one occasion. Margaret and Peter felt that he did not much care for either of them. On the telephone, Colville would take for granted what he had read in the newspapers and challenge her, "Why did you do it?" without checking the truth with her first.

He was trapped whichever way he turned if he tried to respond to *The People*. A denial would be a lie, a confirmation impolitic. In two more weeks, Peter was due to fly with Margaret and her mother to Southern Rhodesia on another empire-holding mission when Bulawayo marked the hundredth anniversary of the birth of Cecil Rhodes, the high-minded British capitalist who administered South Africa. Part of Peter's job had been to organize their end of the tour.

Everyone in the family, Peter, the court, and Commander Richard took cover from the fox. *The People* was told nothing. It was more difficult than ever for the two lovers to be alone with each other now that their intentions were known by everyone around them. During these crucial days, they had greater need for each other than before, but privacy for more than minutes at a time was denied them. The moments when they could touch hands and lips and she could draw strength and comfort from him became very precious.

She was bitterly conscious of the eyes that followed her everywhere and the ears that listened for every word she spoke. She clung to the hope that the storm would blow itself out and reluctantly appreciated why, in a hopeless effort to disguise the situation, Peter's role with her in Rhodesia was cancelled. Captain Lord Patrick Plunket, bachelor, old Etonian, ex-Irish Guards, whose maternal grandfather owned a South African diamond mine, would step into Peter's shoes and succeed him as deputy master. The displaced comptroller was to travel instead with Elizabeth and Philip to Northern Ireland on July 1, the day after Margaret's departure. After that, it was back to duty with the Royal Air Force for him and posting to Brussels as air attaché. He was not seen in the palace again. It would be more than two years before he returned to Margaret.

She knew as well as anybody that she had to have Elizabeth's written permission to marry. Margaret could quote the terms of the one-hundred-eighty-year-old Royal Marriage Act: "No descendant of George II shall be capable of contracting matrimony without the previous consent of the King, and signified under the Great Seal, declared in Council, and entered in the Privy Council books." If she flouted the law, she would be disinherited. Unless she waited for two more years. In 1955, she would be twenty-five, and she would then be legally required only to notify the queen a year in advance that she planned to be married. The happiness that had surged in her such a short time ago was ebbing slowly. But if she learned to be patient, all would be well.

They said their unexpected good-byes to each other in Clarence House. They had no cause to anticipate heartbreak. Like any loyal officer, Peter was reconciled to surprise postings to fresh duties. Nobody in the palace had dared pressure Margaret to give him up for good lest she fly off the handle and stir another constitutional crisis on David-and-Wallis lines. She and Peter were running into obstacles, but they clung to the belief that eventually their love for each other would prevail.

They would bide their time in ignorance of the implacable opposition of the forces ranged against them, led by Winston

Churchill; Elizabeth's highly influential private secretary, Sir Alan Lascelles; and Philip. Elizabeth's mind was not yet made up. She was torn between sympathy for her sister and fulfilling her obligations to the country, as outlined for her by her husband and her counsellors.

Margaret went off on her travels with Peter's photograph, expecting him to be waiting for her on her return, so that they could spend a few more days together. In fact, he was whisked off twenty-four hours before she was back, and anger flared in her at the trick that had been played.

The court's hurried attempts at evading the truth succeeded only in scandalizing half the population as soon as the facts were fitted together. In Parliament, two Labor members, Emrys Hughes and Marcus Lipton, demanded the whole distasteful story. The *Daily Mirror* polled its five million readers on whether Margaret had the right to wed Peter. "Yes!" answered 67,907 of them; "No!" said 2,235.

The Church of England's official position had not changed since David was forced to abdicate. Yet the theory that divorce spelled disgrace to both parties, innocent or guilty, had been strained in the past for some royals and their close relatives. Victoria's granddaughter Marie Louise, for instance, freed herself from her German prince, Joseph of Anhalt, after nine years as his wife. And not too long ago, Elizabeth and Margaret had gone together to celebrate the second marriage of their cousin, the Viscountess Anson, deserted by her husband after bearing him two children, who was trying again with Prince Georg of Denmark.

Winston Churchill, defender of the faith and protector of monarchies, whose own mother, Jennie, had gone through the divorce courts, advised Elizabeth that Margaret should not be allowed to be married to Townsend. What was more, he felt confident that his fellow leaders in the other realms and territories overseas would not argue with his judgment. He trusted that the new Elizabethan age had inspired the country to begin restoring itself to better ways. No breath of dissension or conflict within the church over the claims of a divorce must be contemplated, in case it damaged that opportunity.

Elizabeth, still callow in her job, accepted what he said. Her sister lacked a champion at court with an ounce of Churchill's prestige. Perhaps it was only coincidence that put her to bed for a few days with what was variously described as "a heavy cold" and "severe chill" in her hotel at Umtali, some five thousand miles away.

Before July was over, she fell subject to what was presented only in terms of another coincidence. Until then, her place in the hierarchy made her the understudy of her sister should Elizabeth die or lose her physical or mental health before one of her children reached the age of eighteen. The Prime Minister announced plans to change that disturbing state of affairs. The Regency Act, which established Margaret's position, was going to be amended; his confreres in the Commonwealth had already approved. If catastrophe overcame Elizabeth, Philip would become Regent and guardian of the king or queen among his children. Margaret was not erased entirely. In the improbable event of dual disaster removing both her sister and her brother-in-law, Aunt Margo would be Regent until Charles grew up.

She spent a languid and lusterless twenty-third birthday at Birkhall, with twenty-four months ahead before she could declare that she was set on becoming Peter's wife and twelve more after that before the desire was fulfilled. She settled down to wait as patiently as she could, continuing to carry out the modicum of public duties required of her, shunning the gathering places of what seemed to be a distant childhood.

Her letters to Peter went to Brussels by diplomat's pouch.

Every so often, an inquisitive reporter caught up with him. Interviews were always brief. "I came here," he said, "because the position was impossible for us both." He told another interrogator, "I cannot answer questions because I am not the prime mover in the situation. My loyalty to Princess Margaret is unquestionable. I would undergo any difficulties because of that loyalty."

For six months, Elizabeth was out of reach except by telephone—she and Philip were back at the job of showing the flag in her realms and territories around the world. Margaret took a hand in keeping her five-year-old nephew entertained while his parents were gone. Otherwise, she passed hours alone behind the white door of her Clarence House apartment, occupying herself by playing records from a collection in the thousands, keeping up her correspondence, wrestling with crossword puzzles, which were a family standby. She surprised herself by winning three guineas' worth of books from *Country Life*, the glossy weekly of the squirearchy, for solving a puzzle whose clues were as obscure as the notorious mind-benders published each day in *The Times*.

If the prize was evidence of intelligence she was not always credited with, her pale-green sitting room held a clue to something else. Over the desk that stood between the pink-curtained windows and French doors opening onto the terrace hung an ivory crucifix. There were people who took it as a sign that her audience with Pope Pius may have been more significant than even the fundamentalists suspected. One canard in the perennial crop held that she was contemplating conversion into the Church of Rome, either as a mark of ultimate defiance or, more sensationally, as the initial step toward entering a convent. Contact with Peter in what was popularly known as his "exile" continued without interruption.

With Elizabeth's permission granted in advance, Margaret

was drawn into a winter of rollicking amateur theatricals. Colin Tennant would play the double-dyed villain and Billy Wallace the Scotland Yard inspector in *The Frog*, a time-tested thriller having to do with a master criminal's frustrated attempt to terrorize London. Margaret, assistant producer, understudied the heroine. Patrick Plunket enlisted in the cast, which was enough to convince the tattlers that he had his eyes on her as a bride. The impeccably upper-class performers—a duke, an earl, and a brace of milords included—were joined by Douglas Fairbanks, Jr., and Elsa Maxwell, whose limitations as a singer in a cabaret setting were helped out by a Sophie Tucker record spun behind the scenes. The net result was a donation of £10,000 to the Invalid Children's Association, which impressed Margaret as a worthwhile cause.

When Elizabeth returned, Margaret was rewarded for good behavior. English winters sapped her health. At the end of January, in the year she would be twenty-five and technically liberated from legal restraints on her freedom to marry, she could enjoy a month of Caribbean sunshine, with receptions and the chores involved in being royal held down to a decent minimum.

Her wardrobe was shipped ahead in *Britannia*, Elizabeth's most controversial perquisite. The £2,000,000 yacht, less than two years old, cost an annual £500,000 to operate for an average of seventeen weeks in royal service. When its most distinguished passenger was aboard, crewmen wore canvas-soled shoes and orders were relayed by hand signal or walkie-talkie so that built-in loudspeakers would not disturb her; for the same reason, the palace's thirty housemaids used carpet-sweepers, not whining vacuum cleaners, on their morning rounds. Employing *Britannia* as a seagoing pantechnicon helped to justify the overheads.

Margaret was flown out to Trinidad in the Stratocruiser

Canopus, chartered from British Overseas Airways Corporation, newly decorated in blue, gray, and white, and converted for Elizabeth's comfort with dressing rooms, wide sleeping berths, and a lower-deck cocktail bar. Commander Colville hastened to correct the impression that this was strictly a pleasure trip. "Her Royal Highness will, of course, shake hands with all of the considerable number of persons who are introduced to her."

The itinerary sounded like a travel agent's vision of paradise. From Trinidad, *Britannia* carried her on to Tobago, Grenada, St. Vincent, Barbados, Antigua, and finally Nassau. The schedule blended tours of sugar-cane factories, Government House banquets, and children's rallies with lolling on golden beaches and soaking in the azure sea, perpetually trailed by correspondents and cameramen.

She got carsick and seasick. One afternoon in the sun, sitting through a demonstration by dark-skinned soldier who were drilled like Guardsmen, she suffered a touch of heatstroke. When her hostess in Tobago organized a swimming party, Margaret chose to rest in the shade. "I don't want to spoil my hair and look all wrong for your party," she explained.

All in all, she doted on everything that came along on this first solo tour away from home. The Caribbean was exactly what most people had said it would be—*romantic.* It suited her mood at the time, and the memory would take her back again and again.

The crowd that welcomed her home to London yelled "Good luck!" as she drove by. A Sunday-morning newspaper spelled out what the greeting implied. Double columns of type pinpointed the choice confronting her when she turned twenty-five in August: bow to the dictates of the church headed by her sister or break away to marry Peter.

Her birthday fell on another Sunday. Sightseers in the

thousands turned up to watch her walk into Crathie Church
on the Balmoral estate. The Reverend John Lamb prayed
aloud "that, trusting in Thee, she may find fulfillment of her
heart's desire, that joy may be her heritage and peace her
portion." Peter passed the morning on the opposite side of the
Channel at a riding stable he patronized. In two more weeks,
he would not need to make excuses for going to England.
There were solid business reasons why he should attend the
annual aircraft show at Farnborough, Hampshire, when
British industry was pushing hard to sell more planes to
foreign customers.

During the week he spent in and around London, he dined
twice with a woman who had become as close as a sister to
Margaret. Lanky Elizabeth Cavendish, the Duke of Dev-
onshire's daughter, had played with her on and off as a child.
"We've *always* known each other," they agreed. Still single at
twenty-nine, Lady Elizabeth had been along on the Caribbean
errand. She made a perfect go-between for carrying messages
to and from Margaret when Peter waited for her to tell him
what the plan was now.

At present, she did not know. Her choice might be clear-
cut, but perhaps a compromise could be found somehow if
nobody got too impulsive. He flew back to Brussels without
seeing her. He had four weeks' leave coming up, starting on
October 12. That would be the time when decisions were
made. Meanwhile, he caught the flu.

He came back to London Airport heavy-eyed and in need
of a shave. The press corps quickly got around to the key
question: "Will you meet the princess?" He fenced. "I'm not
answering questions like that. I've told you I'm just here for a
holiday. I expect to be back at my job in Brussels in four
weeks' time."

Did he expect "any startling developments"? He repeated,
"I'm not answering questions of that kind." Bathed and

shaved, he arrived at Clarence House in a little green Renault.

An increasing number of Britons were satiated with the whole affair, which, they decided, had grown as tedious as any soap opera. But no scenario for *Search For Tomorrow* gave the heroine an attack of migraine and the hero a sore throat for their reunion after two years apart. They were left alone for two hours, affection still strong between them, but the power of the bond in question.

They spent the first weekend in the country under the roof of her cousin, Mrs. John Lycett Wills; Peter stayed behind when Margaret went to church on Sunday the 16th. Their meetings in the following weeks were clocked day by day by contingents of reporters eager as their readers to know the outcome of the serial they were writing. Would Rapunzel escape from the tower? Could the Little Mermaid find joy in the end?

On the second weekend, Margaret went without Peter to Windsor for the climactic conference with her sister and brother-in-law. When they left the dining room on Saturday evening to make their way into Elizabeth's sitting room, Margaret's look was still defiant. When she came out an hour later, her eyes were puffy from tears. She kissed them both and went off to her bedroom.

It was not hard for those familiar with the facts to judge what had occurred. Elizabeth had spoken in the name of their father. She accepted his concept of duty as the supreme sacrifice. It was time for Margaret to follow his example. She must not allow the yearnings of her heart to dictate what she did. She owed it to the country and the commonwealth to surrender Peter Townsend. More than that, she could not flout the dictates of her church, which represented the will of God. Philip would endorse every word his wife said, matching her severity with his. There would be no pretense that evening of sisterly affection. Duty superseded sentiment.

Margaret wanted more time to resolve what to do. It was impossible to acknowledge defeat without further brooding. Yet the resolution of the conflict between the sisters was not in doubt. Elizabeth's disciplined strength of purpose overwhelmed her sister. Margaret was what her father had intended her to be, a hunter after happiness so eager for approval that she had to pretend she could make do without it. She could not change her nature. Love for a man was not a universal solvent capable of dissolving the mold in which she was cast.

On Friday the 27th, she called to see the archbishop in Lambeth Palace. "I have made up my mind," she said. He thought her decision was made "purely on the grounds of conscience. When it became clear what God's will was, she did it."

That evening, she went with Peter to the Knightsbridge town house of the John Lycett Wills. By this time, the two of them accepted the inevitable ending of the romance. She had taken it upon herself to break the news to him—that was her ordained obligation, too. Just when and where she told him was their secret, one of the few left to them. To judge by the tears he and she wept on other occasions, tears were not lacking then.

Their pledges that they could love only each other for the rest of their lives had come to nothing. While they waited for the world to turn their way, it had persisted in spinning in its usual direction. The gentleness with which they had always treated each other remained, increased if anything by the harshness to which they had been subjected. There could be no hysteria, no melodramatics. Both were too well-schooled and too profoundly hurt for extravagant outbursts of emotion. Both had a depth of religious faith that made it possible to seek a crumb of comfort in the belief that what they suffered was not entirely due to the hostility of church, government, or royal relatives. Perhaps God's will was also involved.

Throughout the epilogue to their story, Peter was treated with the courtesies due a stranger at the gates. He stayed at No. 19 Lowndes Square with the Marquis of Abergavenny. He was invited with Margaret down to Uckfield House, Sussex, on Saturday the 29th by the younger brother of the marquis, Lord Rupert Nevill, who was as close to Elizabeth as to her sorrowful sister. What must be done next was to spell out for the world what had happened.

The first text was written from the heart, a combined effort of Margaret and Peter. The courtier who was sent to collect it went over the draft word by word, pencilling in changes, cutting heavily, before he suggested what he had been briefed by the palace to say: Wouldn't it be better to issue no statement at all? Margaret was incensed at the idea.

On Monday evening, October 31, the announcement came from Clarence House. The mark of other hands showed in some of its language; the sentiments were hers exclusively:

> I would like it to be known that I have decided not to marry Group Captain Peter Townsend. I have been aware that, subject to my renouncing my rights of succession, it might have been possible for me to contract a civil marriage. But, mindful of the Church's teaching that Christian marriage is indissoluble, and conscious of my duty to the Commonwealth, I have resolved to put these considerations before any others.
>
> I have reached this decision entirely alone, and in doing so I have been strengthened by the unfailing support and devotion of Group Captain Townsend. I am deeply grateful for the concern of all those who have constantly prayed for my happiness.
>
> MARGARET

X

Tide on the River

The true believers had prayed for Elizabeth to reign as a faerie queene who would wave her golden scepter to work miracles for the country, but the harshness of life in a debt-ridden nation could not be wafted away. Margaret avoided company as much as possible for months after renouncing marriage with Peter. Her isolation coincided with the opening of a new chapter of hard times for the country.

Foreign markets for automobiles were being captured by West Germany, which had massive American aid to replace factories wrecked by wartime bombing. Workmen on British assembly lines, put on a four-day week, struck in protest.

Prices of everything climbed as inflation took firm hold, unchecked by the government's fumbling efforts to curb it. London cash reserves grew slimmer, yet the only way to stave off trouble with the unions was to pay higher wages. Neglected workers, like school teachers, protested bitterly, but a round of budget cuts hit school meal services and trimmed the size of Elizabeth's armed forces.

In the spring after Peter's dejected return to Brussels, Britain set off its first hydrogen bomb, cause not so much for celebration as for relief: defenses based on a nuclear deterrent were cheaper than bombers, battleships, and cumbrous armies. The hopes of the faithful rebounded when Elizabeth opened the world's first full-size nuclear power station in Cumberland. But sentimentalists were taken aback when, as a footnote to the economy drive, she stopped paying the bounty of £1 a head for the birth of triplets or quadruplets that Victoria initiated. Fertility drugs were on the verge of making even quintuplets little more than an overnight wonder.

Unrest eroded the kingdom. Engineers put down their tools. Dock workers walked out. Shipyards stood idle. Newspapers and magazines were shut down, most to survive, others to vanish. London buses stayed in their garages for seven weeks on end when the drivers went on strike. At the opposite end of the income scale, a new breed of financier appeared.

Inflation meant soaring land values and stratospheric rents. Speculators in real estate joined the ranks of the latter-day rich. Old-established businesses that fell out of step were grabbed up in takeover bidding by another set of expansive entrepreneurs, the captains of conglomerates, who counted the bottom line on the balance sheet far more important than the product.

The new Elizabethan Age, like most triumphs oversold in advance, was turning into something altogether different from its boosters' expectations. Shrinkage of the realms overseas and the free attractions offered by the welfare state at home resulted in a flood of dark-skinned immigrants from Pakistan and the West Indies. "Skinhead" gangs of teenagers with cropped hair and steel-studded "bother boots" sprang up in the poorer streets of some cities; the beating of Pakistanis and other strangers flourished like an outbreak of smallpox among the non-vaccinated.

Both by its nature and by its pace, change bewildered the older generations. Instead of being restored to former glory, the country was acquiring an altered identity, as if by mutation. A government report, named for its principal author, Lord Wolfenden, encouraged homosexuals to emerge from hiding, and male prostitutes plied their trade around Piccadilly Circus and Kings Road.

Heterosexual Englishmen brought ruin to old-fashioned barbershops by wearing their hair even longer until it overhung their collars. Their taste in clothes turned to peacock variations on Edwardian modes; as a tourist's mecca, Carnaby Street, where gawdy boutiques sold "mod" fashions in velvet and denim, came to rival Buckingham Palace. Four sprightly Liverpool lads who called themselves The Beatles—Paul Mc-Cartney, John Lennon, George Harrison, and Ringo Starr—warmed up in preparation for a peaceful conquest wider ranging than Victoria's armies had ever accomplished with shot, shell, and Bible.

At the palace, adjustment came fitfully. Finding servants was a ceaseless problem when wages stuck at poorhouse levels—nine dollars a week for a new footman. Hotheads talked of organizing walkouts until the money improved. Philip, still barbered as trimly as a naval officer, did put an end to having footmen pomade their hair white with flour and starch, but they kept their red knee breeches and tunics of red and gold. He made his debut on television and persuaded Elizabeth to do the same when she delivered her Christmas message of good cheer in 1957. She had already agreed that next season would be the last for plumed and primped debutantes to make their bow at court.

To the floundering middle class, the royals came more and more to represent an image as trustworthy as Gibraltar in a storm-whipped sea. To their critics, carping at the cost of maintaining them, they appeared to be an increasingly expensive anachronism.

Margaret, bereft of Peter, moped behind her white front door. The sounds of her record player sometimes drifted on a breeze within the hearing of a nearby sentry on duty with rifle and bayonet outside St. James's Palace. Visitors who called on the mother seldom saw the daughter.

She roused herself to fly with her mother to Norfolk for the marriage of Colin Tennant and another friend, young Lady Anne Coke, who lived not far from Sandringham in Holkham Hall with her parents, the Earl and Countess of Leicester. Margaret's pale face showed traces of a long, indoor winter.

The wedding pictures were shot by a member of the up-and-coming generation, four months older than Margaret and no more than two or three inches taller. Antony Charles Robert Armstrong-Jones looked like any other guest in his morning coat and striped trousers, but he was hired for the day on Elizabeth Cavendish's recommendation.

The era of change worked well for professional photographers. Mass-selling magazines for women paid unheard-of prices for color transparencies to dress up covers and inside pages—pretty girls, royals and their relatives at work or play, winsome children, and soft-eyed dogs. Most of the cover girls were sun-bronzed Americans, posed in studios on Manhattan side streets, with the pictures syndicated in London for as much as five hundred dollars apiece, which was double or triple the price usually paid for the less glamorous British product.

One local supplier who cashed in on the market was a firm friend of Philip's in his dash-about bachelor days—Baron Nahum, sepia-hued, crippled in one arm, an engaging combination of commercial skill and suave salesmanship. Tony Armstrong-Jones trained as his apprentice on payment of a five-hundred-guinea premium. At Margaret's first sight of Tony, he was hunched over his camera, strong jaw clamped in concentration to excel in his chosen job. Elizabeth Cavendish thought Margaret might be amused to meet the bouncy little fellow, but he had darted away before she had the chance to introduce him.

Like the current crop of operators in real estate and takeovers, Tony was a postwar product, an upper-class photographer at ease among his peers. There had not been many like him before other than Cecil Beaton, a dandy of many proclivities and gifts who was often summoned to photograph one or other of the family. Tony followed fast in Cecil's footsteps. On the strength of the Holkham Hall pictures, Edward, Duke of Kent, son of Princess Marina of Greece, asked Tony to take pictures of him in readiness for his twenty-first birthday.

Tony was on the fringe of being an aristocrat. His mother, Anne, divorced her lawyer husband when their son was five years old and married the Earl of Rosse. Ronald Armstrong-Jones, a ladies' man, found a second wife in a dizzying Australian blonde, actress Carol Coombe. When he was one month old, Tony's name had been put down for Eton. He was a schoolboy there while Margaret was cooped up like Rapunzel in Windsor Castle. He remembered seeing her with her sister and parents at service in the college chapel the morning after his fifteenth birthday.

Polio threatened to cripple him the following year. It centered in his back and left leg. He spent six months in Liverpool's Royal Infirmary, progressing slowly from confinement in bed to a wheelchair, then into steel braces and onto crutches. Recovery left him with one leg shorter than the other by an inch or more. His fascination with cameras could be traced to his invalid days, when photography was a hobby he could handle. His impulsion to succeed had its roots in his struggle to walk again.

He was late entering Jesus College, Cambridge, planning to become an architect. Competition boxing, which he had gone in for at Eton, was closed to him, but he had the right size, weight, and temperament to make him coxswain for the rowing crew, good enough to steer the university eight in 1950 to a three-and-a-half-lengths' win in the Oxford and Cambridge boat race, an annual April festival held on the Thames, usually as dull as the weather. Tradition called for him to get a ducking to commemorate the victory.

The prospect of a career based on an architect's drawing board was too tame. He was going to make photography his business in spite of Cecil Beaton's murmurs of discouragement. Ronald Armstrong-Jones put up the necessary five hundred guineas, and as soon as Tony graduated from Baron's studio, he started calling on the glossy weeklies, offering art editors shots of his friends and relatives, mostly on his mother's side.

The countess, well provided for with a London town house at No. 18 Stafford Terrace and twenty-six thousand acres of Rosse estates in Yorkshire and Ireland, swam on the social tide along with Cavendishes, Ogilvys, and Montagu-Scotts. All of them enjoyed connections of some kind with royals. Tony had a fond and useful uncle, too, in Oliver Messel, a romantic impresario of theatrical design. The glossies' church-mouse payment rates kept young Armstrong-Jones hungry but happy.

By now, he had his own place, drab on the outside, stylish within, between a laundry and an antique shop at No. 20 Pimlico Road, which before its transfiguration had been a hardware store. It was a decided improvement over former premises in a Shaftesbury Avenue basement, where the darkroom was a converted coal cellar. His father advanced him £1,000 to make over the latest atelier, where the rent amounted to an affordable £5 a week—$14 in unobtainable United States currency.

Margaret saw and thought no more of him for ten months. Elizabeth's concern was to find some way to end her sister's brooding and coax her back into public life. Students of the *Court Circular* noted that Margaret's retreat into reclusion made more work for relatives like Marina. The load increased in times such as these, on the theory that a display of royals on their appointed rounds provided a tonic for national depression. A flareup of rumors that Margaret was in love again irritated the queen. Her sister's husband-to-be this time was reputedly Cousin Christian of Hanover, brother of Greece's Queen Frederika. At present, Frederika was living in Athens, where the on-again-off-again monarchy would finally collapse eleven years later.

Margaret was invited to join her sister and brother-in-law in Stockholm for the Olympics that summer. She missed having Elizabeth Cavendish at her side as a source of comfort, amusement, and gossip, and made sure that she went along on the next venture: Margaret was off to East Africa in September as part of the program to keep her mind off Townsend.

That trip belonged by right in an earlier century. It resembled travel in a science-fiction time capsule set into reverse. The whole African continent was caught up in the throes of change. To the north, Egypt's President Gamal Abdel Nasser had seized the Suez Canal from its British and French owners two months before she landed in Mombasa. Soon after she flew home, Israel invaded the Sinai Peninsula and Anglo-French forces pounded Egypt to induce Nasser to accept a cease-fire. In the aftermath, England got a new Tory Prime Minister. Anthony Eden pleaded ill health, to be succeeded by Harold Macmillan—"Super Mac" to his admirers.

Mombasa schoolgirls in white saris welcomed Margaret

with necklaces of tropical flowers. She sipped syrupy coffee with the veiled ladies in an Arab sheikh's harem. On the spice island of Zanzibar, a British protectorate since Victoria's reign, she spoke in her sister's name with the seventy-eight-year-old sultan. After Zanzibar broke away to form part of a new nation called Tanzania, commando assassins struck down a successor of his, the Socialist Abeid Amani Karume.

She learned what panic meant before Mauritian police clubs drove back a screaming mob of Hindus, Moslems, and mulattoes that smashed through steel barriers to cut off her car. Mauritius was another island due for independence after six generations of British rule. In Nairobi, gastritis laid her low, and Elizabeth Cavendish stepped in as nurse.

When they got back to London, the Suez debacle led to restoration of gasoline rationing for the British. Politically, the country was more bitterly divided than it had been since Neville Chamberlain stooped to Hitler at Munich. Elizabeth awarded her sister more points for good conduct by taking her along when the queen rode in state to Westminster to open a new session of Parliament, in which Super Mac, taking over from Eden, was to prove himself a master at convincing most voters in the next election that, thanks to Tory rule, prosperity was in sight at last.

If the Queen Mother's search for an extra home could be taken as evidence, Elizabeth concluded that Margaret was no longer interested in marriage. Her mother wanted a place where the two of them might get away from London for a spell every summer without imposing on her other daughter and family. Somewhere suitable in Scotland was bound to turn up.

She adjusted to being a widow with the same outward calm that distinguished her as a wife. Her married daughter still referred to her as "Queen Elizabeth" in talking to servants, but she was content to take herself out of the picture and let

Elizabeth II handle affairs on her own. For her part, she had enough to do in trying to mother Margaret.

With her sixtieth birthday not far away, her smile demonstrated peace of mind and her shape a passion for chocolates. She liked to nibble them in bed while she read poetry, the racing form, or a newspaper account of a cliff-hanging murder case. Eleven o'clock struck her as a convenient hour for starting the day after a pot of morning tea, a bite of fruit for breakfast, and a telephone call to each of her daughters. William Blake was one poet who appealed to her. After Bertie died, she quoted a line of Blake to Margaret, "And those who are in misery cannot remain so," which translated into a fragment of her own philosophy: "Well, we must take what is coming to us and make the best of it."

Steeplechasing was another passion of her middle age. There were few outings she liked better than to bundle herself up in fleece-lined boots, sturdy tweed coat, and a scarf or two for a day at the races, with additional accoutrements stowed in the car in case it showered or grew chilly—umbrella, fur rug, hot-water bottle, raincoat, change of shoes, and rubbers.

She owned only half of her first 'chaser, Monaveen, who ran first in four races that season. From then on, she kept a string of them, their jockeys in her colors of blue and buff and a black cap with gold tassel. In 1956, her heart leaped like the horse itself as her Devon Loch cleared all thirty jumps in the punishing Grand National and pounded on toward the post with a fifteen-length lead. One of her new life's ambitions was to win the National. Then Devon Lock faltered and sprawled to the ground with jockey aboard while every entry left in the race galloped by. She would have to wait for another year. "Ah, well," she smiled, "that's racing, I suppose."

Whether Margaret was home or not, her mother dressed for dinner in Clarence House, choosing a gown from a wardrobe that was an affectionate British joke. No outfit could be laden with too many frills, fringes, flounces, and furbelows to suit her. She had no intention of shortening her skirts to keep up with the times no matter what her daughters said or did. When she was dressed to dine with no one around but the servants, she did not spare the jewelry for a few finishing touches. Then she mixed herself a champagne cocktail before she sat down to eat with only the television set for company.

If for no other, more sentimental, reason, the new house had to be in Scotland because the best salmon fishing was found there, and she loved to cast a line and reel them in. For days spent on the River Dee, she wore an old felt hat, held in place by a scarf knotted under her chin, waders secured around her ample waist, and a waterproof top, so that she might brave the current to play a catch. So far as she was concerned, life could be lonely sometimes, but it was meant for enjoyment. She wished Margaret could feel the same way again.

She finished by buying not a house but a castle overlooking Pentland Firth, north of Balmoral. Barrogill Castle had its complement of ghosts, ancient and modern. The daughter of a sixteenth-century Earl of Caithness supposedly remained in residence. Frustrated love for a farm boy had driven her to throw herself over the battlements of the eastern tower. In the Second World War, the place had been used to billet soldiers of the Black Watch. One of them shot himself, the rifle bullet passing through his body and lodging in a plastered wall. No amount of replastering prevented the bullet hole from re-appearing.

Renovating the Castle of Mey, as the new owner renamed it, was laborious work, but time did not count with her. Like her younger daughter, she paid little attention to clocks. She liked to climb the winding stone staircase to the roof, where on a rare clear day she could see the red cliffs of Orkney, twenty miles away. Margaret might enjoy that, too, but she was entering an existence as remote from her mother's as the far side of the moon.

Elizabeth Cavendish arranged a dinner party at her mother's house on Cheyne Walk, which skirts the Thames at Chelsea, and invited Margaret and Tony Armstrong-Jones. Business was rosy for him. He had been commissioned to photograph Rupert Nevill's children. Elizabeth saw the prints and made an appointment for her son and daughter to pose for him in the palace gardens. The results, and the timing—the whole session over in twenty minutes—convinced her that Tony was the man to take the official pictures of Philip and herself that would herald their 1957 tour of Canada.

Making portraits of the right people helped establish a reputation, but he had no desire to specialize at it and finish in a dead end like old Marcus Adams, who took postcard shots of the Little Princesses, or the Bacharachs, with their softly lit flattery of grim businessmen. He wanted to take photographs, as he put it, "that reflect or record moments of life." He had no doubt that he was good and getting better. When he introduced himself and his portfolio to *Vogue*, the editors of that free-spending chronicle of haughty couture agreed with him. They found him "amusing" and "audacious," and signed him to a contract.

A basic ingredient in his pictures for them was the model. Sloe-eyed Jacqueline Chan, part Russian and part Chinese, was eighteen when he met her, an aspiring actress type-cast in a role in the London production of *Teahouse of the August Moon*. *Vogue* was not interested in the kind of girls with flawless smiles and apple-pie good looks who made covers for run-of-the-mill women's weeklies. Jacqui was sultry, pared down, beautiful, and right for Tony's inventive handling of high fashion in action.

The alliance of photographer and model had lasted for two

years at the time of Elizabeth Cavendish's dinner party. Jacqui was an understanding companion. She appreciated when she was wanted, and when Tony needed to be left alone. She had helped him settle into what he referred to mysteriously as The Room.

It was part of a gimcrack brick house in a sooty row that stood across the Thames in dockland, where empty space overgrown with weeds and pitted walls were testimony to German bombing. No. 59, the end house on Rotherhithe Street, was Tony's hideaway. Too many people knew where to find him at his quarters on Pimlico Road. Rotherhithe Street was where he went to make himself scarce or entertain someone special.

The Room was in fact a two-level apartment. Jacqui stitched together some of the square of rush matting that covered the floor of the hallway behind the front door. The hall opened onto a little beamed parlor, whose walls Tony painted fashionable white. A bronze head of Jacqui was included in the decor. The spiral staircase leading down to the cellar was his handiwork, too. This had been a workingman's home, not a smart photographer's pad, before changing times and raised rents made conversions chic and cheerful.

The space downstairs contained a miniature dining room, bathroom, and bedroom papered violet, scarcely big enough to hold a purple-upholstered double bed. An American newspaperman, William Glenton, who lived upstairs over Tony, was as discreet as any courtier until he produced a book about the ménage, *Tony's Room*, eight years later.

Margaret had not come across anyone quite like Tony before they sat at table at No. 5 Cheyne Walk. He was polite with his "Ma'am"s for her, but unabashed about working hard for a living. Tony thought in terms of opportunities, not problems. Life for him was "super," "blissful," "terrific."

He had enough irons in his fire to brand a herd of horses.

He free-lanced for *Vogue*, designed theater sets like Uncle Oliver Messel, and bubbled over with ideas for trendy clothes to try out on the market for mods. An exhibition of his photographs was in the works, together with plans to publish a collection of them in hard covers, and he was going on assignment to Venice.

"Don't you think he's really rather extraordinary?" Margaret said soon after she heard about most of his ventures at firsthand. Some of his circle wondered if he reminded her of Peter. Both men had a gift for making any woman feel important, but Tony had more brashness than Peter. She continued to think about Peter and the loss of him.

Inch by inch, Tony attracted her into unexplored territory, with Elizabeth Cavendish to help as a guide. Margaret went with her for a conventional pot of tea at No. 20 Pimlico Road, served downstairs in another made-over basement sitting room, also painted white, furnished in a facsimile of Regency style with studio props and the bargains he was always scouting for in secondhand shops—a chandelier that might need new crystals, an old poster, a piece of Bristol glass, a picture frame that could stand regilding, or a china rolling-pin. He knew where pickings were good, not forgetting the junkmen's barrows on Petticoat Lane, piled with the detritus of half a century. Chipped Victorian stoneware, Edwardian photo albums, tawdry souvenirs of George's silver jubilee, regimental buttons and tarnished brass shell casings, seashells, perfume bottles, chamber pots—there was no telling what might turn up when everyone, it seemed, had a sudden urge to collect *something* with a scent of nostalgia, washed up on the shores of change.

The next step for Margaret was to see The Room. It was clear now of the temporary lodger Tony had recently installed. Elizabeth Cavendish had asked whether her portly poet friend, John Betjeman, might stay while his own house in

Smithfield was repaired after fire broke out there. Betjeman was a future Poet Laureate on the Queen's payroll at a salary of £70 a year and allowance of £27 in lieu of the 126 gallons of Spanish sack and cask of canary wine which went with the appointment when Elizabeth I invented it.

The gregarious Lady Cavendish called first to tidy up the place before she brought Margaret over. Jacqui's visits had tapered off. "The fire went out" was the explanation of someone who knew both her and Tony. Princess and lady-in-waiting crossed the river on the public ferry at Deptford, Margaret muffled up in a plain wool coat and head scarf that would become standard camouflage on her later adventures. Tony was waiting with a car.

Going through from the dingy street to the back of No. 59 dazzled her. The house was perched on the brink of the murky river, which gurgled against the seal-gray wall under the windows. The only other sound was the occasional hoot of a tug towing a string of barges or the blast from a freighter's horn as it edged among the docks of the Pool of London. She could see the span of Tower Bridge divide and unite again as a tall ship sailed by on the tide, and on the far side of the water, the gilded cross and white dome of St. Paul's. There was no reason for anyone to mention the bronze of Jacqui when drinks were poured.

The relationship with Tony stayed amusing but inconsequential for almost two years. "I believe," he vowed to Bill Glenton, "that a man only really falls in love once. When that happened, I'd marry the girl, whoever she was." Margaret had looked forward to one marriage, and she was not ready to risk it again.

She had crept out of her shell, in contrast with a previous line of forgotten royal sisters, disappointed in love, who settled down to dowdy respectability in an atmosphere of loyalty and lavender water. She had her hair restyled in a smart, shorter cut and tried a different makeup so that she would not appear completely out of date when younger girls were experimenting with white lipsticks and eyes as enticing as Cleopatra's. Snapshots of Peter in a leather-bound triptych kept their place on her desk.

She had known Tony for thirteen months when Townsend came to Clarence House for a cup of four-o'clock tea with Margaret and her mother. Elizabeth and Philip were out of the country—in the Netherlands on a visit to Juliana. At six-fifty, Margaret left, eyes sparkling, for the Carlton Theater—the curtain went up preternaturally early at 7 P.M. While he stayed in London, those teatimes were repeated, and Fleet Street sniffed for smoke from a rekindled fire.

He evaded reporters more successfully than before, letting his attorney, Alan Phillpotts, speak in his name: "There are no grounds whatever for supposing that my seeing Princess Margaret in any way alters the situation declared specifically in the Princess's statement in the autumn of 1955."

The curiously oblique words could be interpreted as meaning—what? In giving him up, she had acknowledged his "unfailing support and devotion." Was he taking a round-about course to repeat that he was still devoted to her? Had she decided to give a second thought to the problem with Peter Townsend, who, a shade nearer fifty than forty, still had no wife?

A Swiss newspaper speculated that she had and that the next act was about to begin. Toward the end of May, Elizabeth ordered a clearing of the air. For once, a flat denial was forthcoming from Commander Colville: "The press secretary to the Queen is authorized to say that the report in the *Tribune de Genève* concerning a possible engagement between Princess Margaret and Group Captain Peter Townsend is entirely untrue. Her Royal Highness's statement of 1955 remains unaltered."

Apart from laying one rumor to rest, the announcement was no more straight-forward than Peter's in focussing again on his devotion as much as on her solitary decision not to become his wife. A question arose that neither the family nor the court was willing to answer: Why didn't Margaret speak up for herself again, assuming that she wanted to?

Peter's photograph went with her when she flew to Canada in July, with Elizabeth Cavendish included in the entourage. A touch of renascent egotism showed up when Margaret first learned of the booking. "It's about time," she said.

Admiration for her sister remained high in the North American portion of the realm under the premiership of John Diefenbaker, who rivaled Winston in his ceaseless tributes to the monarchy. Margaret dabbled again in seeing something of the country incognito. The desire was as strong as in her childhood, when she complained, "I wish we could be visiting these places when royalty aren't." In Vancouver, she skipped out of the service entrance of her hotel to take in some sightseeing on the island that was proud to be British.

She offered herself at a press conference, wielding a gold-banded ebony cigarette holder like a sword to fend off impertinent questions. When it got lost along the line on the journey eastward, it was described by one of her party as a gift from an unnameable "old friend." Townsend?

She had never been in better form. "Canada," she said, "turns me on," which was language she had picked up in Tony's company, where the patois tagged along behind the Manhattan idiom: *Dig you ... I've flipped ... That's real gone ... Cool, Man! ... I got the message.*

Coming down to earthly levels in a bid to be likable more than idolized was not easy when experience was limited, but she tried. Her departure point was Nova Scotia, the peninsula jutting out into the Atlantic Ocean; her final appointment at a banquet in Halifax. Television cameras peered at her as she boarded her homeward-bound flight in the glimmering gown she had worn at dinner. She put off changing it to settle down for the night to call for the stewardesses. "They might like to look at my dress before I take it off."

The decisive move to disentangle the ties between them was made by Peter. She learned from him that he had found another girl he wanted to marry and who wanted to marry him. Marie-Luce Jamagne went to the same Brussels riding club. Her father prospered in the tobacco business. She was twenty-one years old.

The photographs of Peter vanished at last. From now on, he would exchange telephone calls with members of·the family when he came to London, but as one keen-eyed watcher of the royals noted, "They did not accept his invitation to a drink."

Next year, Margaret would be thirty, reaching that meridian which many a woman on its leeward side approaches with more trepidation than the one that follows ten years later. Most of the people who had fluttered around her when her father was alive were already married, separated from her by the intangible barriers that marriage raises around man and wife.

She occupied a peculiar position on the hierarchical pyramid, third in line for the thone. She could not marry a social equal because there was none; no family in the dwindling fraternity of monarchs compared in prestige and splendor with the royal Britons. She could only, in a time-worn phrase, marry beneath herself. The question was how far down the slopes of the pyramid she could choose to reach.

From her restricted viewpoint, Tony fulfilled a remarkable number of requirements. Physically, he did not tower over her, which was important when she was acutely conscious of her modest size. He represented a mode of living that appealed to her much more than hunting, fishing, and opening bazaars. He had tastes and a similar brittle sense of humor that showed in talents akin to hers—decorating rooms, sketching fashions, playing records, appreciating a movie or a play. He had applied his skills with energy she admired, where she had been frustrated. Nipping off to cross the river to Rotherhithe became common practice for her.

For months, Bill Glenton did not recognize her when he answered the front door. He took her to be some new girl in Tony's circle of men and women. Jacqui in bronze disappeared from sight at the same time Tony let Margaret know something of what Jacqueline Chan had contributed for him. The Room could use one bit of home improvement to save Margaret trips on the spiral stairs. There was a cupboard under the main staircase leading to Glenton's habitat. "Don't you think," Tony asked him, "it might be a good place to put in a loo?"

She enjoyed herself in the apartment in much the same way as in The Little Thatched House at Royal Lodge, washing dishes after Tony had coped with cooking on the gas range, sweeping the rush matting. ("You really need a Hoover.") She hadn't had a play house of this kind since her childhood. Buckingham Palace had been singularly lacking in that respect. "Crawfie," she once explained, "even if I wanted to cook my breakfast, I couldn't, because there's nothing here to cook on."

This time, she could not afford to have happiness exploded by probing journalists. Elizabeth was not let in on the secret at first, but Ruby the maid had to know. She helped out by booking theater tickets in her name so that her mistress and future master could slide into their seats after the house lights had dimmed and Margaret, in dark glasses, could shelter behind her program between the acts.

In Philip's forthright opinion, marriage would be good for

her. He did not have too much in common with the young man, but Philip was keen on photography, too. If it was at all possible, Margaret should be given her head and not crushed by the rule book a second time. Her mother held the same conviction. As soon as she was invited, she went over to Rotherhithe to see The Room for herself. Her dress, with the inevitable touch of the Thirties, might have looked ludicrous on anyone else against the setting of Bohemian bric-a-brac. But Mummy, who delighted in new experiences, made herself instantly at home. She spent a contented evening singing along with the tenant while the daughter who was in love with him accompanied them on the battered piano. From time to time, Tony bustled around with refreshments. Gin-and-tonic, champagne, beer? Whatever the others were having would do for her. "I haven't enjoyed myself so much since I was twenty."

He used photography as a cover when he was asked for weekends at Royal Lodge or holidays at Balmoral or Sandringham, turning up with his car loaded with the paraphernalia of the trade, which he would ostentatiously tote into the house. By October, the outcome was taken for granted. Ostensibly, the all-night party for two hundred and fifty guests at Clarence House was given to welcome pretty young Princess Alexandra back from a stint in Australia. The true purpose was to provide a good time for Margaret and her intended husband. Bacon and eggs were served for breakfast.

An event was impending that, on the scale of royal priorities, outweighed anything else on the horizon. Elizabeth's third baby was expected in February. The birth demanded precedence over any announcement regarding Margaret. In any case, Tony had not yet gone through the ritual of asking her to be his wife.

The family as a whole honored superstition as unfailingly as they paid obeisance to the queen. Elizabeth herself shied away from sitting down to a meal with thirteen at table. At Sandringham, when the clocks struck midnight on New Year's Eve, the first man to come in through the front door carried a piece of coal for good luck. In 1960, a leap year, Margaret ignored the provisions of another bit of folklore. Bill Glenton noticed that "although she made it as easy as possible for him, it was Tony who had to propose."

It would have suited her best to be married right away, but the pace to the altar was governed by Elizabeth. An announcement that her little sister was engaged had to wait on delivery of the baby, then be delayed by another week so that cause for one celebration would not step on the heels of the other.

Prince Andrew Albert Christian Edward was born on Friday, February 19. On February 26, Margaret was with Tony at Royal Lodge when, according to schedule, the news was released from Clarence House: "It is with the greatest pleasure that Queen Elizabeth the Queen Mother announces the betrothal of her beloved daughter The Princess Margaret to Mr. Antony Charles Robert Armstrong-Jones, son of Mr. R. O. L. Armstrong-Jones, Queen's Counsel, and the Countess of Rosse, to which union The Queen has gladly given her consent."

Those Britons who made a hobby of studying the royals puzzled over what her married name would be. So far as they could guess, she would become "Her Royal Highness The Princess Margaret Mrs. Antony Armstrong-Jones," but that was such a mishmash that it made no sense at all.

Ronald Armstrong-Jones, Q.C., was in Bermuda on his third honeymoon; Jennifer Unite had been a British Overseas Airways stewardess. He was disturbed by the announcement of his son's engagement. "I wish in heaven's name this hadn't happened," he said. "It will never work out. Tony's a far too independent sort of fellow to be subjected to discipline. He won't be prepared to play second fiddle to anyone. He will have to walk two steps behind his wife, and I fear for his future."

XI

Pet and Tone, Brenda and Brian

Elizabeth supplied the Welsh gold left over from her own wedding ring for Margaret's. It had to be made so small that enough metal remained for another—young Anne's when she grew up. Elizabeth also provided *Britannia* for her sister's Caribbean honeymoon. Margaret deserved to be pampered when she had waited so long to find the man she was being allowed to make her husband.

The marriage of a princess and a commoner struck a responsive chord as the era of rock 'n' roll, ordnance of Elvis Presley, reached its crescendo, the beat of the bands grew fiercer, skirts shrank, men's barbers sank into despair, and faith abounded in the ability of Super Mac to lift the kingdom out of the doldrums.

London was primped like a bridesmaid. Television crews jockeyed cameras, cables, and floodlights into the gray vastness of Westminster Abbey. Fashion-trade spies prowled around Mr. Hartnell's workrooms to ferret out details of Margaret's wedding dress. Fleet Street lit on the secret of The Room, and reporters badgered Bill Glenton on his doorstep. Across from the palace at the top of The Mall, workmen built an arch sixty feet tall of live roses and raised a long double line of white poles carrying monogrammed standards, "M" and "A".

Tony put his Pimlico Road premises up for sale and moved into guest quarters in the palace at Elizabeth's invitation. She sent him with Margaret to look at the house she had in mind for them, No. 10 Kensington Palace, double-fronted, ancient brick, left empty by the death of its previous tenant, one of Victoria's grandsons, Alexander, Marquis of Carisbrooke.

In the morning sunlight of May 6, 1960, the glass coach was rolled out again from the mews behind the palace. In tightly cut white satin, a little coronet to hold her veil, and the longest train to be seen on an abbey bride, Margaret rode with Philip and an escort of a hundred horsemen through a crowd that she could only judge would love her through eternity.

Before the altar, standing next to Tony, who sported a white carnation in the lapel of his morning coat, she exchanged vows of love, honor, and obedience. She had asked that words from the Bible be substituted for a sermon. The archbishop's voice droned from the loudspeakers: *Blessed are the pure in heart: for they shall see God ... Blessed are ye, when men shall revile you, and persecute you, and shall say all manner of evil against you falsely, for my sake. Rejoice, and be exceeding glad: for great is your reward in heaven ...*

There was no argument about it among the fans waiting in the thousands outside the palace for their first glimpse of Mrs. Armstrong-Jones: when she came out on to the balcony for their inspection, she had never looked happier. They expected husband and wife to make their exit in conventional open carriage for the drive to Tower Pier, where *Britannia* was moored. Instead, she borrowed a closed Rolls-Royce from

Elizabeth. The throng surged in for a closer examination. Down The Mall, along The Strand, through the maze of narrow city streets leading down to the river, the car crept, delayed by an hour, its paint so scratched in the process that it needed respraying. That was a fraction of the price payable for the day.

Pursuing launches and circling seaplanes beset *Britannia* as the yacht neared its first port of call. Most of the Windward and Leeward Islands in the vast arc swinging from the coast of Venezuela toward Puerto Rico were Elizabeth's possessions. The inhabitants were learning the importance of voting rights for all as a step on the road to self-government. The islands grew crops of sugarcane, cotton, cocoa beans, spices, and citrus fruit to be shipped out to the mother country. Tourism had not expanded into big business yet. Steel bands on Trinidad, calypso singers on Dominica, rain of flowers on Antigua welcomed the couple. They were put ashore on tinier islands of coral and lava sand to sun themselves and swim in limpid water, clicking away at each other with their cameras under the brilliant sky.

They took time to call at a speck so small—a tenth the size of Manhattan—and so remote that it was lost from the lists in standard gazetteers. The Colin Tennants greeted them when they landed here in the Grenadines. Colin had paid £45,000 to buy Mustique. At present, the eighty or so natives lived in shacks and worked cutting sugarcane and picking cotton, limes, and grapefruit under the eyes of a manager installed in one of the few dwellings of any substance.

The new owner pictured his domain with better housing for the islanders, a village school, an airfield, and, most important, a colony of beach houses for well-to-do escapists and a hotel for tomorrow's tourists. He drove Margaret and Tony to a promontory shaded by coconut palms and flanked by beaches of white sand so fine it clung to the skin. Would they accept it as a wedding present?

Margaret needed no urging. A miniature realm of her own could be something close to an earthly paradise, set in a sheltered corner of the world that spelled escape. Compared with her sister, she was compelled to live on a tight budget. As a married woman, her state allowance went up from £6,000 to £15,000 a year. Tony received nothing from that source. She had a few personal jewels—most heirlooms belonged to Elizabeth. She held title to no property in Britain of the kind that provided £30,000 a year for her nephew Charles until he was twenty-one, when his income as landlord would rise to £200,000. She would be a tenant in the house she and her husband moved into. If she wanted use of one of the fleet of cars, a plane from the royal flight, or *Britannia*, she had to ask first.

As soon as this honeymoon was over, Tony would go back to work by choice and necessity unless they intended to look for extra money from Elizabeth to support them for the rest of their lives.

Bandsmen of the Royal Marines played them ashore when *Britannia* sailed into Portsmouth harbor in the middle of June. "Neither of us wanted to leave," Margaret acknowledged, tanned and gentle-eyed. "We would have gladly lived in a little grass hut."

She was eager to move into Kensington Palace as soon as possible. They went back to using The Room as a hideout. The gawkers had faded from Rotherhithe Street, but guides on the sightseeing launches that plowed down the river to Greenwich continued to announce, "Now look hard over there on your right; that's the little house where Princess Margaret did her courting." Occasionally, she watched in amusement from behind the curtains. "We haven't eaten alone together for six weeks," she told Bill Glenton when they turned up one day with groceries packed in the back of Tony's car.

Cooking was something she dared only experiment with. Tony worked at the stove; she washed dishes at the old chipped sink, painstakingly and contentedly, like a child helping out, careful not to drip suds down her dress, since she had no apron. It was a convenient place for getting acquainted with some of her husband's unusual ring of friends, not all of whom matched up with palace standards.

He knew all kinds of people, starting close to the top of the pyramid and descending some distance down. Dr. Roger Gilliatt, professor of neurology at London University, was one; he had been Tony's last-minute choice as best man at the wedding. Uncle Oliver Messel, who had given him a seventeenth-century Flemish wooden screen, was another. David Hicks' alliance with Tony dated back to Pimlico Road days; David was an interior decorator and something of a personage himself, played up as a counsellor in the pages of women's magazines and recently married to Dickie Mountbatten's younger daughter, Pamela. Dominic and Peter Elwes were two more friends, sons of Simon, the satin-finished portrait painter for whom Margaret had sat during Coronation year. Uncle Oliver was a Simon friend.

Then there were the girls who were a photographer's bread and butter, their faces and bodies reproduced on covers and billboards, in fashion layouts and advertisements. Some were Cockney waifs, others daughters of the squirearchy, having in common photogenic looks, long legs and a taste for liberated living. In the jet-set league, they had taken over the role played by ladies of the chorus in the *Floradora* generation of stage-door Johnnies.

A model looking for a husband—some preferred less restrictive relationships—could usually marry well. One of Tony's circle, Jane Sheffield, did that in becoming Mrs. Jocelyn Stevens, wife of a future managing director of the *Daily Express.*

Besides hiring by the hour the agency girls who posed for him, a photographer needed what the trade called a "dolly girl" to work in his studio, running errands, rounding up props and costumes. A dolly girl was as essential in Tony's business as his staunch secretary, motherly Dorothy Everard, another veteran of Pimlico Road days.

He liked to wear the faded jeans and thick wool turtlenecks that were the uniform of men of his mark at camera sessions, movie sets, and stage rehearsals, who rattled off the same brand of brittle chatter. Among friends, he referred to his wife as "the princess," not the stuffier "Her Royal Highness" or "Ma'am." In private they were "Pet" and "Tone." Loving him, she was willing to try adjusting her style to his.

She saw a side of life—it could be termed "plush hip"—unknown to her before. Its women shopped for such items as orange suede boots and brief tube dresses at boutiques like Glad Rags, Top Gear, and puckish Mary Quant's Bazaar on Kings Road. Margaret had to compromise—she lacked the height and pipestem figure for carrying off *outré* designs, but she adored fancying up to go partying.

Vogue and *Harper's Bazaar* set the pattern for high-tone makeup for the women and some of the men. Margaret wore special cosmetics with more *panache* than any other royal lady and laid in a collection of hairpieces and transformations so that she could change a coiffure as deftly as an actress in a stage blackout.

Tony took her to mix with intellectuals, Bohemians, and beatniks, listening to rhythm-and-blues at recitals where conversation turned to Manfred Mann, George Shearing, and a club known as Eel Pie Island "where they dance in their slips and wear beards instead of shoes." She went to movies, the theater, and ballet, chipping in small talk to fit the circumstances. Backstage at a London Coliseum performance of *The Sleeping Beauty* at a later date, she asked one slender male dancer, "Do you wear tights under your costume?" "Yes, Ma'am," he replied, dropping his trousers so she could see for herself.

Her husband introduced her to the joys of junk. They sallied down the Portobello Road, where an old hand like Tony knew that dealers automatically added forty per cent to the asking price. Camden Passage in Islington was another favorite hunting ground with its little cluster of gossipy boutiques. It was also worth a trip to Inverness Street Market to see Red, junkman supreme, who spread his unsorted gleanings over three or four tables until they overflowed onto the sidewalk on Wednesdays, Fridays, and Saturdays, and barred all haggling with a curt "Take it or leave it." Tony could spot the bargains that sold for a shilling or two when they were worth two or three pounds. Margaret had more unalloyed fun than she ever had when Grandmama took her along on her visits to the plush salons of West End antique dealers, pointing out the finer points of Sheraton marquetry and Chippendale carving.

After their move into Kensington Palace, she saw less of her sister, which bothered neither of them. Telephone calls kept them in touch, and in any event Margaret was convinced she and Elizabeth could read each other's minds. "It's no trick," she said, "It's telepathy. We really can do it."

What her sister's thoughts were about Margaret's entry into this suborder of society only Margaret probably knew. In most respects by now they were polar opposites. Elizabeth, increasingly set in her ways, molded by the demands of her station, preferred to be up at eight and on her way to bed at ten-thirty; Margaret and Tony were night creatures who sat up until the early morning.

Elizabeth resisted emotion and developed, in consequence, an unwavering pride in her abilities. She had purged herself of her mother's winsomeness. Charm, in her opinion, was best left to movie stars, along with their mink coats. Country tweeds and head scarves suited her; clothes on the whole held no personal interest.

When her hairdresser came on Monday afternoons, she wanted only a repetition of the same center parting in her soft brown hair. On her bedroom dressing table, the silver-gilt vanity set and the gold-topped crystal containers were aligned as precisely as an infantry platoon.

In her middle thirties, the woman whose wealth probably exceeded any others' anywhere was a frugal as Grandmama had been. The same carriage served Elizabeth's first three babies and was in storage for the next. When she lost a gold-and-platinum wristwatch on a day in the country, she called on the army to send troops to comb the territory—to no avail. A mislaid dog leash on one outing at Sandringham was enough to have Charles sent back to retrieve it. "Remember that dog leads cost money," she told him.

Her waking hours were as regimented as any sentry's at her gates. Appointments were kept to the minute. Time for the children was staked out every day on much the same schedule her father and mother had kept with her and her sister. Nannies brought them down for a caress and a chat after breakfast, then again at the end of the afternoon for tea, television, and ninety minutes' play before she helped put them to bed. She had no thought of excluding Philip from their upbringing. "Ask Papa—he knows best" was a familiar line of hers.

She *had* thought again about the pliable question of family names. Her children must continue to be Windsors, but the ancestry of her husband and Uncle Dickie deserved some recognition. Another Order in Council took care of the matter. "My descendants [other than descendants enjoying the style, title or attribute of Royal Highness and the titular dignity of Prince or Princess and female descendants who marry and their descendants] shall bear the name of Mountbatten-Windsor." In plainer words, the generations originating with her heir Charles and his sister Anne could always be Windsors, but Elizabeth's great-grandchildren descended from her second son, Andrew, and any other children she bore would be hyphenated Mountbattens.

Sometimes the rein she kept on herself slipped a notch and the same quick temper flared in her as it had in her father. One danger signal was the irritated twisting around her finger of the square-cut diamond engagement ring which his father gave Philip's mother and she handed in turn on to her son. A hint of disrespect brought a glare to Elizabeth's blue-green eyes. She cut down a friend caught powdering her nose before a mirror in a palace corridor: "This is *not* a cloakroom."

Whether or not she was supremely happy was not a question worth considering. Her marriage had survived the strains of its earlier years when her job overwhelmed her and Philip had too little to do. She was a captive of tradition and conscience; he declined to be fettered in the same fashion and complained that in the palace "I feel like a lodger."

He was away from home for days and occasionally a week and longer. His absences hurt when she had no alternative to eating dinner like her mother, alone in front of a television set. The worst time came just before Margaret met Tony, when Philip had been away for more than three months, opening the Olympic Games in Australia and going on to traverse the

Antarctic, where she could never venture into similar hazards. Rumors filtered back to her. He had returned to his bachelor ways with women eager to appeal to his vigor and his vanity; her marriage was threatened, the gossip said.

She turned to the woman whose judgements she valued perhaps more than Philip's. Bobo MacDonald exercised the same strong-minded influence as she had when she took charge of Elizabeth at the time of Margaret's birth. Bobo's pile-carpeted flat, where meals and maid service were laid on as though she herself was a royal, stood directly above Elizabeth's private apartments in the palace. The aging, bespectacled nanny, red hair streaked gray, had never married. Elizabeth remained her extra-special daughter. "How can they say such terrible things about us?" she asked Bobo. But the marriage held firm.

Philip made a sterner father than Bertie had been, but his children looked up to him. Over her mother's fluttering, Elizabeth gave him his way in sending Charles off to board at Cheam preparatory school and then on to Gordonstoun, the Spartan institution in Morayshire, Scotland, where Philip before him was taught the benefits of work and cold showers in growing into manhood.

Dogs and horses kept their accustomed place in Elizabeth's affections. Feeding the corgis settled into an evening ritual. A uniformed footman carried a tray to the door of her sitting room after the children had been brought in. On it sat three dishes separately filled with fresh-cooked meat, dog biscuits, and hot gravy, together with a silver fork and spoon, bowls, and a white plastic mat for the protection of the red carpet. Elizabeth came forth to dole out to each "bloody animal," as one friend described them, its bowlful of supper. When her own eight o'clock dinner was served, they stayed at her feet, chomping the cashew nuts she fed them.

Horses were best ridden for polo, in her husband's estimation, not watched from a privileged box at the track. In her morning reading, *The Sporting Life* took precedence over other newspapers, and after work she relaxed keeping the stud book of her thoroughbreds up to date.

The habitually stolid official face came alive when she trained her binoculars on the course, then jigged with excitement as the field spread out toward the finish. She carried a movie camera as part of her equipment but as often as not forgot to use it. Watching racing on television at home brought on similar exhilaration. "Ride him!" she would cry loud enough to be heard through a closed door. "You're too soon, you fool!"

This was the wife the cynics labeled "Brenda" and her husband "Brian" in the same game of parlor sniping that tagged Margaret "Yvonne." There was a difference in how the upper levels of the pyramid regarded the two couples. Brenda and Brian were accepted as a bit of a bore with all their middle-class virtues, but deserving support nevertheless for what they were doing. Yvonne and "that fellow Jones" were simply not welcome.

Philip undertook to coach his brother-in-law on how to jump some of the hurdles he was running up against. The men were farther apart than their wives, and there was not the bond of understanding that linked Margaret with Elizabeth. Tony was deceptive, tougher inside than out, where Philip came suspiciously close to being the converse. But he had some experiences to share on the subject of the compromises demanded when a husband had to follow two steps behind his wife. A program was shaped up for Tony to do his bit as a royal apprentice in delivering speeches, sitting in on conferences, and escorting Margaret on her duty calls.

"They must give him a chance," she said, protectively. "It's not going to be easy."

When her sister told her she was pregnant, Elizabeth

deliberated over some more name-juggling that could be performed at a wave of the scepter. The child should not be simply an Armstrong-Jones. When she first mentioned to Tony what she had in mind, he was not at all sure he wanted a title. He was soon persuaded otherwise. On October 1 in the first year of his marriage, she raised him to within five levels of the apex by creating him Earl of Snowdon, Viscount Linley. The second half of his new name would automatically pass on to his firstborn son.

No. 10 Kensington Palace was so cramped that many a wedding present stayed in storage. With office staff taking up the ground floor and servants the top, man and wife were sandwiched in on a single floor between. The truth of his comment "This is not a wealthy house" was evident in the guest room, furnished with holdovers from Pimlico. Finding space for a nursery would be difficult. Delivering her baby in the palace, which is what Margaret wanted, did not sit well with her doctors. For a princess to go into a maternity ward or a nursing home was out of the question, so she opted to move back into Clarence House to await the birth.

The month after his earldom was conferred on Tony, she bore him a son who tipped the scales at six pounds, four ounces. "It's much less painful than you think," she assured Bill Glenton's wife, Nenne. "The worst part is waiting weeks beforehand. I used to get a little irritable." She hadn't dared guess how Tony would take to fatherhood. She was delighted to pose for him against the pillows, her cheek snuggled against her newborn's, contented and—the only adequate word—beautiful.

David Albert Charles, Viscount Linley, wore the hundred-and-twenty-one-years-old lace robe handed down by Victoria and bawled bitterly at his palace christening. His godmother was Elizabeth, the noteworthy sponsors Simon Phipps, Elizabeth Cavendish, and Patrick Plunkett.

Tony did some discreet job-hunting to pay his share of household expenses and satisfy his untiring urge to advance himself. Staying in business as a studio photographer was disallowed. When Margaret wanted his mother-and-child pictures distributed to newspapers and magazines, Fleet Street rumbled with protests that he was cashing in on his marriage. His title was a joke in itself to some editors, one of whom announced in print that so far as these pages were concerned Lord Snowdon would always be Tony Armstrong-Jones.

He was already encountering the Clark Gable theory of nemesis, nipped on one flank by the restrictions of protocol, on the other by public derision at the idea that a Jones could ever be a royal. He moved into hostile territory and found himself work on a newspaper, as adviser and photographer extraordinary to the *Sunday Times*. Chubby Roy Thomson, its self-made Canadian proprietor, liked the looks and drive of the new recruit from the day he saw him.

Elizabeth consulted her current Prime Minister, Harold Macmillan, a deceptively languid Tory, about the ground rules to be laid down for her extraordinary brother-in-law. They concluded that he must steer clear of politics, since discussion of politics, sex, or religion was not condoned in her presence. His employers must not benefit from royal scoops in words or pictures as a result of his association. Use of his name was forbidden in promotion or advertising campaigns. And official bookings made for him with or without Margaret must have first call on his time. As a working newspaperman, he had to join the National Union of Journalists, which caused another flurry of nervousness inside the palace and out. He kept his passport in the name of Armstrong-Jones.

The domestic affairs of the Snowdons intrigued the British. Their first butler, Thomas Cronin, resigned in a tiff and straightway sold his memoirs to *The People*. "I was mortified by the strange standards imposed upon me," he huffed. "For the sake of the royal family I must speak." Uncle Dickie's household supplied his successor. Ruby, Margaret's long-term personal maid and confidante, gave in her notice five months after the baby arrived. Tony's mother found a replacement in Dorothy Palmer, whom Tony had known as a handywoman to have around a house for years.

Margaret resented the criticism as much as she detested the press photographers who kept her and Tony under surveillance. "We sometimes think they are just vultures waiting for an accident." Palace rules prohibited her from doing anything more than groan in private. "I used to get appallingly upset," she remembered afterward, "with no way of hitting back. I was an absolute wreck after some of the publicity."

The arrows flew again when the baby was two months old and she went off with Tony for a New Year's vacation in the comforting Caribbean on the island of Antigua with nothing more to do than soak themselves in the warm sea and hot sun. The contrast between the dutiful queen and her pleasure-bent sister overcame some otherwise loyal citizens. Poison-pen letters, usually anonymous, began arriving in the mail for Margaret.

In Parliament, Willie Hamilton, the cockleburr Socialist, was curious to know the price the country was being charged in the fitting out of a new, more expansive home for her in Kensington Palace, No. 1A instead of No. 10. The question still dangled in August when the two sun-seekers flew out again, though this was on business—Margaret stood in for Elizabeth as Jamaica celebrated its brand-new independence with fireworks and fiestas. It was time for Elizabeth to step in and undertake to bear £20,000 of the soaring cost of fixing up No. 1A.

Outwardly at least, Margaret was a changed woman. She gave her husband the credit for making her "twice the person

I used to be." Friends noticed that what they referred to as her "acid drop expression" seldom pursed her lips these days. Tony roared around on a mighty motorcycle in his black leathers and coaxed her to cling to the pillion seat behind him. He lured her into water-skiing off the Antigua shore wearing all-embracing black rubber in the fancy that it would help ward off the chills she was still prone to. She continued to catch colds.

He handled four simultaneous lives like a juggler twirling clubs. The priority of trailing Margaret on her rounds bore down hard, but he was a quick study. The neatly groomed backup man who stood beside her at the head of the reception lines was scarcely recognizable as Tony the photographer, "a good-time Charlie" in the opinion of one of his old enclave.

He needed two engagement books to separate these two segments of his time, one in charge of Dorothy Everard, the other for his state occasions, which were supervised by Margaret's secretary, Francis Legh, whose office was on their ground floor. At the *Sunday Times,* he more than earned his keep. Rival camera hands admitted he turned out professional-quality stuff, but most of them complained that he enjoyed an unfair advantage.

Then he had what he described as "my voluntary work." Every royal was laden with so many patronages and affiliations that remembering precisely what associations listed them as presidents and supporters was a feat delegated to secretaries. Margaret accumulated more than half a hundred official connections; Tony's list grew longer every year, but he sought for himself the first appointment: advisor to the Council of Industrial Design, with its showcase on Lower Haymarket. "I love the whole job. It's super."

He set about making sketches for an airy new birdhouse for the Regent's Park Zoo. Its construction evoked more jeers and mutterings of privilege. "Whiz kid" was one of the gentler gibes aimed at him. Fiddling with aviaries could not be accepted as a suitable pastime for Elizabeth's trendy brother-in-law.

So he retained a toehold on life among the plush hip, where he was safer from ridicule. He realized that he was being type-cast just like Margaret. In contrast to Philip the good, a current family favorite with the British, Tony's role was the arty harum-scarum, and the comparison was odious.

In some respects, the Snowdons behaved like a pair of enthusiastic, well-off suburbanites, setting their style by *House and Garden*. Margaret, who wanted a showpiece kitchen in their new home, shied away from inflating the bill for it and finished by chipping in some of her own money. Tony fancied a rather more majestic bathroom than the one installed in a closet at The Room and tracked down the Gothic molding for it in a junkyard. Together they unearthed an eighteenth-century commode; wouldn't it be *campy* to replace its concealed chamber pot with a flush toilet?

They lent a hand with the moving by running carloads of personal treasures between the old apartments and the new. Margaret by then was two months away from having a second child. On their first weekend in No. 1A, they planted a magnolia by a wall in the garden in hope that its white petals would be out when the child was born.

Lady Sarah Frances Elizabeth Armstrong-Jones arrived on May Day, 1964. Her aunt came punctually as usual to the palace christening. Philip's helicopter landed behind schedule in the garden, leaving him no time to change before he hurried in. A reception followed in the Queen's Gallery in the south wing, the newest exhibition of its kind in London, devised to let her subjects, on open days, see some of her inexhaustible collection of works of art after handing their admission tickets to a footman in a gold-braided top hat.

the wish to give a boost if she could to British export trade and her determination to sample some American joys. Sharman Douglas was the instigator with her invitation for Margaret and Tony to come to see Pontano Farm, her father's ranch near Tucson, Arizona. The rest of the pieces of the itinerary fell in place around that.

British Week in San Francisco: she could usefully appear there. Then on to Los Angeles on a double-barrelled mission, going to parties designed to raise funds for deserving charities and, while she was at it, meeting fellow guests such as Paul Newman, Steve McQueen, and Gregory Peck; Gable was gone from the scene in 1965. Lyndon Johnson would welcome her to the White House. She could travel up from Washington to New York to help with the genteel promotion of British goods on sale in the stores and employ her charm when she met the banking tycoons whose goodwill meant survival to the kingdom. Tony would be with her all the way and, as a sideline, put in a word for his latest collection of photographs bound into a book entitled *Private View.* Three weeks for £30,000? The British Foreign Office considered it a bargain.

She played to sold-out audiences in the best royal performances Americans had seen since Uncle David becharmed the land in the 1920s. Tony lingered the prescribed pace behind her, hiding the vestige of his limp, hair combed into a blond cockscomb over his forehead. Sometimes his face gleamed like hers, with preternatural health; their smiles never wore thin and the handshaking went on forever.

They made a sparkling pair, as engaging as a little bride and groom on top of a wedding cake. "I'll tell you what it is," said one smitten onlooker as they entered the ballroom of their Manhattan headquarters in the Waldorf-Astoria. "It's a put-on; campy; tongue-in-cheek camp. She's doing an impersonation of herself."

XII

Matters of Convenience

How she behaved anywhere was usually determined by the mood of the moment, but the imperious demand for respect seldom wavered. She expected her servants to address her without fail as "Your Royal Highness." She was "Ma'am" to all but her closest friends and in that her sister's equal. She would insist, when she felt inclined, on a police escort of motorcycles to lead her car from the apartment to a railroad station, or on borrowing a helicopter for a ten-minute flight to some duty call.

She had Elizabeth's technique of ignoring any remarks that displeased her and staring down the culprit. Her sister was constrained from counterattack where Margaret might cut down a chosen target with sarcasm. If she felt she was treated too irreverently by fellow guests, she would simply walk out. Unless a party lived up to her expectations, she would leave early, as she abandoned a gala hosted by Rupert of Lowenstein-Wertheim. Mick Jagger was there, but the Rolling

Stones were not one of the three rock groups that kept the walls vibrating and police telephones jangling with complaints from the neighbors. The third sex, she found, was so well represented that night that dancing partners were scarce. Homosexuals, it seemed, had a way of gravitating toward her, fancying she had the deep-rooted sense of insecurity that drew women like Judy Garland, Marilyn Monroe, and Vivien Leigh to their kind rather than to more aggressive heterosexual males.

Margaret's physical beauty had reached its peak as she matured. Whether she was in a simple, sleeveless weekend dress or gowned by Dior for a gala night in town, she was a strikingly handsome woman, with an alert, knowing look in her bright eyes. Her appearance and her reputation as a hedonist combined to make her unique among princesses: she was thought of by many a man as a sex goddess in the tradition of Jean Harlow, Rita Hayworth, and Monroe. Even in photographs, she bore an air of sensuality. She would not have been surprised nor probably the least bit upset had she overheard some of the pub and club gossip among admiring males who concluded that she would make an eminently satisfactory sexual partner.

"I think everybody has the right to stick up for themselves," Margaret said, drawing the line between how she treated her companions and those dignitaries she met on princely business. She claimed that to them she was never less than democratically polite. Not all her relatives thought so. Her first cousin, Alexandra, another royal princess and fifteenth in line of succession, was outspoken in comments about Margaret. "She can never forget she is a princess," she said.

Alexandra, tall, poised, throaty-voiced and six years younger than Margaret, was Aunt Marina's daughter. She was taking over more of her cousin's jobs and revelling in them, which Margaret minded not at all. Alexandra had also married a man with no title and little inherited money. Tense, overworked Angus Ogilvy remembered Tony as a younger boy, keen on boxing, at Eton. Angus' share of the estate of his father, the Earl of Airlie, was a meagre £3,000, but he made a more-than-comfortable living by sitting on company boards. He counted more than fifty directorships at the time of marriage.

The cost of having a wife so eager to help out Cousin Elizabeth and understudy Margaret ran high. Alexandra had no income of her own, and her original allowance from Elizabeth's pocket amounted to £3,000 a year until it was raised to a more realistic £30,000. Angus had to provide at least as much again to cover the expenses of her annual obligations. "You don't think I would allow her to do it on the cheap," he said.

He turned down the offer of an earldom like Tony's—"I don't see why I should get a peerage because I have married a princess"—as well as the rent-free house Elizabeth wanted to hand over to the Ogilvys. In place of it, he bought the lease on Thatched House Lodge, a stately stucco mansion in Richmond Park, for £150,000, much of it borrowed, with interest payments on the mortgage running at £17,000 a year, and staffed it with butler, cook, housemaid, and gardener, and a nanny for the son and then the daughter who came along.

Meeting the bills presented no problem for the time being. One bit of business took him to Rhodesia before Ian Smith, the Prime Minister there, announced that he was pulling out of Elizabeth's commonwealth to maintain white supremacy over the vast black majority that worked the mines and farmlands. Angus' mission was to find a man to put some steam into a trading company known as Lonrho Limited. He recommended a human steamhammer, Roland "Tiny" Rowland, once a porter at London's Paddington Station, now a local farmer-cum-entrepreneur. Within six years, Lonrho profits were hoisted from £150,000 to £90,000,000. When the British government in 1965 declared Rhodesia's independence illegal and embargoed trade with the rebel nation, Lonrho devised its own means to beat the sanctions. Angus remained on the London board, whose chief executive was Tiny Rowland.

But Lonrho's muddied affairs and Angus' part in them were of no concern to most of Elizabeth's subjects; the storm surrounding them built up a decade later. At present, readers of the *Court Circular* totted up the number of gatherings Alexandra attended, always with her husband when he could spare time from his office, and compared her performance with Margaret's. Three a week was par for Alexandra, which left Margaret in the shade.

These comparisons rankled Tony. If he avoided some chores as his wife's consort because they struck him as silly, he held that to be strictly his affair. A loner could not exist without time to himself. He held back from talking against Angus, but he brooded over the contrast in their reputations. Clearly, he would have been much more acceptable if he had elected to become a City businessman.

"I feel very frightened of the City," he admitted once. "You always feel there is going to be some awful rule you don't know about, that you're meant to walk down the street on the right-hand side instead of the left ... I always feel I'm going to be caught out because I don't belong."

At the same, soul-baring session, he tried to justify his attitude. "If I'm attending an official function or an official trip, I never have a camera. I always wear a suit and so on. But in return for that, when I'm photographing, I want to be alone and to wear ordinary jeans or working clothes."

He was stung by accusations that he depended on favors to

further his career. "I will not take pictures or work on stories where it could be said I have an unfair advantage. I hope it's accepted by Fleet Street that I haven't tried to scoop other photographers."

One of his unpaid pastimes stemmed from a Fleet Street friendship and his own months as a polio patient, confined in a wheelchair. Quentin Crewe, a *Sunday Mirror* columnist, could not walk. Wherever he travelled, he needed a muscular companion to heft his bulk into and out of a car and ease him into a chair. The only available self-propelled models that a cripple could manipulate struck Tony as being hopelessly inadequate. He spent hours over the weeks and the years in his catacomb in Kensington Palace, struggling to put together a phototype of something better that would not tip its driver over onto the highway if he made a turn at much speed above a crawl.

The legacy of polio sent him into St. Bartholomew's Hospital for a brief checkup half a year after he and Margaret reached home from New York. He was spreading himself thin by taking on his first television contract with a colleague, Derek Hart, who Tony insisted should have the same £2,100 fee as himself. Columbia Broadcasting System wanted them to shoot a documentary about old age. Uncle Dickie would consent with no great enthusiasm to figure in *Don't Count the Candles* as he approached his seventieth birthday.

One segment of élite society was already looking and hoping for cracks to appear in Margaret's marriage. Like ancient Greeks, the English set great store by the concept of *hubris,* the fate meted out by the gods to those guilty of wanton arrogance. She had flouted the rules, the argument ran, so she deserved to suffer. A story went the rounds that Tony had spent a lonely weekend in the hospital, waiting for a visit from her. In fact, they had gone down to his latest hiding place in the Sussex woods.

Old House consisted of two Tudor cottages knocked together with an extra, Georgian wing attached. Water had to be pumped by hand to fill the bathroom tank. Kerosene lamps supplied the only light when day faded outside the leaded windowpanes. The place was on loan to them from Uncle Oliver Messel. They had laid the matting from Rotherhithe Street on the floors and installed some of The Room's worn furniture. "Tatty" was the word applied by some friends who dropped in, but shabbiness sometimes exercised a deep appeal for Margaret. She wanted them to take their time about making changes to improve the limited comforts. The first stab at having a building contractor tackle the job ran into stalemate when his trucks got bogged down in winter quagmires.

"Our marriage," Margaret said cryptically, "is in the mud." She and Tony both realized that, but young David and Sarah were protected from the sorry truth. They were being reared in accordance with nanny convention, attractive children whose beaming smiles at the sight of their parents simultaneously delighted and troubled both of them when they contemplated the future.

Elizabeth thought her sister smoked far too many cigarettes and dieted too hard to keep Hanoverian poundage away. She seemed unusually susceptible to colds, and the pulsing pain of migraine could make her cry. If Tony's game leg happened to be bothering him at the same time, tempers on both sides were in danger of snapping.

They settled down with inevitable friction into a pattern of living that Tony had woven for himself in the first place. The biggest change came about when, for fear of cancer, he temporarily gave up his acrid Disque Bleu cigarettes, a mark in his favor according to one criterion of Philip, who quit smoking on the eve of his wedding and ordered windows opened and air fresheners brought into rooms he found smelly with stale tobacco fumes. Margaret stuck to her daily consumption of Gitanes.

The Snowdons made a conspicuous target when they were out together in London. They were spotted on the first ride she had taken on the Underground since she was an eight-year-old, clutching Crawfie. Their car was held up in traffic on Kensington Road on the way to Leicester Square for the opening of a rerun of *Gone With the Wind*. She wondered why they and their accompanying detective shouldn't hop out and try the Piccadilly Line. Squeezing into the train after them came the advertising manager of the *Sunday Times*, uncertain whether this could indeed be *them*.

"We'd better cool this tube thing," muttered Tony, who liked to compartmentalize his time.

The clothes she chose usually made her the less conspicuous of the two. She had broken the habit of emulating her mother in the number of brooches, necklaces, and bracelets worn simultaneously. Gaudy shoes were also a thing of the past, like the pearls, which had once been standard equipment. Mr. Hartnell continued to supply formal gowns, but otherwise she shopped for plainer fashions, which had the effect of lowering her visibility. Tony could look like Mr. Dressup in a long velvet jacket, water-silk vest, and black suede shoes, especially if the evening was a family affair, where the cut of men's dinner clothes had scarcely changed by a gusset since Grandpapa's reign.

If Tony was out of the country on assignment, paid or voluntary, she still went out with one of the clique of escorts. Peter Sellers' companionship was hard to resist when he could top any imitation she might come up with. She went with him one night to listen to the international language of jazz in one of the few Soho clubs licensed for real food and drink. Spike Milligan, a comedian with ginger beard and antic wit, stood up to improvise some lines for Sellers' benefit: *"Wherever you are, wherever you be/Please take your hand off the princess' knee."*

When Tony was away, and often when he was not, ripples of gossip spread through the town. *Can you guess who she was out with last night? Did you hear what she did after dinner? They say that the car was parked right there outside KP. You must be joking. It couldn't be true. But then again . . .*

"When I married Tony," she said later, "I thought I would travel, but that didn't work out." He made no excuses for his need to be left alone while he worked. He knew of no other way to do it. "It would be terribly bad," he said, "if every assignment I went on, I took the wife and family."

In retrospect, he endeavored to explain what he ran into. "Being recognized by people often creates problems for my work, because it changes a situation. People react differently. When I photograph someone, I usually try to do justice to the person, to show them as they are and shed some understanding.

"While I was working in Italy, I was pursued daily by about twenty photographers. In Venice, they would wait in front of the hotel for me to come out, and I was forced to leave by the back entrance. Several days later, when they hadn't seen me come out, the newspapers carried stories saying I was in Venice but spent all my time in my hotel room. It was terrible.

"One time, I went out for a boat ride with a fisherman, but I soon realized he was not a fisherman because he had a large bulge protruding from under his shirt. I finally told the poor fellow to take the camera out and sit down and have a drink.

I suppose I could argue with them or become bitter, but I usually sit down and have a drink and try to reason with them, but usually this doesn't work either."

Six months after Tony's checkup, Margaret checked herself into King Edward VII Hospital for Officers for something more searching. "Nothing more than observation and tests for a day or so," was the bland official explanation. "Nothing to worry about." She had, it seemed, lost too much weight.

When the subject of Peter Sellers arose, it was handled equally urbanely by the more roseate chroniclers of life within the family. He was, wrote one of them, "particularly good in making a straight-faced threesome." Diners at nearby restaurant tables who heard strained whispers exchanged were led to believe that it was all in fun.

On the day she came out of the hospital, Tony's *Sunday Times* schedule took him off to Tokyo. He stayed there long enough to grow a beard as an attempted disguise before he arrived in New York on the way home. Gossip had flowered into headlines: the marriage was on the rocks. He was so jumpy that he took it for granted that the telephone line was tapped when he called her. "Let's meet in Reno," he said.

She flew into Kennedy Airport to meet him before they left to go down to Bermuda as guests of Jocelyn and Jane Stevens. "Margaret and Tony," one raconteur reported, "enacted enormous comedy scenes of reconciliation."

There was rather more to it than that. She had recently brushed up against something that developed first into pathos and then into tragedy. During one of her husband's absences, yearning for her overpowered another man. Robin Douglas-Home was the impressionable nephew of an obelisk of the social structure, Sir Alec Douglas-Home, who had served Neville Chamberlain as parliamentary private secretary and the Tory Party as a sturdy linchpin. For reasons of genealogy and personal preference, he had been known variously as Lord Dunglass and Lord Home before he settled on his present title and held office as Prime Minister for close to a year between Super Mac's retirement and the Socialist victory in October, 1964, that put Harold Wilson into No. 10 Downing Street.

Sir Alec was sweetly courteous, true-blue aristocracy, and politically so much a man of the Munich era that he rebelled against approving the Yalta agreements signed by Churchill, Roosevelt, and Stalin in 1945. Sir Alec and a handful of others akin to him constituted a reclusive coterie which owed allegiance to its members over anyone else. Membership was hard to come by. The right school tie helped, but money was no guarantee of admission, since overspending was considered vulgar unless performed by an Edwardian profligate like Lord Derby. Rich or beggared by death duties, a member was expected to act with the indifference of a millionaire.

Neither was virtue rewarded by entry—a number of dukes in the membership were lechers and wife beaters—and Jewishness was a definite impediment. Freshly minted fortunes were regarded with suspicion; members were willing enough to accept food, drink, and tokens of esteem from a self-made captain of industry, but they were rarely returned.

The supreme qualification was arrogance, the certainty that whatever you did, you were superior to ordinary people on the outside. Men of the innermost sanctum were convinced that they alone knew what was best for England, no matter what the government in power might think. George V had been a bore to them, Bertie a commendable example to the less-elevated classes in time of war. Elizabeth was—well, Brenda, and Margaret beyond redemption.

Robin Douglas-Home was a man of delicate sensitivity, privy to a story that had circulated among the coterie since the time of Townsend's exile. According to this account, the breakup of Margaret's love affair had been Philip's doing. Allegedly, it was his means of settling the score with Peter, whom he blamed for questioning his qualifications as a husband when Philip was courting Elizabeth. Peter's doubts had weighed heavily for a while with Bertie, the coterie believed, leading him to hesitate about giving his daughter's hand to young Lieutenant Mountbatten, a man who resented being kept waiting for anything and a man with a long memory.

Robin was infatuated with Margaret. He may have pictured her as a victim of her brother-in-law's vengefulness, encouraged into a marriage whose happiness was wearing perilously thin. He detected her misery and apparently mistook it for desperation. He was no Peter Townsend, but he fancied that he could offer her a chance of greater joy than she was finding now. He underestimated her. No matter how depressed, she could stand aside from herself like an actress playing a role and watch the effect on an audience of one. She wrote him letters in the headlong, sentimental style set by Victoria in her correspondence, and he treasured them as expressions of true love, convinced that she would gladly escape with him.

When the truth finally struck home, he could feel only a sense of abasement. He had made a classic idiot of himself, and the shame was too much to endure. The following year, he carried the plot of the neo-Victorian melodrama to its curtain and killed himself.

The letters she had written emerged in New York, due to be sold as costly curios to the highest bidder. They were withdrawn from the market before sale day, to be returned to England and, in the belief of traders in holography, burned in a Buckingham Palace furnace. Somehow, one of them may have eluded destruction, to reappear when Margaret's affairs reached a turning point almost six years afterward.

At that time, a letter written on stationery bearing a cornet and a curliqued "M," dated February 14, 1967, and addressed to "Darling Robin" appeared in a West German magazine. The script was graceful and fast flowing, the words of gratitude spiced with wit. It conveyed thanks for a "perfect weekend" which, the writer said, had restored her heart.

By that time, more names had been added to the list of men who admired her, and not always in secret. They were all more of Tony's breed than of top-drawer hierarchical quality. Dominic Elliot's fellowship dated back to the heyday of the Margaret set when he squired her to parties, tolerated by Grandmama because his grandmother was one of her ladies-in-waiting. The Earl of Minto was Dominic's father, but Minto did not amount to much in the inner sanctum.

Patrick Litchfield was *Lord* Lichfield, which he found underwhelming; he preferred the reputation he had earned as a professional photographer and competitor of Tony's; Patrick took Margaret nightclubbing. Derek Hart, Tony's television colleague, was another Margaret-follower. Among friends less involved, the tendency was to level the blame on her husband for neglecting her and his stubbornness in clinging to his old ways of living in making a career for himself. "Tony's wandering eye" became the pat explanation for what was happening to the marriage.

When its erosion became obvious to everyone who knew them, the names of the women involved were bandied around London like after-dinner mints. If he invited any one of them to the cottage that stood on the grounds of his mother's house in Sussex, it was taken, rightly or not, as conclusive evidence of something more significant than a photographer's fascination with a pretty face.

Lady Jacqueline Rufus Isaacs, the dazzling daughter of his mother's neighbor, the Marquis of Reading, was a visitor. She also went to London to see him in a hospital there when he was undergoing a minor operation on his leg, and she confessed she was in love with him. The infatuation came to a halt when a blithe young Welshman, Dai Llewellyn, took her on a ski trip to Gstaad. Jacqueline, who earned pin-money as a model, had someone else in mind as a husband—Mark Thomson, son of a Berkshire landowner, Sir Ivor.

Pamela Colin, London editor of *Vogue*, was fond of Tony as a person as well as a source of marvelously chic pictures. "Love" was not a word to apply to the affiliation. She went on to marry Lord Harlech, Elizabeth's exemplary ambassador to the United States. The editor of a less-refined publication, *Playgirl*, carried away by esteem for Tony, asked him, unsuccessfully, to pose in the requisite state of newborn innocence for a center spread in her magazine. Gayle Hunnicutt, an American actress, whose marriage to the actor David Hemmings remained intact as yet, was a steady companion of Tony's, open to view on the dance floor of nightclubs like Chez Maggy.

Margaret kept pace with him on the same orbit. *("Wait for me, Lilibet.")* She had tastes similar to those of Uncle David, who would die in 1972. Raffish comradeship appealed to her so long as she could dominate it. She reveled in the haunts that jet-borne connoisseurs rated as the swingingest clubs on the credit-card circuit, rubbing shoulders with movie stars, diplomats, fashion models, gangsters, call girls, drunks, tired businessmen weary of their wives, and the biggest spenders of all, hairy young kings of pop whose records sold in the millions. The clients of most places were divisible into three sexes, but that was accepted as part of the ambience. The important thing was to be out enjoying herself within walls variously decorated with appliqué velour or psychedelic light, dancing to electric guitars pounding over the amplifiers. Other clients assumed that she and Tony arranged their evenings in advance to avoid bumping into each other on the same napkin-sized floor. While Tony and his partner patronized Chez Maggy, Margaret was out with Patrick Lichfield at Raffles.

The marriage still held together. She carried out a share of calendar engagements—one hundred and seventy-two of them in 1970—and so far as her public could gather, she and Tony had found they could make it work even if love meant something other than what she had hoped it might be. Overseas, she was a bigger crowd-puller than at home. Nobody but Emperor Hirohito drew more attention when she and Tony went to open British week in Tokyo.

The acclaim received in following the line of duty she had chosen in rejecting Peter was not enough to compensate for present anguish. Perhaps part of the problem between herself and Tony lay in the fact that they had been too dutiful, at the expense of personal pleasure. If they could retreat to a private sanctuary far away by the white beaches of the Caribbean, the marriage could be improved.

The plot of land under the palms of Mustique retained its place in her ambitions. She saw the kind of house she dreamed of when the two of them spent a late-winter vacation with Uncle Oliver in the spanking-new home he designed for himself on Barbados. On Tony's thirty-eighth birthday, they hired a plane for the hop due west over the cays and glimmering sea to take a look at their property and make a start on planning what they might build there.

Mustique was taking on a different identity under Colin Tennant's ownership. His new hotel, the Cotton House, was open for business. The shoreline was dotted with the first batch of sparkling white-walled villas with gardens cleared from the tangle of palms and vines. The native population was growing by leaps and bounds toward a total of two hundred,

finding work as cooks, maids, and houseboys instead of slicing
down sugarcane. The age of Aquarius had arrived in the
Grenadines, and what she saw of it enchanted Margaret.

The first house of her own was designed by Uncle Oliver;
she would call it *Les Jolies Eaux*—Lovely Waters: a long house
of stone and stucco with a low profile, coral pink and gray;
big windows to let in the breeze and keep the living room
cool under the scorching sun; four bedrooms, one for the
detective; three baths; and views of the Caribbean a few steps
away. She would have to be patient, though. Construction
advanced at a crawl in this nook of the universe. The last lick
of paint would not go on for another two years. And by then?

Paying for the place could be a problem if Tony's income
fell much below its present £30,000 a year. But before all the
bills came in for *Les Jolies Eaux,* she had a stroke of good
financial luck. Thanks in part to Philip, Margaret's state
allowance was more than doubled.

Bertie had actually handed back to the government money
saved by his drastic pruning of entertainment during the war.
Elizabeth copied his frugality at first, but inflation had
changed that. She was spending roughly £100,000 a year of
her own income beyond her £476,000 allowance, a sorry state
of affairs which court officials hinted stood in urgent need of
review—they used the same technique of dropping the word to
selected newspapermen as the Pentagon exercised when next
year's budgets were being drawn in Washington.

Running into debt and pleading poverty had been something of a habit with Hanoverians in the past. With £800,000
a year coming in, the third George had to be bailed out ten
times by his governments. There was no knowing in 1969
how long Elizabeth and the family might have waited for
purse strings to be loosened if Philip had not intervened.

He repeated on television's *Meet the Press* what he had been
complaining about around the palace for months: "We go into

the red next year, which is not bad housekeeping if you come
to think of it. We've in fact kept the thing going on a budget
which was based on costs of eighteen years ago ... Now
inevitably if nothing happens, we shall either have to—I don't
know, we may have to move into smaller premises. Who
knows? We've closed down— Well, for instance, we had a
small yacht which we've had to sell, and I shall probably have
to give up polo fairly soon. Things like that."

The prospect of Elizabeth being forced to cut corners
dismayed many of her subjects. Prime Minister Wilson
cheered them up by promising a study of the circumstances.
The outcome was a comfortable increase in her bounty, and in
the process Margaret's £15,000 rose to £35,000 before taxes,
plus £125 paid in piecework for every official engagement she
undertook as an incentive to keep on the move. The critics
who begrudged her a penny had twice as much to mutter
about.

Leaner times had sharpened the outlook of the court and its
guardians. Philip was a prime exponent of the argument that
the day had gone when royal mystique should be as
impenetrable as that of the Wizard of Oz before Dorothy and
Toto caught him lurking behind his curtain, manipulating the
machinery to spew smoke and flame.

Lord Cobbold, lord chamberlain by job title, which made
him the latest head of Elizabeth's official household, reported
for duty with conventional qualifications—Eton, Cambridge,
and the Bank of England—but he preached the necessity of
keeping up with the times. "We've entirely got rid of the
idea," he said, "that it's huntin', shootin', fishin' people" who
monopolized senior appointments on palace staff.

After Commander Richard Colville retired from the press
office with his knighthood as a memento, his place was filled
by a more outgoing Australian, Bill Heseltine, who went so
far as to help with a book offering a behind-the-scenes peek at

the royals, while he made members of the family available for judicious interviewing, excluding Elizabeth herself.

Any innovation disturbed the woman who would have been happier living in Victorian seclusion than in being promoted like a package tour in British Airways advertising. She had no illusions about her abilities as a public speaker when she was condemned to plod her way through the dull texts that were put together for her. Her throat dried up in advance unless she sucked on a piece of barley sugar as Alah had taught her to do in nursery days.

Elizabeth protested that publicity had gone altogether too far after her fourth and last child, Edward Antony Richard Louis, was born in 1964 and a smuggled snapshot of her, cuddling the baby in bed with her first three looking on, turned up in *Paris Match* and, worse still, in the *Daily Express*. The investigation launched to discover how this came about got nowhere, but the picture earned something like £5,000 on its publication.

Philip believed in airing his opinions in public, but bridled if they were accepted as less than gospel. "Listen to what this bloody fool says," he would snort, flinging down on the breakfast table a newspaper that faulted him. Apart from the hubbub over Margaret, he sensed that to many people the family was growing as monotonous as his wife's prefabricated speeches.

He took to television to contribute a little common sense to the situation. "You know, we're getting on for middle age, and I dare say when we're really ancient, there might be a bit more reverence again. I don't know, but I would have thought we were entering probably the least interesting period of the kind of glamorous existence ... There used to be much more interest. Now people take us as a matter of course. Either they can't stand us, or they think we're all right."

When irritation got the better of him, he slid into waspishness: "I know as well, if not better than anyone here, that life in Britain is not wholly rational." He scoffed at the tomfools who could not reconcile his enthusiasm for the World Wildlife Fund with his zeal in shooting pheasant: "We seem to exist with a strange morality in this country. Everything which is pleasant must of necessity be sinful."

Some of his outbursts carried him onto thin political ice. With his personal freedom curbed as it was, some government rules provoked him. "Over everything you try to do, there is a control or sanction. I know that in Scotland, we had to get planning permission to block up a fireplace in a cottage ... Really, it's unbelievable."

His comments about behavior in lands abroad were just as pungent. He lectured a gathering of Canadians: "The monarchy exists not for its own benefit but for that of the country. We don't come here for our health. We can think of better ways of enjoying ourselves." America's race to land men on the moon left him skeptical: "It seems to me that it's the best way of wasting money that I know of." A reporter travelling in Philip's entourage on the drive from the airport into Amsterdam heard a mutter, "What a po-faced lot these Dutch are!"

While Philip enjoyed sounding off, Tony withdrew into his shell, steering clear, for instance, of the House of Lords, where he had yet to deliver a pronouncement about anything. The thought of it terrified him. "I never made a speech until I was thirty," he said in justification of his silence. "Anyway, I'm very inarticulate, so if I'm doing something like that, I always write it out in full first. And I can't be funny. I hate jokes and things. If somebody is naturally funny, that's great, but if you're not funny, it's better to remain a bore."

A streak of haughtiness ran through both men. Dr. Salvador

Allende was president of the Chilean senate, a year away from being elected the Marxist leader of his country, when he arrived at a Santiago banquet for Elizabeth and her husband. Allende's lounge suit singled him out in a throng of males otherwise bedecked in tails and white ties.

"Why are you dressed like that?" Philip quizzed him.

"Because my party is poor, and they advised me not to hire evening dress."

"If they told you to wear a bathing costume, I suppose you'd come dressed in one."

His brother-in-law was too tongue-tied in public to deliver a thrust so pointed, but when a flatmate of his bachelor days yelled, "Hi, Tony!" and waved to him as he drove to Kensington Palace, he received a secretary's note in the mail: would he please refrain from a repeat performance?

It was not Tony who talked Elizabeth into starring in a marathon documentary for television but Uncle Dickie, gratified by the success of a serial filmed to relate his own life story. She shuddered at the suggestion. Recording her Christmas Day chat to the kingdom was an ordeal that had her squirming in embarrassment as she recited her lines from the teleprompter. But the court and its guardians considered that carefully supervised TV provided an absolutely first-class means of refurbishing the regal image and making her *interesting* again by showing her as the woman her most loyal subjects conceived her to be.

The new movie might also serve as an introduction for an endless series featuring Charles, twenty now, and eighteen-year-old Anne as the next generation whose job, if they could pull it off, would be to tighten the bonds between the people and the crown. Admittedly, a degree of risk was involved. The general impression to date was that Charles was likable enough but a bit of a namby-pamby, his sister a sloppy schoolgirl enamored with nothing but horses.

Elizabeth grudgingly agreed to appear on camera. She had to force herself to do what was expected even though she could not stand the thought of a production that was to stretch over eleven months of shooting. Philip sat as chairman of the new partnership of BBC and commercial television that was to supervise the venture and sell the show overseas with half the profits assigned for Elizabeth's charitable disposal.

The finished product depicted a pleasant-faced woman coping like an upperclass suburban housewife with a handsome husband, dogs, and brood of well-adjusted children, then handling the social niceties as she chatted at a diplomatic reception and got involved with Richard Nixon on his first visit to the palace. "My sister," Margaret said afterward, "copes very well with presidents." Touches of nostalgia from the Lilibet era padded out the filmed performances, but flag-waving was held down to a minimum.

On its first showing, twenty-three million watched the hundred and ten minutes of *Royal Family*. One executive responsible heralded it as "the most exciting film ever made for television." Lord Cobbold fancied that the attitudes of nine out of ten Britons were "changed overnight." Half the schoolchildren who saw it concluded that Elizabeth had to be the most important person in the wide world. That portion of the population which referred to her as Brenda had its own title for the show: it was *Corgi and Beth*.

Since faded respect for the family had been restored for the moment, nothing was going to be allowed to shadow it. The contentious affair of Margaret and Tony must be ignored in the interests of extending this new chapter in Elizabeth's history.

"Tony is a naughty boy, but I do love him," Margaret said. Palace publicity concentrated on these missions they still undertook as a pair. They flew to Australia; Tony stayed on to shoot pictures. They rode side by side in a coach following her sister's when she and Philip marked their silver wedding anniversary with a service in the abbey. Whatever conditions came up to keep the Snowdons apart, lap-dog journalists were eager to invent excuses. Margaret's feelings over being left to go alone for another spell in the Caribbean amounted only to "comic despair" under that formula.

Their clashes could no longer be concealed. If they appeared at a party, the host and hostess had to be prepared to deal as best they could with an open quarrel. She sniped at Tony along with anyone else in sight when she was in a mood to hurt. He would put up with her gibes until he lost his temper and snapped, "Oh, God, you bore me!"

A host of theirs complained, "It was terribly difficult to entertain the Snowdons. One never knew what was going to happen. She had grown positively skinny in an effort, I suppose, to keep him attracted to her when he was surrounded by pretty girls in the course of his job. The two of them would usually begin the evening on terms of politeness, but gradually she might start needling him as if he could do nothing to please her. It was a toss-up whether she would walk out first, or Tony, or whether they'd leave together to continue the argument elsewhere."

"I'm much nicer in my old age," Margaret smiled, but there was such irony in her that her meaning was the opposite of her words.

The marriage had degenerated into little more than a convenience by the time she reached forty-three. Final efforts to hide the truth needed to account somehow for the obvious squabbling between husband and wife. "On the fun side," according to one apologist, "the couple had been known to stage fearsome outbursts, fists clenched, expletives flying, in a quickening crossfire of improvised Noël Coward wit until they collapsed in impish laughter."

Most of the country knew by then that the Snowdons

pursued their separate ways. Those who venerated Elizabeth found Margaret's conduct unforgivable. The afterglow of *Royal Family* had died away, and Margaret was partly blamed for the letdown. A newspaper polled its readers and discovered that thirty-nine percent of them were in favor of bringing the ancient institution of monarchy to a timely end.

It had been a year or so since she came to the conclusion that, as she put it, "Now I could do pretty well anything." She felt she had outgrown her frustrations. What was likely to happen in the future, she didn't know, she said.

XIII

A Slide Down the Pyramid

Bluff, hard-riding Harry Llewellyn, late of the War-
wickshire Yeomanry, made himself as much at home around a
boardroom table as on the hunting field. On his horse
"Foxhunter," he had won a gold medal in the Helsinki
Olympics in the year of Bertie's death when Harry was forty,
then gone on to be awarded a Royal Society medal for
lifesaving a little later. As a twenty-five-year-old gentleman
jockey aboard "Ego," he placed second in the bone-rattling
Grand National steeplechase.

Colonel Harry took pride in his two terms as joint master
of the Monmouthshire Hounds and put hunting the fox first
among the sports he enjoyed at Llanvair Grange, his two
thousand acres of Wales near Abergavenny at the foot of the
Black Mountains. The clubs he joined—the Cavalry and the
Jockey—and his voluntary job as president of the British Show
Jumping Association were all part of the picture.

He was, in other words, the breed of man Elizabeth
thoroughly approved of. Had he been the eldest and not the

second son of his father, Sir David, baronet, he would have inherited the title, but he had little cause to doubt that sooner or later he would receive a knighthood in recognition of the career he had made for himself after he came down from Trinity College, Cambridge.

Harry presided over a brewing company, Whitbread (Wales) Limited; served as a director of a bank, a building society, an assurance company, an engineering group, a management consulting firm, the Wales Tourist Board, and Chepstow race-course. Llanvair Grange boasted half-a-dozen servants and a fey mistress in his wife Christine, daughter of Baron de Saumarez. She bore him three children: a daughter, Anne, and two sons, Dai and Roddy.

Dai had a lot more of his father's dash than his younger brother, who badly disappointed Harry by showing minimal interest in horses as a hobby. It was Dai, living and working in London, who interrupted Jacqueline Rufus Isaacs' attachment to Tony by taking her off to ski in the Swiss Alps. Tony had no reason to be fond of the Llewellyn brothers. "One of them takes my girl friend," he said as the situation developed. "Now the other takes my wife."

Dai was the extrovert, Roddy the gentler, sensitive one, overshadowed by father and brother. So far, Roddy had not distinguished himself as a working man. Among the string of jobs he had tried was a spell of clerking at the College of Heralds. Compelled once or twice to draw £10 a week in unemployment pay, Roddy sadly deduced in general that he was unemployable.

Both the brothers were bachelors, endowed with Welsh charm, soft voices, and good looks to qualify them as useful extra men at anybody's party. Roddy had been enrolled for that occupation when he met Margaret. In appearance, he could have been a cousin of Tony's, eighteen years younger, an inch or so taller. They had the same lithe build, lean cheeks, and quick bright smiles. She would discover that they chose the same kind of blue jeans, tops and sandals for comfort, but Roddy opted to wear a silver stud in his left ear. The personalities of the two Welshmen were different, too: Roddy lacked Tony's compulsion to succeed.

In middle age she was going through some of the bleakest years she had known. The ceaseless lighting of cigarettes was one mark of tension and another was the Scotch she sipped, with the inherent risk of bringing on migraine. Roddy served as a pick-me-up in the first place. She sent a friend, Lady Violet Wyndham, to Dai's apartment to talk to his brother. Would Roddy care to join another party to the Colin Tennants,' Glen House, Innerleithen, thirty miles outside Edinburgh? Yes, he would indeed; Margaret drove to the railroad station there to meet him off the train.

On the other side of the marriage, stress was showing in Tony. He found himself shaking with anxiety as he held a camera, the trembling of his hands blurring some of his pictures. "I find it gets worse as I get older," he said. "It happens when I go on assignment. I sit outside in my car too terrified to get out."

In search of relief, he applied himself even harder to perfecting something safer than the standard gasoline-driven three-wheeler sold with government approval for cripples. His solution was what he christened the "Chairmobile"—in essence, a mobile platform, operated from a control console. He assembled the first for Quentin Crewe in wood, a second in metal, the third built with a body of Fiberglas.

His goal was to see every three-wheeler committed to the scrap heap and replaced with a perfected Chairmobile. He would argue his cause before any parliamentary committee of investigation that wanted him as a witness. To accomplish this, he needed proof of the hazards built into the older contraptions.

He took one of them out for a test run in the grounds of Kensington Palace. It performed adequately as usual on the straightaway. Then he swung it into a sharp turn at no greater speed than a healthy man could run. It toppled over and trapped him inside, steering column rammed against his chest, gasoline spilling from the tank. If a spark from the wiring touched off the fuel in such an accident, a cripple might die.

He pulled himself clear and went indoors to telephone Margaret, raging over the regulations that encouraged the sale of carriages that he was satisfied could kill anyone more seriously handicapped after polio than himself. He had not escaped unscathed. The pain in his ribs might mean broken bones.

It was a moment when he would have liked her near. Instead, she was off in Munich, opening yet another British Week as a travelling saleswoman. The marriage had come to this. In the past, she had vented her fury on him for being absent when she needed him. This time, it was his turn. There was little she could attempt to say to soothe him or apologize. She was carrying out her duty, like it or not. They passed one more milestone on the downhill road.

She came home to go with him to the wedding of her niece Anne and Lieutenant Mark Phillips, son of a sound county family who made such a sprightly, well-curried bridegroom in regimental dress uniform that he might have marched straight out of the pages of *Vanity Fair*. Tony's injuries were painful enough to take him into King Edward VII Hospital for a surgeon's attention two days later. When the damage to his chest had been repaired, he returned to work, and Margaret made her own way to Mustique.

To some who knew him well it seemed that the desire had sprung up to leave some imprint of his own on the wax of public recognition before the opportunity was lost. His accident was discernible as the impetus he needed after thirteen years of saying nothing in the House of Lords. On April 10, 1974, the Earl of Snowdon put on a dark-blue business suit, picked up the text he had written, and set off to make his maiden speech.

Margaret sat with their enthralled son and daughter in the Peeresses' Gallery, listening to him talk, nervously but tellingly. For thirteen minutes he related his experiences with polio and the built-in hazards of three-wheelers, which he condemned as "intensely lethal machines."

Man and wife were not often seen in each other's company after that. "Whatever month you arrive," the guidebook said, "you're sure to be in time for some interesting event or other. Sports matches, pageantry, exhibitions, old customs . . . they all take place in the course of the London year. Watch the calendar. You could be lucky!"

May brought the running of the Derby at Epsom; the cricket season got under way; choirboys sang from Oxford's Magdalen Tower; Elizabeth in headscarf and tweed watched the riding at the Royal Windsor Horse Show; and the annual flower show opened in the grounds of Royal Chelsea Hospital. Margaret and Tony were there in 1975 among the sea of blossoms, the ladies up from the country in hats that rivalled the exhibits, and grizzled army pensioners in uniforms designed in the reign of Victoria. It was their closing dual act in the royal arena.

The popularity of individual royals in the kingdom rose and fell like counters in a non-stop game of snakes and ladders in which Elizabeth was bound to come out ahead eventually. Philip's following had slipped lately as a result of his determined one-man campaign exhorting British manufacturers to "pull the finger out," cautioning the unions that a welfare state was no substitute for "enterprise and hard work," condemning controls that interfered with "freedom to succeed."

After Anne's launching into public life "with the expertise

used for a new deodorant," as one observer put it, she suffered badly from over-exposure on television. Viewers were treated to unduly generous doses of her on horseback, laced with interviews in which she talked about her favorite subject—horses. Her mother was anxious to find a country home for Anne and her husband. The impression that Elizabeth was spoiling her was fortified when she bought them Gatecombe Park, a Cotswold manor house and 730 surrounding acres, for something in excess of £250,000.

Charles' counter had just been skipped up a ladder by the roll of the dice. It had taken a long time to dispel the general feeling that he was an insipid young man who would never catch up with his father. But Charles' reputation climbed fast after he spoke up for himself on TV, in newspaper interviews, and under his own published by-line.

Reminiscing about the family was his speciality. He recalled that Uncle David referred to his short-lived reign as "drudgery." With a polite "if I may say so" and "it seems to me," Charles disagreed, on camera. He thought the monarchy was "one of the best jobs in the world." Victoria, he wrote, was no "puritanical old she-dragon" but a woman endowed with "a glorious sense of humor" who split her sides with laughter when a German dignitary split his breeches in Balmoral's drawing room.

George III held a particular fascination for Charles. He corrected the picture of a man maddened by disease whose obsessions lost him the American colonies. Farmer George, said his descendant, was simply misunderstood; he was kind, good-humored, and "enormously popular in his old age."

The dice that favored her nephew sent Margaret slithering down a snake to the bottom of the board. More and more of her sister's subjects asked aloud whether the time had not arrived to threaten her with the loss of her £35,000 a year if she persisted in misbehaving.

She sought out Roddy more than any other man to share

her leisure with her. He fancied at first that their relationship amounted to no more than "a bit of fun." He was flattered by her interest, he basked in the sense of status it gave him when he had accomplished nothing spectacular on his own account to date. It was all too incredible to be taken seriously.

Some of his friends and relatives were less reluctant than he to talk about what was developing. Chatty Nicky Harlan, an interior decorator by trade, regarded him as "a lovely, sweet, angelic boy." He interpreted Roddy's responses solely in the light of sibling rivalry. "You must understand that Roddy has always been a bit jealous of his brother Dai. Now I think he feels a bit superior."

In this particular friend's opinion, Roddy "pulled off the best piece of one-upmanship in the world." Nicky offered another thought: "Roddy likes girls. I don't think there was ever any question about that."

A cousin of the Llewellyns, Colin Pritchard, took a more empathic view. "I know that as the relationship developed, Roddy took it seriously. He is a serious person and would not have maintained the relationship for too long just for prestige."

The number of people eager to be identified as friends of Margaret was shrinking. Colin Tennant and his wife remained steadfast. So did the Napiers, Lord and Lady, who also had a house on Mustique. What impelled Margaret was a subject that intrigued everyone who knew her. Speculation ranged far and wide. The resemblance between Tony and this new young man half-way persuaded them that love for her husband had not died; she must be prompted by jealousy to score off Tony.

No, went the opposing argument, they had both given up on their marriage, and Margaret was casting around again to find an alternative mode of living. Neither of the patterns she had known until now fulfilled the requirements of a chameleon personality that intermingled hauteur with insecurity, warmth with frost. She had tried to exist on two levels simultaneously and failed in both.

Serving her sister in royal drudgery did not satisfy her. Margaret had experimented with bridge-building between royalty and a gayer world on the outside, yet she was no more willing to give up her title and forego her privileges than she had been when she loved Peter Townsend. In refusing to become Mrs. Armstrong-Jones, she had lost her second chance of happiness.

A partisan of Tony's summed up this side of the debate. "It may be right and natural to call the queen or her sister 'Ma'am' at a once-and-for-all official function. But for all those authors and playwrights and actors who thought they were being asked to join the royals' own swinging set, the counterpart of the Kennedy's White House era, it must have been extremely tiresome to have to worry all the time about protocol, never being sure whether they could break the ice without going through it."

Tony himself could not be drawn. "I have never over the past fifteen years made any comment about my private life, and I have no intention of doing so now," he said.

Margaret was familiar with two levels of the pyramid. Once more, the only places she could explore lay farther down. She had protested in the past, "When I grew up, it was 'No, darling, I wouldn't do that. I don't think people would understand.'" There was precious little chance that they would now, but she intended to go ahead, anyway, with Roddy to post the way to life among the "trendies."

She was willing to shed a limited amount of her dignity during her search in the company of the man she called "darling angel." She did not ask to be addressed as "Ma'am" any longer, or as "the princess," which was Tony's term for her if other people were present. She settled for "PM" in Roddy's circle.

It was made up in large part of hippies, dropouts from Establishment society, and latter-day flower children whose misty dreams of what tomorrow should bring pictured swords beaten into plowshares, and harvests, grown free of poisonous fertilizers, that would nourish the spirit of love and compassion, one for another. Peace on earth and goodwill to all would prevail. Greed and viciousness were doomed to disappear. The vision was so remote from everyday existence that the only way to begin giving it shape was for a group of kindred souls to band together and set up a commune, which is what Roddy and a handful of the cohort ventured to try that summer.

Their scheme possessed a certain plausibility. The commune would be supported on the profits from a restaurant they would open, and food supplies for the restaurant would come from the commune's sowing and reaping. They came across half the property they were looking for in the ancient city of Bath, a little more than a hundred miles west of London. The city had ties with kings of antiquity. Legend said that King Lear's father, Bladub, founded the place in 863 B.C. after applications of mud from local mineral springs cured him of leprosy. Edgar the Peaceful was crowned in the Saxon abbey there in A.D. 973. Under the third of the Hanoverian Georges, Beau Nash inaugurated the city's golden age; disused Roman baths opened up again, the Pump Room was rebuilt, the streets were cleared of footpads, and the citizens taught to conduct themselves like true ladies and gentlemen.

Roddy and his fellow communards took over an empty Kardomah café. Its previous clientele had consisted in the main of matrons of the distinguished old city in need of a pot of tea and a buttered Bath bun or possibly a plain Bath biscuit. The newcomers dressed up the place with posters and potted palms and renamed it Parsenn Sally. From time to time, the sweet scent of marijuana hung in the air. Later, when business proved slow, the proprietors planned on holding a ten-day festival of movies that would include a screening of "Deep Throat," barred from Britain as hard pornography, but the show was hastily called off.

As the complementary half of their project, Roddy and a syndicate of seventeen others scraped up £40,000 to buy Surrendell Farm, forty-five acres in the county of Wiltshire, in whose hills the limestone for building Bath had originally been quarried. Wiltshire's past predated the record of English kings. Stonehenge stood against the sky to the southeast; Bronze Age burial mounds lay hidden under the coarse grass of the uplands.

The farm laid claim to a little history of its own: Oliver Cromwell's Roundheads battled the Cavaliers of King Charles I on this land as a prelude to beheading him and converting the country into a republic for eleven years from 1649 on. The house on the place, no gem of antiquity, was a monument to neglect, its paint peeled away and its boards stained by the weather of the past twenty years, when nobody lived there except the rats and mice.

A cluster of the latest tenants, Roddy among them but ladies excluded, took advantage of the farm's remoteness by stripping off to relax on a hot August day. "Mad rompings" was how one spectator indignantly described what he spied going on around the unkempt yard. "We are just having a good time in a quiet atmosphere," Roddy explained lightly. "When the weather gets colder, it's back to clothes."

The frequency of his excursions to Kensington Palace increased. Occasionally, he stayed at No. 1A as an overnight guest; among its twenty-one rooms, there was always one to spare. The gentleness in him held a deep appeal for Margaret. "I cry easily," she had once confessed. A woman friend attempted to account for what had happened: "They have turned each other into happy people. They have saved each other's lives. They are both emotional, and if they feel like having a bloody good blab, they sit down and have one."

Under pressure from reconciling his role with Margaret and his part in the commune, Roddy was admitted for a spell in Charing Cross Hospital, suffering from nervous exhaustion, drawing the sickness benefits due him under the national health scheme. After his discharge, Margaret had him go with her to Mustique again to speed his recovery.

Tony had never cared much for the pink and gray villa after it was finished. She had been there without him when the furniture was delivered and waited to be uncrated. Staying with the Tennants until that job was done, she had made up a song in anticipation of moving into her sun-baked sanctuary at last. She could improvise a calypso at the drop of a cocktail napkin: *When you've been unpacking furniture all day, it's sheer delight to sit down and play ...*

Contentment was a built-in fixture in *Les Jolies Eaux*, where a housekeeper and cook looked after the chores incurred in entertaining and a full-time gardener tended the flowers. On Mustique, Margaret was recognized as "Her Royal High Jinks" as she took a dose of sun in thick protective makeup, sipped a tall drink, and sang in pure satisfaction like a lark rising from a meadow. A performance of "Buttons and Bows" to the guitar of a former member of the Mamas and the Papas became a piece of island folklore.

This November of 1975, she had Roddy with her everywhere, trailed by the indispensable detective, Chief Inspector John McIntyre. If a tourist spotted her and tried to break in on them, he was deflected by the instant chill in her clear blue eyes. Roddy showed his generation's unconcern for some of royalty's accouterings by dressing in a pair of Union Jack swim trunks.

She took stock of herself as one year ended and another began. At forty-five she had yet to find her fit in life. Possibly she never would, because circumstances made it impossible. Her marriage was broken beyond hope or desire of repair. Concealing the fact was just as impossible when cameramen had trailed her to Mustique and caught her with Roddy. But there had been instances before when the family cut off discussion of royal misery simply by ignoring it until public interest wore itself out. Her rationalizing ran into a blank wall of frustration. She could not decide what to do next.

"I do not say I want a divorce," she told one close friend. "I do not say I don't want a divorce. But I believe it is my duty to keep my solemn vows—my duty to my family, myself, and my country."

Her plight had already been debated by Elizabeth, Philip, and an increasing number of other relatives. Margaret had applied clear-eyed logic in dividing the problem into its three key elements: how would the breakup affect her son and daughter, herself, and the kingdom. Far from being bewildered by the issues involved, she was prepared to leave the solution to her sister and her counsellors. Margaret had learned as a girl in love the price of taking emotional decisions into her own hands. She would be content if they were to go on leading their present scandalizing existence. She was not concerned about what people thought of her. Life was too short for her to be intimidated by ostracism.

Elizabeth spent restless nights turning over the problem of what might be done about her sister. Philip held Margaret and Tony equally responsible; it would be hard to forgive either of them for the pain they were causing his wife. But it was necessary to make the outcome as smooth as possible for everyone involved. Tony was a reasonable man, who could not be cold-shouldered in any event.

In February, lawyers entered into the discussions; on

Margaret's side, Farrer and Company of Lincoln's Inn Fields, who also acted for Elizabeth; on Tony's, Lord Goodman of Goodman, Derrick and Company of Little Essex Street, a forceful advocate with long-standing connections in Fleet Street.

It would probably have suited his client better if a divorce might be sought without delay, but the stultifying Royal Marriages Act, more than two centuries old now, contained no provision for such a solution. If Margaret and Tony could be treated as non-royals, existing law made divorce possible after two years of separation, provided both of them consented, five years should either raise objections.

Legal separation must be the first step. The timing was important. The announcement would be withheld until Tony had left London on a business trip to Australia in the middle of March. Margaret set her own timetable and flew back to Mustique for another vacation with Roddy.

Exchanging gifts with him called for ingenuity when there was such disparity in what each could afford. She made one— "a private message," in his words—by taking a wooden board and pasting on it a fragment of tapestry, a pheasant feather, a child's fan, marbles, a bow tie, a corner of burned parchment, a moth, a pen nib, and an old Dinky car. What did it signify? Psychologists could interpret the symbolism as they wished. Neither Margaret nor Roddy would provide a clue.

The court feared that the news would break prematurely during the month she was away. One weekly magazine that fed on scandal and bare bosoms raced into print with "Secrets of a Royal Marriage," concentrating on "Tony and the Jet-Set Beauties." Newspapers in Germany reported a palace crisis brewing in London.

A twelve-hour flight brought her back on March 3 from Barbados, where Roddy stayed on, head low, in a house of his father's. Two more weeks remained before Tony's departure for Sydney. After Roddy slipped back into England, she went with him for her first sight of Surrendell Farm. No lady-in-waiting travelled with her this time, nor did her detective.

Once they had left the highway and the car had started winding through the lanes of Beaufort Hunt country, they might have been back in the previous century. Only a television antenna by a smoking cottage chimney or a power line strung among the freshly-leaved trees told of the passage of time. At a turn in the road by a wall of mellow brick in Grittleton village, a signpost pointed the way up a climbing, single track of blacktop to Surrendell.

At the top of the rise, a mile or so along, the track ended, and they turned into the rutted entrance to the farm. Birdsong sounded as the engine died. Chickens scurried among the weeds that grew by the broken-down fences. A roving sow, bought cheap because she was lame in one hind leg, would bear a litter soon. The lean Irish wolfhound was no shaggier than most of the males in the bits and pieces of clothing they wore to express disdain for dress as a symbol of conformity.

Living creatures of any species had the run of the place as a matter of principle. "It's a way of letting them do as they please," a later visitor was told by a clear-eyed girl in a home-made, brown print dress whose hem barely cleared the mud. Money was tight already; Parsenn Sally was running at a heavy loss. They would have to cut their hay, the only crop, early and sell it for perhaps £40 a ton if they were to continue eating. A local businessman wanted to buy what was left of the soft-red tiles on the stable roof, but that would be sacrilege. "We're going to restore everything as it used to be," the girl promised. The going was hard. One young man of the commune on another day was found with a bullet in his head.

Margaret picked her way through the March mire to the steps leading up to the battered front door. The old house wore boards like bandages over most of its windows, whose glass had long since been shattered. Great holes gaped in the plaster of the inside walls, covered here and there by a frowzy fabric hanging. The ground floor was largely open space, with lumpy mattresses laid on the bare planks by the outer walls. The one bed in the place, iron framed, was reserved for her up the flight of stairs, which had been repaired with roughly-sawn oddments of raw lumber.

The whole house exhaled the odor of grime, mold, greasy cooking in the littered kitchen, and stale smoke of assorted flavors. "Have a joint?" was the amiable greeting extended to another guest. There was no heat, no hot water, no telephone. Placing a call meant traipsing over to Mays Farm, which backed on to Surrendell, and using an extension line in a shed near the pigsty.

"We live and let live," said the farmer there, John Rawlins, though telephone charges piled up when one communard, an Australian, now and then called home. They counted on paying off their debt in hay as soon as it was cut, which Mr. Rawlins accepted at first, but he found that was all they could offer.

"Maybe I'm a bit old-fashioned," he said, "but they don't appear to like parting with checks or money, though that's what I'm holding out for." He still let them use his extension.

They brewed tea for Margaret over an open fire. She was "P.M." to them, and they considered her, as they said, "a nice lady." She was obviously enjoying herself in young company. She went up to change for dinner and came down in a sedate dress and the pearls which had been put aside under Tony's influence. The meal was served on the kitchen table, an item of furniture a junkman would have chopped up for firewood. Then around a campfire, they circulated the wine, and she joined in the singing. "Chattanooga Choo-Choo"—thirty years, forty years old?—was one item in her repertoire. "She is," a companion of Roddy's decided, "extremely intelligent, sensitive, and forward looking."

The next day, she pulled on rubber boots to help in the vegetable garden. The villagers had caught on to who the visitor was at Surrendell Farm, but they were not quite sure how to handle the sudden onset of the age of Aquarius in Grittleton except with restraint. "Naturally, she doesn't speak to us," said one of them with recollections of how royals were supposed to conduct themselves, "and we on our part let her get on with her own life."

Before the business of the palace announcement was over with, she would be back for another weekend.

Tony left London Airport on the first leg of his flight on March 16. "I am," he said, just turned forty-six, "a very old man." The pared-down look of his face supported his words. "I love my work, just love it. It will take a long time before I give up, although I sometimes feel like a yo-yo. I seem to be flung around all the time."

The official pronouncement sounding the knell of his marriage was not due to be issued for four days more, but the clamor for information could not be stilled. Someone had to speak for Elizabeth immediately. It was left to one of the household staff to say, "Everything possible has been done to make the couple patch up their differences. But the situation has become untenable, not only for the Snowdons. It has also become a cause of great distress for the queen."

Fleet Street asked for nothing more to justify the headline MARGARET AND TONY: DIVORCE on March 17. Elizabeth called a meeting of the Privy Council for the end of that morning in the 1844 Room of the palace. The Councillors numbered some three hundred in all, including Philip and Margaret, but only those needed for the current discussion were summoned, sworn to customary secrecy and, in accordance with another tradition, expected to speak on their feet. No precedent applied to the business in hand. Never before had public admission been made that a royal marriage had collapsed. Meanwhile, the police prepared a security check on the farm and its inhabitants.

One or two of them declined to let principle stand in the way of making money off the reporters and photographers who patrolled the area. A sense of loyalty to Roddy was as alien as clean laundry to some of those who exploited him. One intimate of his peddled pictures and information indiscriminately to the *Daily Express,* the *News of the World* and *The Sun* for a total of £12,000 in cash to pay off his debts. John, his fellow inmates decided, had never been the best of influences on Roddy. But perhaps he was right, after all, to grasp the opportunity when Parsenn Sally was going under, weighted down by unpaid bills. Some of them went on to say that they were fed up with Roddy for "exposing us to the attention of journalists."

Anybody prepared to talk about Roddy was fair game for the probing pressmen. Cousin Colin Pritchard ventured to say, "If there was a divorce and he felt it would be expected of him to marry the princess, then he would go ahead and do it." A friend of Margaret's ("you're not to mention my name") pooh-poohed the idea. If she ever married again, "it will not be Roddy Llewellyn." Actress Diane Cilento, once married to actor Sean Connery, lived not far from Surrendell, succeeding in what the commune had foozled—growing and selling fresh vegetables to the neighbors. Since she knew Roddy, watch was kept on her.

Hounded like a fox, Roddy fortified himself with a glass or so. He was tracked down one night at Diane's house, where a group of her friends had gathered. One of them, a young playwright, helped him escape through the back door to elude the inquisitors waiting outside the front. The two of them would beat a retreat across the dark fields to the home of another lady whose discretion could be trusted.

Roddy played paratrooper as they wove their way over pastures, a stream that detained him, and stone walls that had to be scaled somehow. Their intended hostess kept a large, guardian ram behind the walls of her estate. He had once left the mark of his horns on Harry Llewellyn, when he lured the beast into charging him, a make-believe matador. After Roddy had dropped into the last field separating him from refuge, the ram caught him in the rear and spread-eagled him.

On Friday, March 29, 1976, the palace finally confirmed what the world had already been told. The accent was laid on obligation: "Her Royal Highness the Princess Margaret, Countess of Snowdon, and the Earl of Snowdon have mutually agreed to live apart. The Princess will carry out her public duties and functions unaccompanied by Lord Snowdon." Surmise about an early remarriage was momentarily put to rest. "There are no plans for divorce proceedings."

In Sydney, Australia, Tony could not control the tremor in his hands or the tears from welling in his eyes. He was, he said, "desperately sad in every way that this had to happen." He listed three things he had to do. "Firstly, to pray for the understanding of our two children. Secondly, to wish Princess Margaret every happiness for her future. Thirdly, to express with the utmost humility my love, admiration, and respect I have always felt for her sister, her mother, and indeed her entire family."

Margaret said nothing, except to those dearest to her, but she let only four days pass before getting on with the job of being royal. The chubby face encircled by the silk scarf that covered her hair was as impassive as a peasant's as she took

Linley down to the Pool of London. She had sailed from there on her honeymoon.

This morning, she wanted her son to go aboard the destroyer *Hampshire*, which she had launched on another dutiful day fifteen years ago. At the end of the week, Roddy emerged into view, dancing at the Tramp, a nightclub on Jermyn Street. Margaret was not with him, but the T-shirt he wore was a token of amity. The letters on its back spelled out RODDY FOR PM. Keeping in touch by telephone, they decided against breaking off their meetings.

His father concluded that Roddy must be heard from and shown in a more favorable light than the glare of present publicity. While Colonel Harry drafted a statement for the newspapers, his son added some final explanatory lines of his own: "I much regret any embarrassment caused to Her Majesty the Queen and the Royal Family for which I wish to express the greatest respect, admiration, and loyalty. I thank my own family for their confidence and support, and I am very grateful for the help of my friends at the farm, who, with myself, share a common interest in restoring a house to its original order and beauty and in farming land which it is hoped will provide food for our Parsenn Sally restaurant in Bath."

With that much said, Roddy returned to the commune. Margaret had to survive one more blow to her standing. The letter she had purportedly written Robin Douglas-Home was printed in *Stern*, the German news magazine. The story was scissored out of every copy imported by the British distributors in the same fashion as all references to Wallis Simpson had been excised forty years ago, but *The People* came to hear of what had been done and told its readers about it on the following Sunday morning.

Tony came back that weekend, wheeling his own luggage

on a handcart through customs, anxious to be known from now on only as Armstrong-Jones, snapping at reporters, and "a bit under the weather," according to Dorothy Everard. He would move in with his mother in Stafford Terrace, a stone's throw from No. 1A, while he looked for a new home. He would see Margaret again if for no other reason than to arrange times for their children to spend with him.

He had his own life to lead and his work to do. In the coming summer, he would see another house of cards quiver, possibly bolstering his relief that he had never fallen into the trap of becoming a businessman. A government probe into the delicate affairs of Lonrho Limited singled out Angus Ogilvy as a weakling, too submissive to Tiny Rowland, and "negligent in fulfilling his duties as a director . . . to an extent that merits severe criticism."

The "only honorable thing to do," Ogilvy answered bitterly, was resign all ten of his directorships in much the same way he had quit the Lonrho board in 1973 after Prime Minister Edward Heath, Tory champion of free enterprise, branded the company as the "unacceptable face of capitalism" for breaking the ban on trading with white-ruled Rhodesia. But public opinion did not turn against Angus as it had against Tony and Margaret from the moment of their marriage. Angus deserved another chance to restore himself to good grace for his own sake and Alexandra's.

Roddy laid low for weeks, first at Llanvair Grange, then on the island of Sark, staying with an uncle who owned part of the territory. Colonel Harry bought him a ticket to Australia, in an echo of long ago, when Botany Bay was the destination chosen for prodigal sons, but Roddy did not go there. There was talk around the commune of getting Mick Jagger, his diamond-studded tooth, and the Rolling Stones to put on a fund-raiser in the barn, the only building on the farm capable of withstanding the uproar. Roddy, said the companions of his salad days, was "crazy" over Jagger's tooth, but no rock concert was ever staged.

Margaret went back to wearing a crucifix as she had in previous times of trouble—the death of her father and the embargoing of Peter Townsend. She also sought out Simon Phipps, Bishop of Lincoln now, for counselling. Roddy was still not excluded from Kensington Palace.

The newspapers savaged her. "Her life," said one of them, "is in urgent need of a rescue operation. Sixteen years ago, the talk was all about getting her a job. It ought to be about getting her one now." Another questioned the claims of all the royals other than Elizabeth herself to special favor. "If Princess Margaret's undignified behavior now provides the formal occasion for divesting the Royal Family of its aura of holy dignity, so much the better for members of that family and for the rest of us besides."

Doubt and darkness over Margaret had the effect of intensifying the light that gleamed over her sister. Elizabeth's handling of the Roddy episode and her evident compassion for Margaret no matter what she did marked her as a woman of distinction in most of her people's estimation. A fresh note of sympathy was added to the chorus of praise.

Her trip with Philip to see Gerald Ford in the White House and open the Olympics in Montreal evoked some of the most fragrant prose since Victoria's diamond jubilee. "The Queen's presence," one overawed correspondent wrote, "gave Americans a new perspective on their own history and accomplishments, and also a new conciousness of how well they have succeeded in adapting their British heritage to achieve their very own greatness."

Most of the riddles encompassing Margaret remained unsolved. What drove her into persistent trouble? Why couldn't she settle down as a responsible assistant to her sister?

Was it wilfulness or because her father and Elizabeth both pampered her shamefully? Did she ever intend to stop being the blackest sheep in the flock?

Some members of the medical profession believed they had found most of the answers to these questions by reaching back to the days of George III and beyond.

XIV

A Royal Malady

It served the interests of both sides in the American Revolution to call Farmer George a madman. The rejoicing winners could justify rebellion by claiming they had been compelled to start the fight for independence in 1775 and again in 1812 to throw off the rule of a lunatic enthroned in London. The losers could look back in sorrow and blame defeat on a psychotic king who insisted on personally directing the strategy of war.

Was George really insane? History books published in either country did not raise the question. One generation after another, the stereotype was of a babbling monarch, confined in a straitjacket by doctors he hated in order to curb his restless pacing through the rooms of his palace, or when he sweated so much that he threw his wig away, or refused food because he could not swallow.

He was pictured as having been deranged most of his life, certainly from the time he turned twenty-two and succeeded his grandfather, the second George. Only a maniac, the argument went, would have permitted Parliament to pass the Stamp Act of 1764 to defray the cost of keeping royal troops in the North American colonies and then the Townsend Acts, levying further inflammatory taxes on glass, painter's lead, paper, and tea.

His physicians were hard put to know exactly what was wrong with him. Protocol ruled that before they ventured to ask about his symptoms, he must speak. They had no stethoscopes for listening to his chest, no sphygmometers to measure heartbeat, not even accurate clinical thermometers. If he permitted it, they felt his pulse, checked his tongue, heard his complaints, and inquired about his bowel movements.

One of them confided to his records the outcome of an audience in the sickroom: "His Majesty appears to be very quiet this morning, but not having been addressed, we know nothing more of His Majesty's condition of mind or body than what is obvious in his external appearance."

Medical opinion, operating with its usual infallible hindsight, used to hold that early warnings of derangement showed up in 1765 when he had been king for something short of five years. The profession could not explain why for the next twenty-three years England knew him as a benign, devoted patriot. Farmer George, lover of the countryside, books, and music, patron of science and the arts, gave no sign at all of mental disturbance.

A century later, Dr. Isaac Ray, president of what was to emerge as the American Psychiatric Association, restudied the skimpy evidence then available and concluded, "Few men would have seemed less likely to be visited by insanity. His general health had always been good; his powers were impaired by none of those indulgences almost inseparable from the kingly station; he was remarkably abstemious at the table and took much exercise in the open air. Insanity had never appeared in his family, and he was quite free from those eccentricities and peculiarities which indicate an ill-balanced mind." Dr. Ray, however puzzled, went along with the accepted notion and diagnosed George's condition as "mania."

So that was the description applied to George's recurrent illness from then on: by dictionary definition, "the manic phase of manic-depressive psychosis, characterized generally by abnormal excitability, exaggerated feelings of well-being, flight of ideas, excessive activity, etc."

Some of the symptoms in his first crushing attack qualified as mania under those terms. He was fifty years old; for the past sixteen the Royal Marriages Act, which was to bedevil Margaret, had been law.

The seizure in his abdomen struck in June, 1788. His chief physician, Sir George Baker, ascribed it to "solidified bile" and prescribed a curative spell at Cheltenham Spa, imbibing the local spring waters. Four months later, Farmer George's troubles returned with such vengeance that doctors feared for his life. Vicious pain in his bowels, constipation, a racing pulse, weakness in his arms and legs—these were his physical afflictions.

They persisted for weeks, then were matched by insomnia, headaches, disturbance of vision, and delirium. One weekend in November, he fell into convulsions which left him in a stupor, drifting for days between life and death. After the travail subsided, the physicians watched his moods alternate between tranquillity and wild excitement, when his mind wandered and his words made no sense. Fever, they judged, had "settled on the brain," which gave rise to doubt whether he would ever be fit to rule again.

They saw little significance in one manifestation that appeared at the onset of the illness: his urine had changed to the color of port wine.

Everything possible, or impossible, had to be tried before the country was told that he had lost his reason. The business of

Parliament slowed toward a halt as members cross-examined his doctors on George's chances of recovery and Prime Minister William Pitt, anticipating constitutional crisis, laid plans for setting up the fourth George as regent in his father's place.

The physicians called in dubious allies for help. One of them, Edward Sutleffe, set great hope by what he termed a "herbaceous tranquillizer," but it was not tried out on George. Instead, the Reverend Dr. Francis Willis, theologian and medico, was brought into the case, along with a team of strong-armed assistants.

The bushy-browed disciplinarian ran his own private madhouse. There, in the practice of the day, he treated obstreperous patients like George by strait-jacketing them or swaddling them from head to heels in damp winding sheets. George's objections when he was submitted to such indignities were dismissed as delusions. Down to the present decade, his recovery by the following March was credited to the treatment of Willis, nicknamed "Doctor Duplicate," who had a medal struck in his honor.

George's popularity with his subjects soared on the news that he was well again; drafts of a Regency Bill were set aside. A dozen years elapsed before he was stricken with the same symptoms as before. They, too, disappeared in due course, to strike him for a third time three years afterward and for a fourth time in 1810, which prompted Parliament to fix on a decisive step. The Regency Bill passed into law, replacing Farmer George with his heir—fat, fatuous Prinny. The third George was adjudged permanently insane, the cause attributed to the death of his favorite daughter, Amelia.

Hanoverian energy kept him living, blind and senile, to within five months of his eighty-second birthday, stirred by fleeting fits of tears and gales of laughter. The final attack came a month before he died, when he went for more than two days without sleep, writhing in a ferment of excitement, mad in the belief of the kingdom and the world.

The diagnosis was not challenged until the late 1960s. Then two British psychiatrists, Ida Macalpine and Richard Hunter, mother and son, laid hold of his doctors' notes and records, preserved in Windsor Castle, the British Museum, Lambeth Palace Library, and the archives of some of his descendants. They had his published letters to guide them, too. Applying up-to-date medical knowledge, they worked like masters of detection, weighing each shred of evidence after the trail had cooled. They came to a startling conclusion: George was by no means mad. He suffered as the victim of an agonizing hereditary disease that had gone unrecognized by mankind until the advent of the twentieth century: *porphyria*.

Not one in a thousand laymen knew so much as the name, and among doctors in general, recognition of it spread slowly. The word came from the Greek *porphyra*, meaning purple-red. It made its first appearance in medical literature in 1871 after researchers in European laboratories set out to discover what gave blood its distinctive coloration. Iron was not the cause, as had been the original belief; they found it was a pigment they labelled porphyrin.

That initial chink of light on a disorder hitherto shrouded in darkness led to identification of suspected cases of porphyria before the turn of the century, but forty years went by before the first description of the disease was published. Its origins remained ambiguous, its treatment undetermined. Only the symptoms could be stated with any precision, and they existed in bewildering profusion.

George had most of them, as Dr. Macalpine and Dr. Hunter perceived when they reexamined his case history. The most common was a seizure of prolonged abdominal pain so fierce that only narcotics could relieve it. Constipation and nausea were likely to be included in the attack, which might be triggered by a mild infection, like George's at the age of twenty-two. Fever rose and fell over a period of days. Blisters erupted in the skin.

From its apparent site in the abdomen, porphyria advanced on the nervous system controlling the muscles of arms and legs. George, for example, felt so weak he could not stand. He broke into heavy sweats; he had difficulty in swallowing or focusing his eyes. All these indicated the root of his supposed derangement.

Then the inexplicable excess of porphyrin affected the brain. A patient either could not sleep or else suffered terrifying nightmares. His head throbbed as if with migraine, and his agitation mounted. Unable to formulate a coherent word, his mind seethed with delusions.

The mother and son investigators came upon a tell-tale quotation from George's physicians: "Delirious all day ... impressed by false images ... continually addressed people dead or alive as if they were present ... engrossed in visionary scenery ... his conversation like the details of a dream in its extravagant confusion."

The onslaughts followed the classical development of the disease toward its climax. He writhed in convulsions before he fell into a coma, close to death, which came in something like twenty per cent of cases when chest muscles were paralyzed. But George's illnesses adhered to another, more usual pattern. He made a spontaneous but slow recovery every time.

The clue that originally spurred the two doctors' studies was the color of his urine, almost always an infallible sign of porphyria. Too much porphyrin in the body usually shows up there as an attack progresses, then fades again when the crisis is over. Less noticeably, bones and teeth may turn a permanent reddish-brown.

Ida Macalpine and Richard Hunter did not end their explorations with Farmer George. Porphyria was a hereditary disease, so why not look into the whole Hanoverian inheritance as far as they could? The results convinced them that he passed it on to some of his children.

His daughter Charlotte, named for her mother, died in childbirth, probably of porphyria, though most women were free of attack during pregnancy. More eventfully, his heir, Prinny, the fourth George, must surely have been afflicted. His doctors put down the trouble in his legs to "unformed gout." When they could find no better term for his otherwise unaccountable malady, they advised him to go to take the waters in Bath's Pump Room.

He was too ill to attend his father's funeral. By 1828, he needed steady dosing with laudanum to ease abdominal pain. During the closing years of his life, he was stupefied by drugs, with legs so swollen that he could walk only on crutches, sight lost in one eye and impaired in the other. He found it difficult to breathe and impossible to lie down. He spent his nights sitting up in an armchair, his head resting on his hands.

The Macalpine-Hunter search took them backwards as well as forwards. Accessible records disclosed that porphyria—"a royal malady," in their description—was traceable in James V of Scotland's daughter, Mary, queen of Scots. Her son, James, first of that name in England but the sixth in Scotland, vowed that the colic tormenting him was a legacy from his mother. His urine was regal purple-red.

The two researchers charted a tentative course of inheritance of the disease, which could lurk in latent form throughout a lifetime or reveal itself at any age. One of James' sons showed signs of it, but King Charles, executed to Cromwell's order, seemed to be only a transmitter, like his sister Elizabeth, queen of Bohemia.

As a progenitor of kings and queens, she had few rivals until Victoria reigned in England. Elizabeth's grandson, the first George, and her great-grandson, the second George, were marked down as transmitters of porphyria. So was her nephew, James II, while his daughter, Anne, who became queen of England in 1702, was a suspected sufferer.

Most specialists in genetics accepted the findings of Ida Macalpine and Richard Hunter. In a subsequent exhaustive study of porphyria, Dr. Donald P. Tschudy, senior investigator in metabolism research at the National Cancer Institute, in Bethesda, Maryland, listed the royal suspects and noted, "In 1938, the reigning sovereigns of Denmark, Great Britain, Greece, Yugoslavia, the Netherlands, Norway, Romania, and Spain all descended from Elizabeth of Bohemia, daughter of James I."

The two pioneer probers into the medical histories of British monarchs over a span of more than two centuries wrote: "The disease has persisted in descendants of George III up to the present day. We examined some of them and found the characteristic signs ... Our laboratory tests showed that the family had a form of porphyria that makes the skin sensitive to the sun and to injury."

Neither of them cared to say more after their accounts of solving a medical riddle were published in 1969. Other doctors recalled that Victoria's husband, Albert, lived in dread of an unspecified "hereditary malady" in his wife. After the fact that she carried hemophilia emerged, it was taken for granted that this was what he was referring to. But the mutant gene she passed on to her son Leopold arose spontaneously in her. It was more probable that Albert was haunted by the thought of her Hanoverian predecessors' affliction with the disease which then had no name.

When the troubles of Margaret and Tony ran as a front-page serial, a Fleet Street reporter named Jack Warden, who specialized in covering events in the palace, picked up a lead that promised fresh headlines; he heard that Margaret had inherited porphyria. He relayed the word to his newspaper, and a second reporter, Tom Brown, was assigned to obtain verification.

He approached a British specialist on the subject and was granted an interview. The doctor confirmed what Warden had been told. An additional piece of information was supplied: Margaret's great-grandfather, Edward VII, had also shared in that legacy. After answering the newsman's final questions, the expert added one thing more: If the interview were to be written up and appear in print, he would deny ever having talked to Tom Brown. But there were others, familiar with porphyria, who began putting together their long-range observations of Margaret and arriving at the same provisional diagnosis.

The disorder assumed a baffling variety of forms and degrees of severity. The more that doctors learned about it, the more remained to be clarified. At one end of the scale, it could kill, at the other, produce only moods of irritability and highly sensitive skin, which seemed to apply to Margaret. One problem lay in foretelling when a mild case might flare into a massive, potentially murderous seizure.

"In the extreme," Dr. Tschudy wrote, "an attack of acute porphyria can be one of the most terrifying experiences imaginable. A patient can become almost completely paralyzed from eyelids to toes, unable to breath, swallow, or whisper, unable to communicate, experiencing pain, yet mentally lucid and aware of his plight. The unpredictable nature of the disease, as to both the onset and outcome of the acute attack, makes it particularly treacherous."

The pages of the *British Medical Journal* carried a report about one contempory but unnamed descendant of Elizabeth of Bohemia who suffered from what in her early twenties was thought to be colic. In her fifties, it was detected as porphyria, and she spoke of its thrust as "unspeakably severe—worse than labor pains—as if one's insides were sealed off."

Some doctors tabulated as many as thirteen distinct classifications of the disease, questioning how all the clinical findings could possibly be related to only one genetic mutation when it affected body and mind alike. Others argued that a single difference in the DNA molecule, which dictates the characteristics of living cells, was enough to produce the inborn disarray. "The gene mutation varies from family to family, though remaining constant within each family," an Australian expert, Roderick McEwin, decided. "Each family has its own peculiar pattern of the disease."

The sun's unscreened rays were hazardous for any sufferer. They caused welts, blisters, and, in extreme cases, disfigurement of hands, face, and limbs not unlike leprosy. Infrared light at one end of the spectrum tanned the average skin. Ultraviolet light, which passes through window glass, had to be avoided by victims of porphyria. Medical men noticed in passing that Margaret always wore special, heavy makeup for protection.

One difference between the affliction and that other royal malady, hemophilia, was that the lines of inheritance were unpredictable. Women carried the aberrant sex-linked gene of hemophilia and passed it on as a disease in their sons. Porphyria displayed no such orderliness. If numerous varieties of it did exist, men were more prone to some, women to others. Studies were made of identical twins aged sixty-five. One suffered, the other did not. Another patient went through only one attack in fifteen years; a fellow invalid was stricken eight times in twelve months.

There was no mystery about the sparks that could ignite the incredible pains. A cold in the head might do it, or too much alcohol. Taking any barbiturates as sedatives, steroids such as cortisone, or sulfa drugs to fight infection was likely to fan the symptoms into fire.

Doctors cited the example of a nineteen-year-old Australian

girl admitted to a remote country hospital with what was imagined to be acute appendicitis. She was in a state of such agitation that she was dosed with barbiturates to calm her. The effect was disastrous. Her mind and emotions became so disturbed that she was sent by ambulance to a psychiatric hospital in the nearest city. Puzzled physicians there conducted the standard test and discovered the telltale overplus of porphyrin. She was taken off sedatives immediately, but her depression lingered on for six more weeks. Health authorities would have liked to check the rest of her family after they discovered she had two brothers, one convicted of violent crime, the other of murder.

Something else was capable of stirring an attack—stringent dieting to shed weight. Students of Margaret's case, who saw significance in her shunning of sleeping pills, were curious about her 1967 spell in a hospital, which had been explained away at the time on the grounds that she had "slimmed too well," smoked too much, "and caught cold too frequently."

One prescription for averting assaults is the same as for fending off migraine: the patient is put on a high-carbohydrate diet, as much as five hundred grams a day in meals and snacks spread throughout the waking hours. Fashionable London derided the pounds that Margaret had gained and censured her because "she has let herself go." More objective observers believed that she was following advice from her doctors.

They conjectured, too, that Charles' often-expressed admiration for Farmer George was related to sympathy for his Aunt Margot. Elizabeth's compassion for her sister could be interpreted exactly in the same way.

The incidence of porphyria is uncertain, like so much else involving the royal malady. In one sampling, less than two per cent of men and women with symptoms suggestive of it showed positive test results. In most countries, doctors hesitate to guess how many cases there might be when the disorder may go undiagnosed for a lifetime.

The meager statistics disclose a curious link between levels of porphyria and violence in a community. It has been calculated that one in every 13,000 Swedes aged fifteen and older has the disease, while the figure for Northern Ireland is put at one in 5,000. In parts of South Africa, porphyria turned up in one of every 233 adults admitted into the hospitals, leading to the estimate that three per thousand of the population harbor the defective gene, all traceable to a white couple who were married at the Cape of Good Hope in 1688.

A typical patient is fretful and easily provoked, sometimes to the point of seeming mentally disturbed. United States doctors conducted a check at a mental hospital, involving twenty-five hundred people. Thirty-five proved to have porphyria, though it had not been originally identified in any one of them. Ten had been judged to be schizophrenics, six of them alcoholics. As for the rest, admission records read as follows: "psychotic depression," two; "neuroses," four; "personality disorder," one; "acute and chronic brain syndrome," ten; and "miscellaneous," two.

Laboratory research presents a special problem. Experiments span the gamut from psychiatry to genetic biology. Investigations continue around the civilized world, using guinea pigs, monkeys, mice, rats, rabbits, liver cells, and chick embryos. But porphyria is unique to man; it does not occur naturally in animals, so the condition must be induced in every test of them.

Doctors agree on what causes porphyria, though they know of no means to prevent or cure it. A living cell works as a factory, building up its supply of nutriments or breaking it down into simpler substances or waste matter. The process is complex and continuous, progressing stage by stage as one kind of self-manufactured compound transforms itself into another, in a miracle of biochemistry. No electron microscope or other laboratory instrument can peer at the action itself. The cell must be dead before it can be examined and photomicrographs made of an object whose size is measured in millionth parts of a millimeter.

Science calls this step-by-step progression "the metabolic pathway." Porphyria somehow interrupts the process in the cells of the liver and bone marrow. The result is an imbalance in body chemistry, generating a superabundance of porphyrin to act as a toxin in the nervous system.

Geneticists can supply the answer to *why*. A child may inherit the aberrant gene from either the mother or the father. Whether every child of the mating will be affected is not known but doubted. When no animal carries the disease except artificially, research is heavily dependent on surveys of human families and their medical histories. Too few have been available for conclusive studies to be performed.

How porphyria operates to break the steps of the metabolic pathway is a mystery. Until this can be resolved, it continues to be what Professor C. Rimington of London's University College Medical School cautiously described nine years ago as a "rare and still incompletely understood disorder." A current handbook popular with general practitioners as a working guide says merely, "Treatment is non-specific ... Overall mortality rate is 15-20%; death may occur as a result of motor paralysis during a acute attack, but the prognosis for life is much better than was formerly believed."

The gravest risk stems from mistaken diagnosis like the errors Farmer George's physicians made in dealing with him as a maniac. Porphyria exhibits so many contradictory symptoms that a Scandinavian doctor has accurately labelled it "the little imitator." Patients have been treated for lead poisoning and migraine. Others, gripped by misleading abdominal pains, have been hurried into surgery for appendicitis or intestinal obstruction, with the drugs administered paralyzing their muscles and hastening them into coma.

The Danes came up with a means of minimizing such catastrophes in 1942. They began to compile a national register of all identified cases, under a law that allowed investigators to test families in which porphyria emerged. On the basis of Danish experience, a movement quickened among medical men to have every known bearer of the abnormal gene supplied with a bracelet recording the fact, in the same fashion as a diabetic carries notification of his condition in event of emergency need for insulin. In porphyria, wrong medication is a primary cause of needless premature death.

A patient can look forward to an extended life so long as precautions are taken to ward off acute attacks. That involves keeping to the right kind of diet, shielding from sunlight, and the care of doctors aware of the perilous sensitivity to a specific list of drugs.

"Merely warning members of the family of precipitating factors may be a life-saving procedure," Dr. Tschudy wrote, reviewing the general problems inherent in the disease.

Among most families affected by a heritage of illness in the past, the traditional method was to conceal it. Ignorance of the cause led to dark dread that it represented a kind of curse, a punishment of the gods for some ancestral wrongdoing. The Pharaohs of Egypt responded to hemophilia by prohibiting a woman from bearing more children if her first son died from hemorrhaging after an insignificant wound.

Signs of insanity were kept as secret as a skeleton in the closet. The motive was understandable: confinement in a madhouse was worse than prison when inmates were treated like ferocious animals. Attitudes toward genetic ailments have proved slow to change. Researchers find a high refusal rate when they seek to examine living members of a family and delve into the records of grandparents and generations earlier than theirs.

While the chronicles of most families are scanty, royalty is much better endowed. British archives abound with details of royal living and dying, meticulously preserved except on the rare occasion when they were destroyed on command, as they were in the case of Edward VII's. But kings and queens, raised in the belief that they must show themselves to be infallible, if not divinely appointed, have been even less willing than the commoner run of people to divulge family secrets for contemporary medical research.

Porphyria introduces a fresh argument in the medical profession, anxious to advance its studies into the royal malady in hope of someday coming to grips with one of the most perplexing legacies of mankind. Every doctor would be better served if the public were made aware of the existence of porphyria and the available means of coping with it. For one thing, it would stimulate funding for research. For another, it would save lives. Only a tiny minority of British medical men, however, would go so far as to recommend disclosing Margaret's health records as one way of focussing light on an area of medical mysteries.

Those few contend that as a side benefit it would clear up much of the misunderstanding enveloping her, possibly revitalize respect, and, who knows, restore some of the sympathy that has been lost for her.

In the absence of routine testing for early signs of the disease, only an exceptional general practitioner is likely to reach an accurate diagnosis of a patient's symptoms. Until this has been done, the doctor is bewildered by symptoms beyond his ability to treat them, while the patient can suffer agony. This ignorance was part of Margaret's upbringing. On the unrecorded day when the root cause of her physical suffering was discovered, and her "moods" simultaneously explained, she could begin to understand herself.

To live with porphyria requires discipline, and in the matter of discipline she was better experienced than most non-royals. If she adhered to a strict set of rules covering what she could or should not eat, what she should avoid or the precautions she must take to avert an attack, then she might be able to exist as something other than a shut-in, fearful of more pain.

That she conditioned herself to live as a free being in harrowing circumstances of health is demonstrated by her passion for the hot sun of Mustique, even if the sun could prove her undoing. A sign that she has come to terms with her physical inheritance? No other explanation fits. There is one impact of the disease which no amount of courage can alleviate. Since its genetic occurrence remains mysterious, if Margaret were a sufferer, she could only trust that her son and daughter would be spared.

On Sunday, February 6, 1977, Elizabeth drove through the rain to Windsor Castle chapel to kneel in prayer to mark her silver jubilee. Elsewhere, Prime Minister Callaghan praised "a quarter century of devotion and public duty." John Grigg, otherwise Lord Altrincham, once critical of the court and what it stood for, purred, "She has been absolutely solid, a wonderful example of permanent social and moral values as well as a really good wife and mother." Margaret was overlooked, but she was used to that.

In Parliament, bickering broke out again over whether or not Elizabeth deserved another increase in her allowance as a reward when times were so hard that she would do without a jubilee ball and set the style for low-key celebration. Two thousand hilltop bonfires blazed when Grandpapa reached the score of twenty-five years as king; this year there were plans for no more than a hundred. Commemorative coins and stamps bearing her likeness, touched up to hide her weariness, would go on sale, but most festivities were to be paid for not by government but by private business and charity organizations. Travel agents rubbed their hands in anticipation nevertheless; the bargain pound wavered around the $1.70 level, and they expected a boom year, with something close to nine million visitors coming in to see the sights and buy the souvenirs after Elizabeth got back from touring her realms and territories along a route that had shortened drastically since 1952.

At the Sunday chapel service in Windsor, the chaplain, the Reverend Anthony Arbuttle, said, "During the shifting sands and changing times of the last twenty-five years, the royal family has advanced and adapted in a most remarkable way, and the debt we owe to the queen and Prince Philip is incalculable."

Among those who knew her circumstances, a question arose: is it not Time to let the world know that, whatever the future holds for Margaret, the little princess in middle age has fallen into line with most of the rest of the human race in the matter of suffering and exploring life in roughly equal measure?

Index